254

THE
CHAIN OF
TRADITION
SERIES

Volume IV:
Jewish biblical exegesis

Frontispiece by

Eleanor Schick

THE
CHAIN OF
TRADITION
SERIES

Jewish biblical exegesis

BY LOUIS JACOBS

Behrman House, Inc.

PUBLISHERS   NEW YORK

In memory of my mother-in-law:
Jane Lisagorska

Published by Behrman House, Inc.
1261 Broadway, New York, N.Y.

Library of Congress Catalog Card Number: 73-1487
International Standard Book Number: 0-87441-225-0

Manufactured in the United States of America

Introduction

THIS book contains selections from the best-known Jewish Biblical commentators of the eleventh down to the twentieth century. Only commentators who wrote in Hebrew are studied and only the most popular, popularity being determined either by the fact that the commentary was printed together with the text in editions of the Bible or that it was frequently quoted in Jewish literature. There is no selection from Saadiah Gaon (882-942), for instance, although he can be considered in many ways the true father of Jewish Biblical exegesis. Saadiah wrote in Arabic, so that his work can only be appreciated against the Arabic background. Moreover, only fragments of his work have come down to us and he is not a popular commentator within our definition of the term. The whole area of Rabbinic legal interpretation has been excluded because this is really a separate field, but examples of Rabbinic exegesis will be found in the first volume in this series, *Jewish Law*, and also scattered through the comments in this volume.

The works studied here are all premodern in the sense that they rely on the Biblical text or on its interpretation by the Rabbis, without any of the considerations that are essential features of modern critical and historical Biblical scholarship. Thus there are very few investigations into the authorship of the Biblical books (but see the section on Ibn Ezra) and very little treatment of the historical background (but see the section on Abravanel). The increase of knowledge about the Biblical period brought about by archeology, comparative Semitic philology and the application of scientific methods of investigation, was unobtainable by these writers. Even the *Biur*, the commentary produced by Mendelssohn's school at the end of the eighteenth century, has been excluded from consideration in this volume because, while hardly critical, it is indicative of the objectivity typical of modern scholarship, in which the Bible is studied as one would study any other work of literature. All the writers treated of in this book (even those belonging to the nineteenth and twentieth centuries) would have vehemently repudiated the view that the Bible, as the word of God, can be studied like any other literature.

The significance of the writers we study lies, therefore, in the evidence they afford of how the Jewish spirit, nourished by the Bible, was constantly at work in explaining the Bible. For an accurate understanding of Biblical texts against their historical background we must turn to modern scholarship. But it is to our authors that we must go if we wish to discover how Biblical ideas became fruitful in Jewish life and thought. These men were far more engaged in trying to discover what the Bible means for them than to know what the Bible means in the abstract. This quest for relevance is an ongoing process, to be undertaken anew in each generation. But if we wish to undertake it we can learn much from the way in which our authors attacked a similar problem.

This leads us to a central theme discussed by practically all our commentators. Two terms are used by the Rabbis in connection with Scripture and its interpretation. These are: *Midrash* or *Derash* (from a root meaning "to inquire") and *Peshat* (from a root meaning "plain" or "simple"). The *Peshat* is the "plain meaning" of a verse, what it says on the surface. The *Derash* is the meaning read into the verse. The Rabbinic Midrashim, of which there are a large number, contain many thousands of examples of *Derash* (hence their name *Midrash*, plural Midrashim). Frequently *Derash* is far-fetched, at times consciously so, for the sake of dramatic effect. The main intention of *Derash* is generally to find a kind of peg in Scripture on which to hang an idea. For instance, we read in the book of Exodus chapter 13 verse 17 that when God led the people out of Egypt He did not lead them "by the way of the land of the Philistines." The *Peshat* of this verse is simply that God did not lead them by this route out of Egypt. But the Midrash disregards "of the Philistines" and reads: "God did not lead them the way of the land," i.e., He did not lead them in a natural way but in a miraculous one. The "way of the land" is that bread comes from the ground and water from on high, whereas when God led the people in the wilderness He gave them manna from Heaven and water from the rock. He did not lead them "by the way of the land." Now obviously the Rabbi who put forward this novel interpretation must have known that it could not have been the real meaning of the verse. He knew this, yet he presented his *Derash* because he wished to read his idea into the verse. The problem is, however, complicated by the fact that laws of conduct are at times derived by the *Derash* method and since these are binding, the *Derash* cannot be ignored as harmless fancy or poetry. The Karaites, the anti-Rabbinic medieval literalist interpreters, in fact rejected many of the Rabbinic laws for this very reason. They could not find them directly stated in Scripture. Many of our authors, under the influence of the Karaites, acknowledged the legitimacy and urgency of the search for the *Peshat*. But since they were loyal to Rabbinic law they drew the line at a departure from the *Derash* and a return to the *Peshat*, where to remain with the *Peshat* would involve the rejection of a law based on the *Derash*. The whole problem will become clearer when the actual selections are studied. Here it may be said that the commentators can be divided into those who stress the *Peshat* and those whose fancy encourages them to turn to the sometimes implausible but poetic realms of *Derash*.

The names *pashtanim* and *darshanim* are used respectively for those who favor the *Peshat* method and those who favor the *Derash* method. Of the commentators studied in this book the division is roughly as follows: *Pashtanim*: Ibn Ezra, Rashbam, Kimḥi, Naḥmanides, Gersonides, Abravanel, Sforno, Malbim; *Darshanim*: Daat Zekenim, Ḥazzekuni, Jacob ben Asher. Arama, Alsech, Lunshitz, Ḥayim ibn Attar, Kalonymus Epstein. Combining the two methods are: Rashi, Baḥya ibn Asher and Baruch Epstein. However, there is considerable overlapping and one should speak of a general tendency rather than try to fit each of the writers into a neat category. Philosophical exegesis is favored especially by Gersonides, Arama, Abravanel, Sforno and Malbim. Mystical exegesis is favored by Naḥmanides, Baḥya, Ḥazzekuni, Ibn Attar and Kalonymus Epstein. Interest in philological detail is evinced especially by Rashi, Ibn Ezra, Rashbam, Kimḥi, Naḥmanides and Malbim.

Although it is advisable to study the book right through, the contents have been so arranged that any section can be studied on its own. Brief biographical notes are given at the beginning of each section. For further information on the authors the articles in the standard Jewish encyclopedias should be consulted. The long article by W. Bacher, on Bible Exegesis, in the *Jewish Encyclopedia* is an excellent account of the history of Jewish Biblical interpretation. This book seems to be, however, the only attempt there is at providing the reader with actual texts from over 900 years of Jewish Biblical exegesis. The passages quoted have been chosen for their intrinsic interest and for the typical stance of each of the authors. It will help to have an English translation of the Bible at hand when studying a text. Moreover, since the commentators deal with words or phrases, it is a good idea to read through the Bible verses as a whole before going on to see how they were interpreted. It will be noticed that our authors often differ considerably from the standard English versions and where this happens the reason for it has been examined in the notes. It should be remarked that the King James version was greatly influenced in its renderings by some of our authors, particularly by Rashi, Ibn Ezra, Rashbam, Kimḥi and Naḥmanides.

Rashi

"The Lord is my shepherd"
The judges and their duties
"The Prayer of Moses"

Rashi (born Troyes in France in 1040; died there in 1105) is, many would hold, the greatest, and he is certainly the most popular, of all Biblical commentators. He is called Rashi after the initial letters of his name: Rabbi Shelomo ben Yitzḥak (son of Isaac). Rashi wrote commentaries to most of the Biblical books, but best-known is his Commentary to the Pentateuch. This was first printed in Reggio in 1475 (incidentally, this seems to be the first Hebrew book ever printed). It has since been printed many times together with the text so that the term "Ḥumash and Rashi" has become part of the Jewish vocabulary. A later Derash playfully applied the curious name Parshandatha (Esther 9:7) to Rashi, taking it to mean parshan ("interpreter") data ("of the Law"). Since Rashi's Commentary to the Pentateuch has already been translated into English with helpful notes by M. Rosenbaum and A. M. Silbermann (London 1929), we offer here his comments on some of the Psalms.

A. "THE LORD IS MY SHEPHERD"—PSALM 23

[1] "A Psalm of David." Our Rabbis say that whenever it says "A Psalm of David," it means that David first played on his harp and then the Divine Presence rested on him. A Psalm to bring the holy

spirit upon David. But wherever it says "Of David a Psalm," it means that the Divine Presence rested on him first and then he sang. "The Lord is my shepherd." I trust that I shall not want anything in this wilderness through which I journey. [2] "In green pastures." In pastures where grass grows. Since he began by comparing his sustenance to that of an animal which feeds, as it is said: "The Lord is my shepherd," he continues to play on the idea by speaking of "green pastures." David sang this Psalm in the forest of Hereth (I Samuel 22:5). Why was it called "the forest of Hereth"? Because it was as dry as clay (ḥeres) but God irrigated it from the good things of the world to come (Midrash to Psalms). [3] "He restoreth my soul." My spirit dulled by misfortunes and flight he restores to its former state. "In straight paths." In straight ways so that I do not fall into the hands of my enemies. [4] "The valley of tzalmavet." A land of darkness. It refers to the wilderness of Ziph (I Samuel 23:14). Dunash ibn Labrat explains every instance of this word tzalmavet to mean "darkness." "Thy rod and Thy staff." The sufferings I have met with and the staff of trust in Thy mercy both afford me comfort. The sufferings will cause my sins to be forgiven and I have trust that Thou wilt prepare a table for me (verse 5), the table being that of kingship. [5] "Thou hast anointed my head with oil." I have been anointed king at Thy command. "My cup runneth over." This means the satisfaction of man's needs.

Rashi first comments on the fact that sometimes in Psalms we find the heading Mizmor le-David (A Psalm of David) and sometimes le-David Mizmor (Of David a Psalm), as in Psalm 24. Now le-David can mean "to David." The Rabbis observe that where the word mizmor is mentioned first, as here, David had to rouse himself before he could become inspired; he had to play on his harp before the holy spirit could be awakened. But when it says le-David first, this denotes that his inspiration came to him without effort. Rashi is very fond of quoting the Rabbinic Midrash although at the same time he pays proper attention to the Peshat, the "plain meaning" of the text on which he is commenting. Note how Rashi here understands the Psalm as referring to actual incidents in David's life. In his comment to verse 2 Rashi quotes the Midrash to Psalms in which there is a play on the word Hereth as if it were written ḥeres, which means dry clay. God made the desert fruitful by bringing down to us

*some of the goodness of Paradise. In his comment to verse 4
Rashi understands the word* tzalmavet *(frequently rendered into
English as "shadow of death") as "darkness." Most modern scholars
accept this interpretation except that they point the word to read*
tzalmut. *Dunash ibn Labrat was a tenth century grammarian and
poet whom Rashi quotes frequently. Note Rashi's clever interpretation of "rod" as the stick with which God had beaten David, referring to his sufferings, and the "staff" as David's trust in God on
whom he leans. In verse 5 anointing with oil is taken literally. David
had been anointed with oil as the king of Israel (see I Samuel 16:13).*

B. THE JUDGES AND THEIR DUTIES—PSALM 82

[1] "God standeth in the congregation of the judges." To see if they
render just decisions. Therefore, O ye judges. [2] "How long will ye
judge unjustly?" [3] "Do justice." If he (the afflicted) has right on
his side, do not declare him to be in the wrong in order to "respect
the persons of the wicked" (verse 2). [5] "They know not." These
judges who pervert justice. "Neither do they understand." That
because of their sin "They go about in darkness" and "all the
foundations of the earth are moved." [6] "Ye are godlike beings."
Angels. For when I gave you the Torah I made a condition that the
angel of death would have no dominion over you. [7] "Nevertheless
ye shall die like *adam*." Like Adam, the first man, you too shall
die since like him your ways have become corrupt. "And like one of
the princes" of old, so shall you fall. But the Midrash understands
it to mean "like one of the heavenly princes," as it is said: "The
Lord will punish the host of the high heaven on high" (Isaiah 24:21).
[8] "Arise, O God." Asaph (verse 1) began to pray that God should
arise and cut off these corrupt judges from Israel. "For Thou shalt
possess all the nations." Therefore it is in Thy power to judge
everyone.

*Rashi translates verse 1 as "God standeth in the congregation of the
judges" (el), hence the connection he draws between the verses.
In verse 7 the Hebrew reads* ke-adam, *translated in English as "like
men." But Rashi takes it to mean "like Adam." The reference is to a
Rabbinic saying that although death had been decreed on Adam, yet
God's intention when He gave the Torah was for the decree to be
cancelled for those who keep the Torah to live forever. But since*

they had sinned, as did these corrupt judges, they are doomed to die as Adam did. Two explanations are given of "princes." One refers to the great princes of ancient times, the other to wicked angels. The idea of fallen angels is common in Jewish folklore and medieval thought. Milton makes use of it in his "Paradise Lost."

C. "THE PRAYER OF MOSES"—PSALM 90

[1] **"A Prayer of Moses."** The eleven Psalms from here to "A Psalm of David" (Psalm 101) were all composed by Moses and they correspond to the eleven blessings he gave to the eleven tribes as related in the portion beginning "And this is the blessing" (Deuteronomy 33:1). **"Thou hast been our dwelling-place."** A dwelling-place is a place where one can live and find refuge. **"In all generations."** and forever for Thou art before all else. [2] **"Before the mountains were brought forth."** Were created. And before **"Thou hadst formed the earth and the world"** and from the first world *(olam)* to the last world *(olam)* Thou art God. [3] **"Thou turnest man to contrition."** Thou bringest sufferings to a man until Thou makest him weak in power and near to death. **"And sayest."** To him through these sufferings, **"Return, ye children of men."** From your evil ways. [4] **"For a thousand years in Thy sight."** A thousand human years are equivalent to a day of the Holy One, blessed be He, together with a portion of the night ("and as a watch in the night"). For a day of the Holy One, blessed be He, together with a small portion of the night of the Holy One, blessed be He, is a thousand years. For Scripture does not say that a day of the Holy One, blessed be He, is a thousand years unless some of the night has been added to it and then there is a complete day and this is a thousand years. This is why Adam had to die before he had reached a thousand years (Genesis 5:5), for if he had lived a thousand years it would have been longer than a day of the Holy One, blessed be He (in which a thousand years is composed of a little of the night as well as the day). It is possible that the length of this "watch in the night" is that of the years which Adam lived (930) subtracted from a thousand years. We have no real information about the length of this "watch" but we can make a plausible guess. So have I found it written. **"For a thousand years in Thy sight . . . "** When Thou didst at the beginning think of repentance Thou didst judge the matter correctly, creating repentance and the years proper to its effective-

ness. For at first the years of man's life were long (giving him time to repent) and Thou didst decide that a thousand years would be in Thy sight only as a day that has passed together with a small portion of the night. For Thou didst say to Adam: "In the day that thou eatest thereof thou shalt surely die" (Genesis 2:17), yet he lived for 930 years. It follows that a thousand years equal a whole day together with a small portion of the night. "Are but as yesterday when it is past." When it has gone by. [5] "Thou carriest them away as with a flood." But now Thou hast seized hold of these years and reduced them to a few days so that they seem only like a short nap. For the years of the generations are only seventy years, as it is stated later on: "The days of our years are three-score years and ten," and they are treated as if they formed one act of sleeping. As it is said: "When the Lord brought back those that returned to Zion, we were like unto them that dream" (Psalm 126:1). This refers to the seventy years of the Babylonian exile for they were in exile in Babylon for seventy years. *Zeramtam* (carried away) means "swept away" as in the expression: "The tempest *(zerem)* of waters floweth over" (Habakkuk 3:10). "In the morning it passeth away." One born during the night dies in the morning when his sleep is ended. But if [6] "In the morning it flourisheth," then it immediately begins to fade so that "in the evening it is cut down, and withereth." Why? [7] "For we are consumed in Thine anger." As if to say: Yet [8] "Thou has set our iniquities before Thee" and *alumenu*, that is, "the sins of our youth in the light of Thy countenance." *Alumenu* means "our youth" as in the verse (I Samuel 17:55) "Whose son is this youth *(elem)*?" "In the light of Thy countenance." Before Thine eyes to gaze at them. [9] "Are passed away in Thy wrath." They have become emptied and have passed away and have gone in Thy wrath. "As a *hegeh*." As a word that is soon spoken and done with. [10] "The days of our years are threescore years and ten." These days of our years and these sins of ours and these youthful sins of ours all total seventy years. "Or even by reason of strength." If by reason of great strength a man lives longer, yet his days are only "four-score years." "Yet is their pride but travail and vanity." All the greatness and power that a man has during these years are but travail and vanity. Why? Because "It is speedily gone *(gaz)*, and we fly away." In anger we hasten to fly away and die. The word *gaz* means to pass away, as in the verse: "they shall be cut down *(nagozu)* and he shall pass away" (Nahum 1:12), and as in the verse: "And brought across (va-yagoz) quails" (Numbers 11:31). [11] "Who knoweth the power of Thine anger?" In the few days he has who can acquire the heart to know the power of Thine anger and to fear Thee? "And Thy wrath is as Thy fear." Just as Thou art feared, so is Thy wrath fierce to punish sinners. [12] "So teach us to number our days." As at the beginning Thou didst make known that the number of our days would be long. If we knew that we would live long we would be able to acquire a heart and to "get us a heart of wisdom." Ve navi (get us) means "to bring." [13] "Return, O Lord." From Thy fierce anger. "And let it repent Thee." Think well of Thy servants. [14] "O satisfy us in the morning with Thy mercy." On the day of the redemption and the salvation, which is the morning after all the misfortunes, the groaning and the darkness. "That we may rejoice and be glad all our days." This means in all the misfortunes which happened to us in those days. [15] "Make us glad according to the days wherein Thou hast afflicted us." In the days of our Messiah let us rejoice for as many days as the days in which we have been afflicted in exile and as the days in which we have seen evil. [17] "And let the graciousness of the Lord our God be upon us." His Divine Presence and His consolations. "Establish Thou also upon us the work of our hands." Konanah (Establish Thou) is in the verbal form used to suggest prayer, as in the forms shamerah, shafetah. The words "Establish Thou upon us" are repeated because one is a reference to the work of the Sanctuary, when he (Moses) blessed them that the Divine Presence should rest on the work of their hands in the building of the Sanctuary, and the other that there should be blessing on the work of their hands in general.

Note Rashi's interesting interpretation of this Psalm as a plea to God to give us a longer span of years. Our life is too short. If only we could live longer, as man did at the beginning, we could acquire wisdom and we would not sin. The rest of our comments here follow Rashi verse by verse. 1. A skillful Midrashic note. There are eleven Psalms from here to Psalm 101, the next ten of which are not ascribed to any author, they are anonymous. So the Midrash ascribes them to Moses, the author of this Psalm. 2. Olam can mean "everlasting" (its original meaning) but also "world," hence Rashi's comment. 3. Note Rashi's fine interpretation. Where does God say: "Return?" He "says" it when He brings sufferings to men. The noble man sees in the sufferings God brings to him a "call" from God to him to lead a better life. 4. Rashi understands "and as a watch in the night" to mean that this portion of the night is counted together with the day the Psalmist has mentioned. The idea of a "day of God" is, of course, Midrashic. 5-6 Rashi translates: "In the morning it passeth away" (yaḥalof). 9. The usual English translation of hegeh as "a tale that is told" is not too different from what Rashi says. 10. Rashi's point here is that the Hebrew says: "The days of our years are with them (bahem) three-score years." Rashi understands this to mean the years together with the sins. 13. God cannot "repent," hence Rashi's paraphrase. 14. Note Rashi's fine comment on "be glad all our days" to mean that if we know that at the end of it all we shall find God's mercy, then even in our sufferings we shall rejoice. 17. The verbal form to which Rashi calls attention is known as the cohortative.

Ibn Ezra

How should the Bible be interpreted?
Why was Moses adopted by Pharaoh's daughter?
"Thou shalt not covet." How is this possible?
Did Moses write the whole of the Pentateuch?

Abraham ibn Ezra (died 1167), Spanish thinker and Biblical commentator, wrote one of the greatest of all commentaries to the Pentateuch, the Sefer Ha-Yashar, "Book of the Upright," as well as commentaries on the other books of the Bible. The Sefer Ha-Yashar was first printed in Naples in 1488 and has since been reprinted many times together with the text in various editions of the Pentateuch. The work has as its aim the understanding of the plain meaning of the text. Ibn Ezra has a cryptic style, often conveying elaborate ideas in two or three words, and this frequently makes it difficult to know exactly what it is that he is trying to say. A number of super-commentaries have therefore been written to explain his meaning.

A. HOW SHOULD THE BIBLE BE INTERPRETED?

The following is Abraham ibn Ezra's introduction to the Sefer Ha-Yashar. This is a most important document for the history of Biblical exegesis because in it Ibn Ezra describes four methods of interpretation which were used in his day and which he rejects and a fifth which he accepts. This introduction is written in rhyme but, of course, it is impossible to reproduce this in translation.

In the name of God, Great and Tremendous, I begin to expound the Torah. I pray Thee, O God of my father Abraham, do kindness to Thy servant Abraham. And let Thy words be a light to Thy servant,

son of Thy servant Meir (meaning "light"). And from the salvation of Thy face let help come to the son of Thy handmaiden who is called Ben Ezra (the family name). This is the *Sefer Ha-Yashar* of Abraham the poet. It is bound with the cords of grammar and improved by the eye of knowledge. Whoever lends it his support will be made happy.

The aforementioned Abraham the Sephardi declares that commentators to the Torah adopt one of five methods.

The first method is lengthy and diffuse, remote from the souls of the men of our generation. If we use the illustration of a circle and place the truth at its center point, then this method can only be compared to the periphery of the circle, which goes round and round only to return to the place where it began. Great men have adopted this method, among them the sages of the academies in the Arabic kingdom like Rabbi Isaac who compiled two whole books on the first section of Genesis up to "were finished" (Genesis 2:1) and he had still not finished, so diffuse was he. On the verse: "Let there be light" (Genesis 1:3) he mentions those who believe in two gods, one of light, the other of darkness, but he himself walked in darkness without knowing it. When he came to comment on the verse: "The earth brought forth vegetation" (Genesis 1:12) he quoted foreign sciences. Rabbi Saadiah, Gaon of the Exile, trod this path. On the verse: "Let there be lights" (Genesis 1:14) he introduced the opinions of others, describing the movements of the heavenly bodies according to the views of the astronomers. The same applies to Rabbi Samuel ben Hofni who gathered wind in his fists when he came to comment on the verse: "Jacob left Beer-sheba" (Genesis 28:10). Here he mentioned at length each prophet by name and how many times each had gone into exile. Whatever value there is in knowing the travels of the prophets, the only value of this commentary is in its length. On the verse: "He had a dream" (Genesis 28:12), he wrote a treatise on dream interpretation and on what people see when they are asleep. If one wishes to study external sciences let him study them from the works of the experts in these matters and let him examine the proofs they offer and test if they are valid. The Geonim only quote from these works without recording any of the proofs offered. Some of them had no knowledge of the ancient sages and of their deductive methods.

It is not too clear to which Rabbi Isaac he alludes here. The "sages of the academies in the Arabic kingdom" are the Geonim (Excellences), the heads of the great academies at Sura and Pumbedita in what is now Iraq (and was then Babylon). Such a Gaon was Saadiah (882-942); another was Samuel ben Hofni (died 1034). Ibn Ezra puns on the latter's name which can mean a "fist." "Gathering the wind in his fists" is a verse in the Book of Proverbs (30:4). Note Ibn Ezra's strongly developed critical sense. For all the respect he has for these famous teachers, he derides their approach to Biblical exegesis. They are too diffuse. Instead of getting to the truth and coming to the point they go on about it and around it. A good commentator, says Ibn Ezra in so many words, should confine himself to the matter in hand and not introduce all kinds of interesting but irrelevant material. A comment on Jacob's dream is not the place for a detailed examination of dreams, nor is a comment on the verse dealing with the creation of sun, moon and stars the appropriate occasion for a lecture on astronomy. If someone wishes to study astronomy let him do so by reading the books the experts on the subject have written and not rely on ill-digested material quoted from astronomical works by Biblical commentators. So the first method, of which Ibn Ezra strongly disapproves, is that of cumbersome, irrelevant exposition. He now turns to the second method of which his disapproval is far more severe.

The second method is that chosen by the distorters, albeit they are Jews. They imagine that they have reached the very point of the circle but in reality they have not the faintest idea where it is to be found. This is the way of the Sadducees such as Anan and Benjamin and Ben Mashiaḥ and Joshua and the way of whoever does not believe in the words of the bearers of religious tradition, turning from it either to the right or to the left. Each of these men interprets the Bible as he sees fit and this applies even to the commandments and the laws. Such persons are ignorant of the forms of the Hebrew language so that they are even guilty of grammatical errors. How can anyone rely on their opinions in connection with the precepts since at every moment they change their minds, going from one extreme to the other, because you will not find a single precept explained fully in the Torah itself. I shall give you only one example but it is of great significance, involving the penalty of *karet* with regard to eating on the Day of Atonement, eating leaven on Pass-

over and bringing the paschal lamb to the Temple when one is unclean. It involves, too, the seven rest days of the festivals, the festival sacrifices, the *sukkah* and blowing of the shofar. Nowhere in the Torah do we find rules governing the calendar, so how do we know the method of calculating the months? These castaways, poor in learning, rely on the verse: "they shall serve for signs and for the set times" (Genesis 1:14), but they are evidently unaware that "they shall serve" is in the plural and refers to both the luminaries and the stars. Furthermore, they argue that the "and" in the verse is superfluous, so that "for signs" is connected with "for the set times." But anyone who argues thus will only be defended by one biased by friendship. Even though we do find a superfluous "and" in two or three places in Scripture, how do we know that this is one of them since the number of necessary "ands" runs into thousands? The meaning of "Who appointedst the moon for seasons" (Psalms 104: 19) is not as these whose loins totter (Psalms 69:24) would have it. Even if Scripture had said: "And the moon shall be for a sign for the set times" (which it does not), who will give us the sign that the reference is to the sacred set seasons of the Lord? For there are numerous references to set times in the Pentateuch, the Prophets and the Hagiographa (i.e., not to sacred set times) and if the reference were to the set seasons of the Lord, Scripture would have stated this explicitly.

The most powerful challenge to Rabbinic Judaism in the Middle Ages came from the sect of the Karaites (from the root kara, "to read," i.e., those who read Scripture as it stands while rejecting all the Rabbinic interpretations). Ibn Ezra calls them here Sadducees, but this is the name of a much older sect which flourished in the period of the Second Temple, though many of the ideas of the Sadducees reappear later in the writings of the Karaites. Ibn Ezra as a staunch Rabbinic Jew takes the strongest exception to the second method of Biblical interpretation, that of the Karaites. This ignores entirely all that the Rabbis had taught by tradition and tried to discover unaided the meaning of the Biblical verses. Thus the Karaites believed that they were right at the center of the circle since they tried to discover the meaning of the Biblical texts without any preconceived notions. Ibn Ezra retorts that without traditions many of the Biblical verses are obscure. It is impossible to know what they mean unless we rely on the tradition of the Rabbis, which, Ibn

Ezra believed, goes back ultimately, as the Rabbis say, to Moses himself who received the Torah from God. (There are still a few Karaites left, some of them in the State of Israel, and these still follow the Karaite interpretations of the laws). Ibn Ezra mentions here four prominent Karaite teachers: Anan ben David (middle of Eighth Century); Benjamin ben Moses Nahawendi (Eighth-Ninth Centuries); Hassan ben Mashiaḥ (Ninth or Tenth Century); Joshua ben Judah Abu Al-Faraj Furkan (middle of the Eleventh Century). Ibn Ezra proceeds to show how the Bible is unintelligible without the traditional interpretation. Karet means to be "cut off," understood by the Rabbis as a kind of decree of death by God. This is the penalty stated in the Pentateuch for a number of offenses which have to do with the festivals, e.g., eating on the Day of Atonement, eating leaven on Passover, bringing the paschal lamb, in Temple times, in a state of impurity, i.e., when one had been in contact with a corpse. There are moreover seven restdays of the festivals in the Pentateuch, i.e., the first and last days of Passover and Tabernacles, the day of Pentecost, the day of the New Year (Rosh Hashanah) and the Day of Atonement, and there is the duty of eating in the sukkah (the tabernacle) on the festival of Tabernacles and of blowing the shofar on Rosh Hashanah. All these, of significance also to the Karaites since they are all mentioned explicitly in Scripture, depend on a knowledge of the Jewish calendar—for if we do not know how to work out the calendar we do not know when any of the festivals fall. Now, argues Ibn Ezra, we know the calendar by Rabbinic tradition, but what do the Karaites do in the absence of any such tradition? They must perforce rely on the Scriptural verses themselves, but there are no detailed descriptions of the calendar in the Bible. Ibn Ezra knows that the Karaite reply to this is the verse in Genesis which means, as they understand it, that one calculates the calendar according to the movements of the moon. The Karaites read the verse: "They (the moon) shall be for signs (for a sign) for the set-times." Ibn Ezra objects that, first, the plural is used so that the verse must refer to sun, moon (the "luminaries") and stars and not to the moon alone. Secondly, the verse does not say "for signs for the set times" but "for signs and for the set times" (the Hebrew letter vav is used for "and"). The Karaites reply that the vav is superfluous. Now Ibn Ezra does admit that here and there in Scripture one does find a superfluous vav, but such a thing is very unusual and unless there is clear evidence to the contrary one must interpret every vav as necessary since the necessary vav occurs in thousands of instances, while the superfluous vav is exceedingly

rare. A further point Ibn Ezra makes is that in the absence of tradi-
tion the Karaites have no evidence that "set times" means the
festivals, since this term is used frequently in Scripture for all man-
ner of purely secular occasions. Ibn Ezra now embarks on a lengthy
but brilliant astronomical refutation of Karaite views on the calen-
dar. We have omitted this as too technical and beyond the scope of
this book. Ibn Ezra concludes this part of his introduction by re-
peating that we must rely on tradition and that therefore any
exposition of the Bible which claims to be authentic must take the
Rabbinic tradition into account. We take up the argument with Ibn
Ezra's refutation of the third method.

**The third method is a way of darkness and obscurity. It lies en-
tirely beyond the circle. This is the method of those who invent
mysterious interpretations for all the passages in Scripture. It is
their belief that the Torah and the precepts are riddles. I shall not
spend much time in refuting this thoroughly confused method. The
words of the Torah are never less than straightforward. In one
thing only are these people right. This is that every precept of the
Torah, whether great or small, must be measured in the balance of
the heart into which God has implanted some of His wisdom. Therefore if there appears something in the Torah which seems to contradict reason or to refute the evidence of our senses then here one
should seek for the solution in a figurative interpretation. For
reason is the foundation of everything. The Torah was not given to
men who cannot reason and man's reason is the angel which
mediates between him and his God. It follows that wherever we
find something in the Torah that is not contrary to reason we must
understand it in accordance with its plain meaning and accept it
as saying what it seems to say, believing that this is its true
meaning. We should not grope about as the blind in the dark grope
for the wall. Why should we understand as mysteries things which
are perfectly clear as they stand? Even though there are instances
where a verse has two meanings, both of which are clear, one referring to the body and the other to the mind, such as "circumcision of the flesh" and "uncircumcised of heart," and even though
the narrative of the tree of knowledge, for instance, can only be
understood in a figurative sense, yet in these instances the figurative meaning is evident on the surface. It may be that the meaning**

is not too evident but will become clear when the wise man opens his eyes to see more deeply into the text. For even certain organs of a man's body have more than one function such as the nostrils, the tongue and the two legs.

The third method with which Ibn Ezra takes issue is that of the allegorists. These refuse to understand the Torah literally, but argue that beneath the surface there are mysteries and secrets which they try to uncover. For instance, the story of Abraham sending away his maidservant Hagar is interpreted by Philo to mean not what it says but to be a figurative way of stating that the perfect man must send away his desire for worldly things. Ibn Ezra considers such a method to be unreasonable. It has nothing to do with the text and is way out beyond the circle. If nothing is what it seems in Scripture, then the human reason has no part to play in the interpretation of Scripture. Note Ibn Ezra's remarkable definition of the human intellect as the angel which mediates between him and his God. In one thing only are the allegorists correct, continues Ibn Ezra. This is that there are some Scriptural passages which cannot possibly be taken literally. Here the figurative interpretation is certainly called for. For instance, the story of the tree of knowledge seems to cry out for a figurative interpretation since one does not "eat" knowledge. Also the Biblical references to "circumcising the heart" can hardly have been intended literally. But in these instances the figurative interpretation is the plain meaning of the verse and can clearly be seen as such. But, argues Ibn Ezra, we have no right at all to take verses which are perfectly clear in the literal meaning and interpret them allegorically.

The fourth method is near to the point. A whole group of commentators have followed it. This is the method pursued by the sages in the lands of the Greeks and Romans who are not overmuch concerned with a balanced view but rely on the homiletical method such as is found in the works *Lekaḥ Tov* and *Or Enayim*. But if we already have Midrashim in the works of the ancients, what purpose can the later authors have in simply repeating them? Actually we find that frequently one Midrash contradicts another. Other Midrashim have to be understood figuratively, not literally, such as the Midrashim saying that the Torah existed two thousand years before the world was created. This is perfectly true, but only if understood figuratively. Many do not understand it in this way, but

it can hardly be taken literally. This is because a year is composed of days and the measurement of days and minutes depends on the sphere—so how could there have been a day, to say nothing of two days or a year or two thousand years, before the creation of the sphere?

The Rabbinic Midrashic method frequently uses the Scriptural text merely as a peg on which to hang certain ideas. The concern of the Midrash is not so much with the text itself as with the ideas that can be read into it. The word Midrash is from the root darash, "to investigate," i.e., to uncover various layers of meaning in the text. But this method is homiletical; that is to say, it is the method of a preacher who uses his text with the primary object of teaching his listeners ideas valuable in themselves to be sure but not necessarily conveyed by the text. The "lands of the Greeks and Romans" are the countries of Christian Europe. Ibn Ezra traveled widely throughout his life and was familiar at first hand with Jewish life in different communities. Lekah Tov and Or Enayim are late collections of earlier Midrashim. Ibn Ezra feels that there is not much point in having such collections, since those who wish to read Midrash can avail themselves of the earlier Midrashic collections. Ibn Ezra is not opposed to the Midrashic-homiletical method as such. He remarks here that it is near to the point at the center of the circle. But he argues that this method should be seen as a rather fanciful attempt to read ideas out of the text, as a kind of poetry rather than a true exposition of the Bible. We find, for instance, that Midrashim frequently contradict one another so that they cannot all be true. Some Midrashic ideas cannot possibly be taken at their face value. For instance, there is a Midrashic saying that the Torah existed for two thousand years before the world was created. Ibn Ezra argues that this is a piece of poetry, it has to be understood figuratively, e.g., that the world is based on the truth of the Torah and so forth. But it is quite impossible to take literally the idea of two thousand years before the world came into being. Ibn Ezra speaks here in terms of the astronomical knowledge of his day in which the heavenly bodies were seen as attached to a great "sphere" which revolved around the earth. We have a different picture today, but his argument is not affected. Time, in the sense of days, years, hours and minutes, is measured by the movements of the sun and the earth so how can one possibly speak of "two thousand years" before there was a world at all? We omit the rest of Ibn Ezra's consideration of the fourth method because it is highly technical.

*Briefly, what he does is to quote further Midrashim which are fine
as poetry but become absurd if taken too seriously. For example, the
very first letter of the Torah is bet. The Midrash remarks that this
is because the word for "blessing," berachah, begins with a bet.
God created the world with His blessing. Quite a pleasant idea, but
if taken literally it is ridiculous since, as Ibn Ezra points out, there
are numerous Hebrew words which begin with a bet and yet express
the exact opposite of any idea of blessing. Ibn Ezra concludes this
section: "The end of the matter is that there is no end to the
homiletical method." He has now described four methods: 1) That of
lengthy exposition of irrelevant topics; 2) The literal exposition of
the Karaites which rejects Rabbinic tradition; 3) The method of the
allegorists which strays far from the plain meaning; 4) The
Midrashic-homiletical method. Ibn Ezra finds all four inadequate
and he now turns to the fifth method which he finds sound and
which is the one he adopts in his Commentary.*

**My Commentary is based on the fifth method. This is the method
that seems right to me in the presence of the Lord. Him alone do I
fear and in matters concerning the Torah I shall show no favoritism.
First I shall investigate with all the power at my command the
grammatical form of each word and then I shall explain its meaning
to the best of my ability. You must look for the explanation of each
word in the place where that word first occurs. For instance, you
will find my comment on "heaven" in the first verse of Genesis. This
is the method I shall adopt. I shall not refer to the reasons given by
the traditional scholars why a word is sometimes written in full and
sometimes defectively, since all they have to say is merely homiletics. It simply happens to be the case that Scripture sometimes
writes a word in full and sometimes omits an unpronounced letter
for the sake of brevity. If they persist in giving a reason for full
and defective spellings, perhaps they would be good enough to
teach us how to rewrite the Scriptural books. Moses, for example,
writes: *Yimloch* ("the Lord shall reign," Exodus 15:18) without a
vav whereas the editors of the book of Proverbs write the same
word with a *vav* in the verse: "For a servant when he reigneth"
(Proverbs 30:22) and the lapse of time between Moses and the editors of Proverbs was of many years. The reasons given by the traditionalists are all right for children. Also a correct interpretation does**

not involve any textual emendation. The Targum of the Torah in Aramaic is accurate. The author of this work explains every difficulty for us. Even though he is addicted to the Midrashim we recognize that even more was he devoted to the true sense of the Hebrew language. It is only that he wished to add further reasons since the plain meaning can be grasped even by the stupid. For instance, he does not render the word *iroh* (Genesis 49:11) as "foal" but in terms of "building the city" and he renders *atono* (ass's colt) in the same verse in terms of "the gate of the entrance" to the Temple (Ezekiel 40:15). The plain meaning of a verse is not affected by its Midrashic interpretation for there are seventy faces to the Torah. But in connection with the laws, rules and regulations, where there are two differing interpretations of a verse and one of them is in accord with the views of the bearers of the tradition (the Rabbis), all of whom were righteous men, then with all the strength we have we must rely on the accuracy of what they say. God forbid that we should have anything to do with the Sadducean claim that the tradition contradicts Scripture and grammar. It is rather the case that our ancient teachers were true and all their words true. May the Lord God of truth lead His servant in the way of truth.

Ibn Ezra says that he will allow no favoritism, that is, he will be critical of other commentators when he feels that they do not do justice to the text. Ibn Ezra's point about full and defective texts is this: In Hebrew the vowels are not written in the scrolls, only the consonants, but some consonants serve as vowel letters. The letter vav, for example, frequently serves as an indication that the "o" sound is to be pronounced. It sometimes happens that these vowel letters are omitted as not really necessary. When a word is written in "full" it contains the vowel letters. When it is written "defectively," it is written without the vowel letters. Why is a word written now in one way and now in another? Ibn Ezra believes that this is not a legitimate question. It just happens to be the case that there is no consistency in spelling. Those who recorded Scripture simply did not concern themselves with this matter and their choice of whether a word is to be spelled full or defectively was purely arbitrary. Consequently, the efforts of the "traditionalists" to give in each instance a reason for that particular spelling is futile. Some of their "reasons" are pleasant homiletics and they provide an innocent amusement for children but, Ibn Ezra suggests, for the mature student it is all a waste of time. He proves this by referring to the word *yimloch, written one way by Moses and another way by the editors of Proverbs. Now here surely, he argues, the search for consistency is ridiculous since so much time had elapsed between Moses and the editors of Proverbs. It is as if someone today would try to discover a clever reason why Shakespeare spells "colour" with a "u" and in the United States it is spelled "color" without the "u." There is no "reason." It simply happens that the spelling has changed over the years. Moreover, the search for consistency will at times demand that a word spelled one way in the scrolls should be altered to another, whereas the "correct interpretation," i.e., Ibn Ezra's, does not involve any textual emendation. In Rabbinic times the Torah was translated into Aramaic so that people could understand it, Aramaic being their normal, everyday tongue. The Aramaic translation that has come down to us from those days is called the Targum (translation). Ibn Ezra is impressed by the translator's great accuracy and knowledge of Hebrew, even though he is very fond of the Midrashic tradition. For instance, he feels obliged at times to give a less obvious interpretation, as he does when he interprets a verse dealing with a "foal" and an "ass's colt" as referring, in fact, to the building of the Temple (taking* iroh *to mean "his city"—Jerusalem). There is no great harm in this since the Torah does have seventy "faces," i.e., each verse, say the Rabbis, can be interpreted in no fewer than seventy different ways. But the plain meaning must never be lost sight of except where to accept the plain meaning would contradict a law as handed down by the Rabbinic tradition. If we followed the plain meaning even here, we would be like the Karaites whose opinion Ibn Ezra has previously attacked. Thus Ibn Ezra's method involves a keen search for the plain meaning of Scripture, aided by a sound knowledge of Hebrew grammar and the Hebrew language.*

B. WHY WAS MOSES ADOPTED BY PHARAOH'S DAUGHTER?

The thoughts of God are so deep, who can know the mysterious way in which He moves? By Him alone are all actions weighed. It is possible that God brought it about that Moses would be raised in the royal palace so that his soul would be able to attain to a high degree through education and study there provided and he would not have the base, ignoble soul of those raised among slaves. You see that Moses slew the Egyptian (Exodus 2:12) when the latter had been guilty of oppression and Moses also saved the daughters of Midian from the shepherds (Exodus 2:15-19) when the shepherds

aggressively used the water the girls had drawn from the well. There is a further possible reason. If Moses had been brought up among his own brethren, who would then have known him from his infancy, they would have had no respect for him, looking on him simply as one of themselves.

Ibn Ezra is fond of psychological observations. Moses, as the future leader of Israel, had to be given an aristocratic training to equip him to fight oppression and not to be servile to the aggressors. Furthermore, familiarity breeds contempt. The Israelites required a leader whom they could respect and so he had to be one of them and yet not one of them. What was required was a prince who was at the same time a brother.

C. "THOU SHALT NOT COVET" (EXODUS 20:14). HOW IS THIS POSSIBLE?

Many people are puzzled by this commandment. How is it possible for a man not to desire in his heart whatever is pleasant to his eye? I shall now give you an illustration. Imagine a peasant of intelligence who sees a beautiful princess. His heart has no desire to live with her for he knows such a thing to be quite impossible. He is not a lunatic who, though he knows it to be impossible, longs to have wings to fly in the sky. No man has a desire to marry his mother, even if she is a beautiful woman, for she has trained him from his infancy to know that she is forbidden to him. In the same way every sensible person must know that a beautiful wife or wealth are not provided for a man by his wisdom and knowledge but are apportioned to him by God. As Ecclesiastes says: "shall leave it for his portion" (2:21) and as the Rabbis say: Children, life and sustenance do not depend on a man's merit but on his good fortune. Consequently, the wise man will not covet or desire something that belongs to his neighbor. Since he knows that God has forbidden to him his neighbor's wife, she becomes even more remote to him than the princess to the peasant. That is why such a man will rejoice in what he has and it will never enter his head to covet or desire something that does not belong to him. He appreciates that since God does not want him to have it, no matter how much he uses power or plans or schemes he will be unable to obtain it. So he will trust in his Creator to sustain him and will only do that which is good in His sight.

An interesting understanding of the tenth commandment. The problem is how can the desires of the heart be controlled, how can a man help himself from coveting the wife or the property of another man? Ibn Ezra replies that a man only desires that which he believes he can attain. The psychological motivation of coveting is that a man believes that if he tries hard enough he can get that which he wants so badly even though it does belong to his neighbor. But the man of faith, with complete trust in God, will lack the psychological motivation to covet. For such a man has come to see that no matter how much skill he exercises and how subtle his schemes, he can never get that which God has given to someone else. God in His wisdom gives to each person that which He wants to give. It is not a matter of "merit" but of each person having his God-given "portion." Thus the tenth commandment is, for Ibn Ezra, a command for a man to have trust in God, to be the kind of person who is so convinced that he can never have that which God has allotted to his neighbor, that he has no desire to attain it any more than a sane person has a desire to fly with wings or a peasant to marry a princess.

D. DID MOSES WRITE THE WHOLE OF THE PENTATEUCH?

Comment on the verse: "These are the words which Moses spoke unto all Israel beyond the Jordan" (Deuteronomy 1:1). The difficulty here is that if, as the tradition holds, Moses wrote the whole of the Pentateuch including this verse, why did he call the side of the Jordan on which he stood "beyond the Jordan"? This expression only makes sense to someone writing in Israel, which Moses never entered. This would appear to suggest that some parts of the Pentateuch were written after Moses. Ibn Ezra accepts this, but because it is a very radical departure from the tradition he remarks on it only by hint. This interpretation of Ibn Ezra is given in the fourteenth century commentary to Ibn Ezra written by Joseph Bonfils (Zaphnath-paaneah, Heidelberg, 1911) and, centuries later, by Spinoza. It was also understood by the Sixteenth Century historian Azariah de Rossi (Maor Enayim, Vol. 11 ed. Cassel, p. 324) who takes Ibn Ezra to task for daring to make such a suggestion. Some commentators have, however, given the passage a more orthodox interpretation, e.g., that Moses was transported across time when he wrote certain parts of the Pentateuch, so that he wrote as one observing the events at a later period, but it is unlikely that this is what Ibn Ezra meant.

Beyond the Jordan **If you understand the secret of the twelve, and of "And Moses wrote," and of "And the Canaanite was then in the land," and of "In the mount where the Lord was seen," and of "Behold his bedstead was a bedstead of iron," you will discover the truth.**

The secret of the twelve probably refers to the last twelve verses of the Pentateuch (Deuteronomy chapter 34). These describe how Moses went up to die on the mountain and he did not come down again so that he could not have written this chapter. The words "And Moses wrote" (Exodus 24:4; Numbers 33:2; Deuteronomy 31:9) suggest that someone other than Moses wrote the words "And Moses wrote." "And the Canaanite was then in the land" (Genesis 12:6) suggests that they were no longer in the land when this was written, but in Moses' day they were still there. "In the mount where the Lord is seen" (Genesis 22:14) is understood as referring to the Temple which had not yet been built in Moses' day. "Behold, his bedstead was a bedstead of iron" (Deuteronomy 3:11) speaks of the bedstead of the giant Og, king of Bashan, who was slain by Moses toward the end of the latter's life, while the words seem to imply that the bedstead was pointed out as an exhibit in the equivalent of the local museum long after Og had been dead. It is because of passages such as this scattered through his commentaries that Ibn Ezra is sometimes said to be the forerunner of modern Biblical criticism, that is the literary analysis of Scripture in order to determine who wrote what and when he wrote it.

Rashbam

How should the Bible be interpreted?
The meaning of Moses' argument
How are the Ten Commandments to be understood?

*Rabbi Samuel ben Meir was born near Troyes in France around 1085
and he died around 1174. He is known as Rashbam (after the initial
letters of his name: Rabbi Shemuel ben Meir). His mother was
Rashi's daughter. His Commentary to the Pentateuch has frequently.
been printed together with the text. We have seen that Rashi,
although very fond of the Midrash, tries to get at the peshat, the
"plain meaning" of the text. Rashbam, as he says in the first piece
we quote, is not convinced that Rashi really succeeded in uncovering
the peshat, and he seeks to make good this lack. He is, consequently,
of all the medieval commentators, one of the two or three whose
findings really tell us a good deal about what the text actually says.*

A. HOW SHOULD THE BIBLE BE INTERPRETED?

Comment to Genesis 37:2: "These are the generations of Jacob.
Joseph, being seventeen years old . . . " Rashi, in his comment to
the verse, quotes the "plain meaning," that the words "These are
the generations of Jacob" are a kind of heading to the later
narrative in which the history of Jacob's offspring is told. But Rashi
goes on to quote a Midrashic interpretation which reads: "These
are the generations of Jacob-Joseph . . . " and the meaning is said
to be that Joseph's life story closely resembled that of Jacob. Rashi

*knows full well that this is only Midrash but he records it
nevertheless. Rashbam, on the other hand, is more impatient of
Midrashic method. In this section he first stresses the importance
of understanding the "plain meaning" and then proceeds to give it
in connection with our narrative.*

Lovers of reason should understand it well that, as our Rabbis tell
us, no Scriptural verse ever loses its plain meaning. Although it is
also true that the main aim of the Torah is to teach us laws,
doctrines and rules of conduct which are derived by hint or by the
use in Scriptural verses of superfluous words or by means of the
thirty-two rules of Rabbi Eliezer ben Rabbi José the Galilean or
the thirteen rules of Rabbi Ishmael. In their piety the early
scholars devoted all their time to the Midrashic explanations, which
contain, indeed, the main teachings of the Torah. But, as a result,
they became unfamiliar with the deeper aspects of the text's plain
meaning. Furthermore, the Sages say: "Do not allow your children
to meditate too much on the Bible." And the Sages also say: "It is of
value when one studies the Bible, but there is no greater value
when one studies Talmud." As a result of all this they were not so
familiar with the plain meaning of Scripture. As it is said in the
Talmud: "I had reached the age of eighteen and by that time I
was intimately acquainted with the whole of the Talmud, yet I had
not realized that no Scriptural verse ever loses its plain meaning."
Our Master, Rabbi Solomon, my mother's father, who illumined the
eyes of all those in exile, and who wrote commentaries to the Torah,
the Prophets and the Hagiographa, also set himself the task of
elucidating the plain meaning of the Scripture. And I, Samuel, son
of his son-in-law Meir, may the memory of the righteous be for a
blessing, argued it out with him (Rashi). He admitted to me that if
he had the time he would have written new commentaries in accordance with the fresh interpretations of the plain meaning which
are thought of day by day.

*Rashbam here considers a problem which exercised the minds of
many of the commentators whose work is quoted in this book. They
were impressed by the demand for an understanding of the plain
meaning of Scripture and they know, moreover, that the Midrash
(or derash—"exposition," "homily") was frequently fanciful and
remote from the plain meaning (the peshat). But, on the other hand,*

many of the laws as understood by the Rabbinic tradition were derived from Scripture by the Midrashic method. The Karaites (see the section on Ibn Ezra) resorted to the plain meaning, but their findings were completely at variance with Rabbinic law. The general attitude of the medieval commentators was to accept the Midrash when a law was based on it, but otherwise to accept the plain meaning. But in practice, this did not always work out so well. As Rashbam says here, the piety of the earlier scholars made them more than a little apprehensive of simple reliance on the peshat, even where no law was at stake. Rashbam appears to argue that in the narrative portions, where no laws are involved, the plain meaning should always be preferred to the more fanciful exegesis of the Midrash. (This is not very different from Ibn Ezra's point of view, as can be seen from the section on him in this book). Rashbam remarks that the Rabbis themselves say that for all the Midrashic ideas read into a Scriptural verse, that verse never loses its plain meaning, i.e., we still have to understand what the verse says without any Midrashic elaborations. This is so, even though it is admitted that from the point of view of the laws and practises of Judaism it is the Midrash which counts ultimately. The thirty-two rules of Rabbi Eliezer ben Rabbi José and the thirteen rules of Rabbi Ishmael are means of uncovering deeper layers of meaning than the peshat. Rabbi Eliezer's rules are applied to the non-legal portions of Scripture and Rabbi Ishmael's to the legal. (Both these Sages lived in second century Judea, though many modern scholars consider the thirty-two rules to be, in fact, much later than Rabbi Eliezer, but fathered by him). The passage about undue meditation on the Bible is not very clear in the original, but Rashbam's interpretation that this is what it means was widely held in France in his day. According to Rashbam, Rashi admitted that his work would have been improved if he had devoted less time to Midrash and more to peshat. Rashbam now goes on to state his own understanding of the narrative here.

Now let the intelligent reader observe the comments of the earlier scholars to this verse. They explain it as meaning: "These are the events which happened to Jacob." But this is nonsense. For, as I have indicated in my comment on: "These are the generations of Noah" (Genesis 6:9), whenever the expression "These are the gener-ations" occurs, whether in the Torah or elsewhere in Scripture, the meaning is either a man's children or, in many instances, his grand-

children. Above in the Genesis portion it is written: "And Noah was five hundred years old; and Noah begot Shem, Ham, and Japheth" (Genesis 5:32). Scripture then goes on to explain that the world sinned but "Noah found grace in the eyes of the Lord" (Genesis 6:8). Scripture then goes on to record: "These are the generations of Noah" (Genesis 6:9), referring to his grandchildren. How so? Noah had three sons, says Scripture, and God commanded him to take them into the ark for twelve months. When they came out again sons were born to them after the flood (Genesis 10:1) until they totalled seventy and became seventy nations. As it is written: "and of these were the nations divided in the earth after the flood" (Genesis 10:32). The same applies to the Esau saga. The first section details the sons of Esau born to him in his father's place (Genesis 36:1-5). Then it says that he went into a land . . . (Genesis 36:6) and he settled in the mountain-land of Seir (Genesis 36:8). The narrative continues: "And these are the generations of Esau the father of the Edomites in mount Seir" (Genesis 36:9). And the whole portion deals in this way with the sons of Esau. Now, just as we find it stated of Esau that his sons were born in the land of his father before he went into a land away from his brother Jacob (Genesis 36:6) and that his grandchildren were born in the mountain-land of Seir, so, too, is it said of Jacob. Above it is written: "Now the sons of Jacob were twelve" (Genesis 35:22). And at the end it explains: "These are the sons of Jacob, that were born to him in Paddan-aram" (Genesis 35:26) and that he came unto Isaac his father (Genesis 35:27). So that Scripture has explained where the sons of Jacob were born, just as it explained where the sons of Esau were born. Now it goes on to explain: "And these are the generations of Jacob," namely, his grandchildren who were seventy in number (Genesis 46:27), and it describes how they were born. How so? Joseph was seventeen years old, says Scripture, and his brethren were jealous of him. As a result Judah went down from his brethren (Genesis 38:1) and he had sons in Adullam and in Chezib—Shelah and Perez and Zerah (chapter 38). The events transpired that Joseph was brought down to Egypt (Genesis 39:1) and in Egypt there were born to him Manasseh and Ephraim (Genesis 41:50-52). And eventually Joseph sent for his father and his household until there were seventy souls there. Moses was obliged to write all this because later on he rebuked the people by referring to this very thing: "Thy fathers went down into Egypt with threescore and ten persons . . . " (Deuteronomy 10:22).

Note Rashbam's grasp of the plain meaning in which our narrative is connected with the rest of the Pentateuch. This is an important idea, widely utilized in modern scholarship. It is no use explaining each little section on its own. Obviously a recurring expression like "These are the generations" is intended to present a pattern. Rashbam tries to demonstrate that there is a scheme of "generations" and, he claims, once this is grasped, it can be seen that our portion fits neatly into that scheme. There is no need to give any fanciful meaning to "generations." The word always means either children or grandchildren and in obedience to the scheme that has been detected we must here give it the meaning of grandchildren.

B. THE MEANING OF MOSES' ARGUMENT

Commentary on the verses: "And Moses said unto God: 'Who am I, that I should go unto Pharaoh, and that I should bring forth the children of Israel out of Egypt?' And He said: 'Certainly I will be with thee; and this shall be a token unto thee, that I have sent thee. When thou has brought forth the people out of Egypt, ye shall serve God upon this mountain'" (Exodus 3:11,12). The great difficulty here is the meaning of the final words. Many of Rashbam's predecessors explain the reference to the "mountain" to be to the Ten Commandments given later on Mount Sinai. But Rashbam finds this impossible. How would the fact that later on Israel received the Ten Commandments on the mountain, be a "token" to Moses for Pharaoh's benefit to demonstrate to Pharaoh that Moses had been sent by God?

Whoever wishes to grasp the plain meaning of these verses should pay heed to what I am about to write, for my predecessors completely failed to understand them. Moses replied to the things God had ordered him to carry out: to go to Pharaoh and to bring Israel out of Egypt by the command of Pharaoh. Moses replied to each of these in turn. He said: "Who am I, that I should go unto Pharaoh?" That is to say: Is it proper for a foreigner like me to enter the king's palace, even for the purpose of bringing him a gift or a present? "And that I should bring forth the children of Israel out of Egypt?" This means: Even if I were suited to enter Pharaoh's

presence, I am ignorant of what to say in order to convince him. Is Pharaoh so stupid that he should listen to me to set free from his land a great populace of useful slaves? What possible argument can I present to him to convince him to let me take them out with his permission? God replied to each objection in turn. First He said: "Certainly I will go with thee." This means: I will give thee the grace to find favor in the king's eyes, so that thou wilt enter Pharaoh's presence without fear. And in respect to this fear of Pharaoh, "this shall be a token unto thee, that I have sent thee." Thou hast seen from the burning bush (Exodus 3:2) that I (the angel speaking to Moses in God's name) am God's messenger. This is a token to thee to trust me that I will be with thee. As for thy second objection: "And that I should bring the children of Israel out of Egypt?" namely, what argument can I present to Pharaoh that he should listen to me to let them go free? My reply is that when thou hast brought forth the people out of Egypt, I now command thee, ye shall serve God upon this mountain and offer up there burnt-offerings. This, then, is the argument thou canst present to him, that thou desirest to lead the people to serve God, and when he hears this he will let them go. It is true that all this is not stated quite explicitly at this stage but it is so stated at the end of this portion: "And they shall hearken to thy voice. And thou shalt come, thou and the elders of Israel, unto the king of Egypt . . . And now let us go, we pray thee, three days' journey into the wilderness, that we may sacrifice . . . " (Exodus 3:18). And whenever Moses came to Pharaoh he said this to him. We find exactly the same thing recorded of Samuel. When God commanded him to anoint David, Samuel said to God: "If Saul hear it, he will kill me" (I Samuel 16:2). But God replied: "Take a heifer with thee, and say: I am come to sacrifice to the Lord" (ibid.). Here, too, in order cleverly to forestall the objection, He commanded Moses: "When thou hast brought forth the people out of Egypt . . . " and since I have now commanded it thou canst say so to Pharaoh. Those who offer any other explanation of these verses are completely in error.

Evidently, the dialogue between God and Moses received, as we have seen, many interpretations at the hands of the commentators who preceded Rashbam. Note his brusque dismissal of his predecessor's attempts both here and in the previous section and how confident he is of the correctness of his own views.

C. HOW ARE THE TEN COMMANDMENTS TO BE UNDERSTOOD?

Comment on the Ten Commandments, Exodus 20:2-14. The numbers are those of the verses on which Rashbam comments.

3. "Thou shalt have no other gods before Me." Because I alone brought thee out of Egypt (verse 2).

5. " . . . visiting the iniquity of the fathers upon the children unto the third and fourth generation of them that hate Me." If the children hate Me.

6. "and showing mercy unto the thousands of them that love Me and keep My commandments." This means to the third generations of the children, the fifth generations of the children, the tenth generations, the hundredth generations, the thousandth generations of the children, so that the term "thousands" refers to the thousandth generation of children. Thus there is no contradiction between the verses. According to the plain meaning, Scripture here speaks of the children and children's children. Children are one generation and children's children are a second generation, so that the children of the thousandth generation are referred to as the "thousands." In Deuteronomy, on the other hand, where there is mentioned neither children nor the third generation nor the fourth generation, it states: "Know therefore that the Lord thy God, He is God . . . that love Him and keep His commandments to a thousand generations" (Deuteronomy 7:9). The "thousand" referred to here is the same as the "thousands" of children in our verse.

7. "Thou shalt not take." All this belongs to the honor due to God, as does the command to keep the Sabbath in the next verse and the command to honor parents (verse 12) for their honor is compared to the honor of God, as it is written: "Honor the Lord with thy substance" (Proverbs 3:9).

8. "Remember the sabbath day." Wherever Scripture uses the expression "remember," the reference is to something that happened in the past. For example: "Remember the days of old . . . When the Most High gave to the nations their inheritance" (Deuteronomy 32:7,8). "Remember this day" forever, since in the past you went out of Egypt on this day (Exodus 13:3). "Remember, forget thou not, how thou didst make the Lord thy God wroth in the wilderness" (Deuteronomy 9:7). "Remember, O Lord, Thy compassions and Thy mercies; for they have been from of old" (Psalm 25:6). Here, too the meaning is: "Remember the sabbath day which came after the six days of creation" (Genesis 2:1-3). As the verse goes on to say: "for in six days the Lord made . . . " (verse 11). Remembering is mentioned here in order to sanctify the Sabbath and rest from work.

11. "Wherefore the Lord blessed the sabbath day." As I have noted in my commentary to Genesis, God blessed the Sabbath day in that when the day arrived God had already brought all His creatures into being with their needs provided for so that the Sabbath was blessed with all good things. Therefore He sanctified the Sabbath that we should rest on it as witnesses to God having rested, in that He first created all things and then rested.

13. "Thou shalt not murder (tirtzaḥ). Whenever Scripture uses the root ratzaḥ it refers to wanton killing. For example, "The murderer (ha-rotzeah) shall surely be put to death" (Numbers 35:18). "Hast thou murdered (haratzaḥta) and also taken possession?" (I Kings 21:19). "Righteousness lodged in her, but now murderers (meratze-him)" (Isaiah 1:21). But where Scripture uses the expression harigah ("killing") or mitah ("putting to death"), the meaning can either be wanton killing, as in the verse which speaks of Cain (Genesis 4:3) va-yahargehu, "and slew him," or it can mean judicial execution, as in the verse: "Thou shalt kill (ve-haragta) the woman" (Leviticus 20:16). As for the verse: "And this is the case of the murderer (ha-rotzeah) . . . whoso killeth his neighbor unawares . . ." (Deuteronomy 19:4), since the passage speaks of intentional homicide it says, but if the murder was committed unawares the perpetrator is not condemned. I argued this out with Christian scholars and they agreed with me. Even though in their translation of the Bible on the verse: "I put to death (amit), and I make alive" (Deuteronomy 32:39) they used the same Latin word as in "Thou shalt not murder," this is simply because they failed to grasp the subtleties of the language.

3. Rashbam reads this verse as following on the previous verse.

5. It would be unjust to visit the sins of the fathers on the children if the children are not themselves sinners. Hence Rashbam understands "them that hate Me" as referring to the children, not the fathers.

6. Rashbam's difficulty here is that the Hebrew uses the plural form la-alafim, which means literally "unto the thousands," whereas in the verse in Deuteronomy only one thousand is mentioned. Rashbam's solution is that "thousands" in our verse does not mean "thousands of generations" but "the thousands," i.e., those children (hence the plural) who will live in the thousandth generation. The usual English translation of this verse reads "unto the thousandth generation," but the Hebrew has only "the thousands."

7. The verse in Proverbs uses the term "honor" of God and the same term is used in our verse for parents, hence, say the Rabbis, God compares the honor of parents to His honor. Those who honor their parents honor God.

8. Rashbam's difficulty is why the term "remember" should be used of the Sabbath. The Sabbath comes round every week so one would not normally forget it. Rashbam's interesting explanation is the "Sabbath" referred to in our verse is the first Sabbath of creation.

11. What does it mean to say that God "blessed" the Sabbath? Rashbam replies that it refers to the first Sabbath which came after all creation was complete and there was only blessing.

13. Rashbam gives here an acute analysis of the three terms. Rashbam's reference is to the Latin version of the Bible known as the Vulgate. The Vulgate renders our verses as Non occides and uses the same word in Deuteronomy: Ego occidam. But, says Rashbam, this is due to a failure to distinguish between the precise meanings of the two words, the one referring to murder (tirtzaḥ); the other to natural death (amit). Rashbam was evidently familiar with the Vulgate and discussed Biblical interpretations with Christian scholars.

Kimḥi

How is Isaiah's Messianic vision to be understood?

David Kimḥi (1160-1235) lived all his life in Narbonne in France. He is called Redak *after the initial letters of his name (Rabbi David Kimḥi). Kimḥi is especially renowned as a Hebrew grammarian and as the author of commentaries to various books of the Bible. There is a passage in* Ethics of the Fathers *which reads: "If there is no kemaḥ ("flour"), there is no Torah," i.e., the scholar has to be able to earn a living, to eat, if he is to study the Torah. So influential did Kimḥi's commentaries become that this saying was applied to them: "If there is no kemaḥ (Kimḥi), there is no Torah," i.e., the Bible remains a closed book without Kimḥi's elucidation. Kimḥi's teachers were his father, Joseph, and his brother, Moses, both of whom he refers to in his commentaries. Kimḥi's commentary to the prophets is printed in many editions of the Bible. The following is his commentary to the book of Isaiah, chapter 11.*

A. HOW IS ISAIAH'S MESSIANIC VISION TO BE UNDERSTOOD?

"And there shall come forth a shoot out of the stock of Jesse, and a twig shall grow forth out of his roots" (Isaiah 11:1). Scripture places this portion, which speaks of the future Messianic age, next to the promises given to King Hezekiah mentioned in the previous chapter.

This is to say: Do not be astonished that such a great miracle was performed in the days of Hezekiah, the whole camp of the Assyrians meeting with its downfall in one moment, for an even greater miracle will be performed for Israel in the days of the Messiah, when the Israelites will be gathered in from exile. This will take place through the Messiah who is of Hezekiah's family. The reason Jesse is mentioned is because the first king of the dynasty (David) came from him. The meaning of *hoter* ("shoot") is a shaft, as Jonathan translates it. The prophet here speaks of the "stock" and the "roots" to signify that the tree which has been cut down will renew itself to produce shoots from its stock and roots. The "stock" is that part of the tree which remains above the ground. Shoots will spring up around this stock. They will also blossom forth from the roots that are beneath the soil. Since Israel has been exiled from its land for so many years and since its kingdom ceased, it is as if the tree had been cut down. But the stock and roots remain in the soil so that the prophet declares his hope that the stock will renew itself. The prophet declares that from the roots of Jesse and from his stock another fruitful branch will emerge. Once again there will be a king of Israel as before and even more than before. And he continues: "And the spirit of wisdom and understanding, the spirit of counsel and might, the spirit of knowledge and of the fear of the Lord" (verse 2), because it all comes from God. First, the prophet speaks of the spirit of the Lord and then he goes on to explain that this means "the spirit of wisdom and understanding, the spirit of counsel and might, the spirit of knowledge and of the fear of the Lord." "Wisdom" refers to that which a man has studied and knows and can draw on at any moment. "Understanding" is man's capacity to derive by deduction things he has not studied from those he has already mastered. "Counsel" refers to acquaintance and training in ethics and patterns of social conduct. "Knowledge and the fear of the Lord" both refer to God, i.e., that he will know God and fear Him.

These comments are self-explanatory. The Messiah is to be descended from Hezekiah and through him from David and David's father Jesse. Note Kimhi's method, used everywhere in his commentaries, of giving precise definitions, e.g., of the "stock," the "roots," "wisdom," "counsel" and so forth. In Talmudic times the Bible was read together with an Aramaic translation, which the

people, who spoke Aramaic, could understand. This is called the
Targum, "translation." The Targum to the Prophets is attributed to
the first century teacher Jonathan ben Uzziel, though modern
scholars are unanimous that the text we have of this Targum
cannot possibly be his; there are even references in it to such late
events as the rise of Islam. Kimḥi is fond of quoting this Targum
as he does here.

"And his delight *(vahariḥo)* **shall be in the fear of the Lord" (verse
3). Of anything easily sensed it can be said that it is smelled, since
to smell something is to experience a sensation easily attained, as
in the verse: "And he smelleth the battle afar off" (Job 39:25) and
the verse: "As a string of tow is broken when it smells the fire"
(Judges 16:9). And so the prophet says: "And his sense of smell
(from** *reaḥ,* **"smell") shall be acute in the fear of the Lord," namely,
without much reflection he will be able to sense which men are
good and which bad. He will not need to see things with his eyes or
hear them with his ears when he judges and rebukes men, for
without much reflection but by his knowledge and wisdom he will
be able to understand their deeds. My master and father, may his
memory be for a blessing, explained the word to mean "And his
speech," that is, the spirit of his mouth, as in the verse: "at my
sighing, at my cry" (Lamentations 3:56). The meaning would then be
that his speech will always be of the fear of the Lord.**

These verses speak of the qualities that will be found in the
Messiah. In verse 3 it is said: "Vahariḥo in the fear of the Lord."
This unusual word is sometimes rendered in English as "And his
delight shall be." Kimḥi, however, connects it with the word reaḥ,
"smell." The interesting interpretation which emerges is that the
Messiah will have such a keen "nose" for justice that when acting
as a judge he will be able to discern immediately who is right and
who wrong. Kimḥi gives another explanation of the word in the
name of his father. This connects the word with ruaḥ, "breath,"
hence "the breath of his mouth." Joseph Kimḥi's interpretation is
then: "And his speech shall be in (or of) the fear of the Lord."

**"But with righteousness shall he judge the poor, and rebuke with
uprightness for the meek of the land; and he shall smite the land
with the rod of his mouth, and with the breath of his lips shall he**

slay the wicked" (verse 4). The prophet refers to the "poor" and the "meek of the land" even though he (the Messiah) will judge all men with righteousness and uprightness, because it is the way of the world to show favoritism to the rich and powerful. Therefore it says that he will not do so, but in righteousness he will demand justice for the poor from the rich and he will rebuke the powerful on behalf of the meek to prevent them being wronged or oppressed in their weakness. The *lamed* of *le-anveˊ* means "for," like the *lamed* of: "*Imri-li* (say of me): He is my brother" (Genesis 20:13) and other such instances. "And he shall smite the land" means "he shall smite the wicked of the land." Since he has previously mentioned "the meek of the land," the opposite of those mentioned here, he relies on the intelligent reader to draw his own conclusion that this part of the verse has the same meaning. The end of the verse also makes it clear: "shall he slay the wicked." Apart from this it is obvious that the meaning is "the inhabitants of the land" (and not the land itself), namely, those who deserve to be smitten, because he has already stated "and rebuke with uprightness for the meek of the earth." The meaning of "the rod of his mouth" and "the breath of his lips" is that he will curse them and they will die, as it is written of the righteous: "Thou shalt also decree a thing, and it shall be established unto thee" (Job 22:28). Of Samuel the prophet it is said: "All that he saith cometh to pass" (I Samuel 9:6). And it is said of the prophet Elisha: "And he cursed them in the name of the Lord. And there came forth two she-bears out of the wood, and tore forty and two children of them" (II Kings 2:24).

The English translation of le-anveˊ *rightly renders the word as "for the meek of the land," i.e., for the sake of the meek of the land. Lamed generally means "to" but this does not make sense here. He will not rebuke the meek of the land, but rebuke the powerful who oppress them. (Note that Kimḥi's understanding of the verse is different from the usual English translation "And he shall decide with equity for the meek of the land"). Kimḥi points out that there are instances in Scripture of the lamed meaning "for" or "on behalf of." Abraham did not say to Sarah: "say to me" but "say of me," i.e., "for my sake." Kimḥi understands the end of the verse as referring to the Messiah cursing the oppressors and he quotes other instances in Scripture of the curse of a holy man taking effect.*

"And righteousness shall be the girdle of his loins, and faithfulness the girdle of his reins" (verse 5). The righteousness and faithfulness to which he holds fast will give him strength to prevent his loins from tottering. The verse describes the same thought twice, each time in different words.

Kimḥi, here and elsewhere, makes an important observation. This is that Scripture frequently repeats the same idea but in different words, as here: "And righteousness shall be the girdle of his loins," and the same thought in other words: "and faithfulness the girdle of his reins." Some commentators would try to discover a different meaning for each of these clauses but, according to Kimḥi, such an attempt is pointless and fails to appreciate the nature of Hebrew poetry which presses an idea home precisely by repeating it in different words. This feature of Hebrew poetry to which Kimḥi calls attention is called by modern scholars "parallelism."

"And the wolf shall dwell with the lamb . . . " (verse 6). Some understand this verse to mean that in the days of the Messiah the nature of the beasts and cattle will change, reverting to what it was at the beginning of creation and in Noah's ark. For at the beginning of creation, if the lion had eaten the lamb a part of creation would have been destroyed. What then did the lion and the other carnivores eat? If they ate the meat of other animals, then the creation would have lacked those animals. For all animals were created only in single pairs of male and female and surely the carnivores did not wait until their victims had multiplied before they ate. It is obvious that until their victims had multiplied the carnivores ate the grass of the field and only from that time (when the other animals had multiplied) did it become their nature to eat meat. Similarly, in Noah's ark, if the carnivores had eaten other animals, then the species of the victims would have become extinct for the animals only entered two by two, unless it be argued that when Noah brought into the ark seven by seven of the clean animals (Genesis 7:2), these were to provide food for the carnivores. Others, however, understand the whole of this section as a parable. The wolf, the leopard, the bear and the lion, referred to here, are, figuratively speaking, the wicked oppressors and robbers who bear the same relation to the weak as the carnivores to their victims.

And the lamb, the cow, the calf and the kid are, figuratively speaking, the meek of the earth. The prophet would then mean that in the days of the Messiah there will be peace on earth and no man will hurt his fellow. But this interpretation is incorrect, since it says: "They shall not hurt nor destroy *in all My holy mountain*" (verse 9). But in the days of the Messiah there will be peace all over the world (not only in God's holy mountain), as it is written: "And they shall beat their swords into plowshares, and their spears into pruning-hooks; nation shall not lift up sword against nation, neither shall they learn war any more" (Isaiah 2:4; Micah 4:3). And it says: "And the battle bow shall be cut off" (Zechariah 9:10). And of the Messiah it is said: "And he shall speak peace unto the nations" (ibid.). The correct interpretation is that the nature of the beasts will not change and they will prey on other animals and eat their meat just as they do now, but these verses are a promise to Israel that in the whole of the land of Israel the beasts will do no harm. That is why it says: "They shall not hurt nor destroy in all My holy mountain," the reason being "for the earth shall be full of the knowledge of the Lord" (verse 9). This means that since they are righteous and keep the way of the Lord no evil beast will have any power over them nor over their animals nor over anything that belongs to them, just as they were promised by Moses our Teacher, on whom be peace: "I will cause evil beasts to cease out of the land" (Leviticus 26:6), and even if they do happen to pass through the land they will do no harm.

The first interpretation takes the verses literally, understanding them to mean that in the Messianic age the carnivorous beasts will change their nature, reverting to the state of innocence that was theirs at the beginning of creation and in Noah's ark. The second interpretation understands the reference to be not to animals but to wild men who wage war on others. Kimḥi cannot accept this interpretation because in the Messianic age they will not wage war anywhere in the world, whereas the verses speak of the "beasts" not hurting only in God's holy mountain, which Kimḥi equates with the land of Israel. His third interpretation, which he accepts as the correct one, is that the victims referred to are the property of the Israelites. Wolves will still eat lambs, but not if the lambs belong to Israelites in the holy land because God will protect the lives and property of those who conduct themselves righteously as the

*Israelites will in the days of the Messiah. But in his next comment
Kimhi is aware of the difficulty in the verse: "And the lion shall eat
straw like the ox" (verse 7) since according to Kimhi the nature of
the carnivores will not change. His explanation is that the verse
means the lion will not eat other animals belonging to the
Israelites in the holy land, so that it will be as if it ate only straw.*

"And the cow and the bear shall feed . . . " (verse 7). The same
thing is said by the prophet Hosea: "And in that day I will make a
covenant for them with the beasts of the field, and with the fowls
of heaven" (Hosea 2:20). When the prophet says: "And the lion shall
eat straw like the ox," he means as if it will eat straw like the ox,
for the lion who will not find a carcass ready to hand will not prey
on the animals in the land of Israel. Furthermore, it is possible to
explain the whole vision figuratively, the lion, the bear and the
snake referring to evil opinions. The meaning of "And the cow and
the bear shall feed" would then be that the whole activity of the
animals will be only with the aim of serving God, not in order to
pursue worldly vanity. Therefore it says: "For the earth shall be full
of the knowledge of the Lord" (verse 9). Some say that the word
meri (verse 6) means a species of large animal, but as others understand it the fatlings of animals are called *meriim*. The Targum of
Jonathan renders the word as *patim* (fatling). "And the cow and the
bear . . . " The word *dov* (bear) is feminine, as in the verse (II Kings
2:24): "And there came forth two *dubbim*" (she-bears). Similarly,
when Scripture refers to *ez* (goat) the meaning is "she-goats."
That is why the feminine verbs are used in: "Their young ones shall
lie down together" (verse 7).

*Kimhi's fourth interpretation is not too clear. He may mean that
the verses are to be taken figuratively in the sense that there will
be a state of innocence among men so that they will no longer be
"bear-like" or "snake-like." Their animal nature will never get the
better of them.*

"And the sucking child shall play on the hole of the asp" (verse 8).
"And the weaned child shall put his hand on the basilisk's *meurat*"
means "on the basilisk's den." This is a hole and is so called because through it there is an entrance to the place of the snake. A

similar reference is in the verse "the *minharot* which are in the mountains" (Judges 6:2), which we have explained as meaning the "dens," so called because they have a hole through which the light (*or*) comes through. In this verse, too, the same idea is repeated in different words. The meaning of *gamul* (weaned child) is the same as that of *yonek* (sucking child) except that a child is called a *gamul* when his mother weans him. The reason he refers to the weaned child and the sucking child in connection with snakes is because snakes are often found in the holes of a house and little children play on the floor of the house and in its holes. The meaning of *hadah* (put) is as if it were written *yadah*, namely, "send forth his hand" (*yad*—hand). Now behold the snake's hatred for man, which had been decreed from the beginning (Genesis 3:15), will vanish in the Messianic age through all the land of Israel. Wherever the Israelites will go, neither the snake nor any other evil beast will harm them. Jonathan translates *meurat tzifoni* as "The pupils of the basilisk's eyes." He means that when the snake is in its hole the pupils of its eyes sparkle in the dark. When the infant sees the sparkle from outside he imagines that a bright stone or a piece of glass is there so that when he reaches into the hole to grasp the thing he imagines to be there, he seizes hold, in fact, of the basilisk and yet no harm will come to him. The prophet refers to the asp and the basilisk because these are the most venomous of snakes. If these will do no harm the others will certainly not do so.

Kimhi connects the word meurat *with or, "light," hence his interpretation that the snake's den is so called because it is the place where the light enters. The Targum of Jonathan also connects the word with or, "light," but understands it rather as referring to the sparkling eyes of the snake.*

"They shall not hurt nor destroy in all My holy mountain; for the earth shall be full of the knowledge of the Lord, as the waters cover the sea" (verse 9). The whole of the land of Israel is called "My holy mountain." The reason it is called a "mountain" is because it is higher than all other lands. The reason why they shall not hurt nor destroy is because the earth shall be full of the knowledge of the Lord. This applies to the land of Israel, as the prophet Jeremiah says: "For they shall all know Me, from the least of them unto the greatest of them" (Jeremiah 31:34). "As the waters cover the sea." The place of the waters is called the "sea" so that the reference here is to the waters covering all that place until the bottom of the sea cannot be seen.

The saying that the land of Israel is higher than all other lands is Rabbinic. The Rabbis may have believed that the land of Israel was actually the highest spot on earth or the saying may have been intended figuratively. Kimḥi translates eretz (earth) as "land" and understands it to mean that the land (of Israel) will be full of the knowledge of the Lord. In this respect, Kimḥi takes a sublime, universalistic passage and interprets it in a somewhat narrow fashion, but it must be realized that Kimḥi lived in an age of fierce religious polemics when each side tended to be exclusive. Kimḥi finally finds difficulty with the expression "as the waters cover the sea." Surely, the waters are the sea? No, says Kimḥi. The term yam (sea) is used for the sea basin, which the waters cover.

"And it shall come to pass in that day, that the root of Jesse, that standeth for an ensign of the peoples, unto him shall the nations seek; and his resting-place shall be glorious" (verse 10). The "root of Jesse" means the one who comes out of Jesse's root, as it says earlier: "And a twig shall grow forth out of his roots" (verse 1). For Jesse is the root. As Jonathan translates it: "The grandson (descendant) of Jesse." "That standeth . . . " This means that the Messiah will stand on that day in which the exiles will be gathered in and he will be for all the nations like an ensign for an army. The whole army follows the one who carries the ensign. In the same way all the nations will seek the Messiah and follow him to do all he commands. They will all obey him so that he will have glory and have no need to wage war. He will have rest and glory for all the nations will serve him. "And it shall come to pass in that day, that the Lord will set His hand again the second time to recover the remnant of His people" (verse 11). The reference to the "second time" means that the first time He recovered His people from the house of bondage in Egypt and on the day of ingathering of the exiles He will set His hand a second time to recover them from all the nations where they have been scattered. This cannot refer to the Babylonian exile for at that time only the tribes of Judah and Benjamin, who were exiled to Babylon, returned and the ten tribes were not gathered in. Consequently, the expression "the second time" cannot refer to the ingathering from Babylon for in the first gathering from Egypt all Israel went out, not a single one remaining behind. The term "the second time" can only have been intended to compare it with the Exodus from Egypt. Therefore this ingathering will be a repetition of the Exodus when all of them went out. And from this exile, too, all of them will go out. Therefore it says: "from Assyria, and from Egypt, and from Pathros, and from Cush, and from Elam, and from Shinar, and from Hamath, and from the islands of the sea." As for the references to "the remnant of His people that shall remain," this is because many of them perished in exile. "And from the islands of the sea." This means also from the lands of Edom and Ishmael which are beyond the land of Israel and these are the islands of the sea.

Kimḥi in his comment on verse 11 is at pains to stress that the vision is Messianic and cannot refer to the return of the Jews from the Babylonian exile. At the time of the return from Babylon, the "lost" ten tribes did not return. Moreover, many Jews remained in Babylon. But the verse speaks of a "second time" and must refer to an ingathering like the "first time," i.e., as at the time of the Exodus from Egypt when all went out. The "lands of Ishmael and Edom" are the countries under the rule of the Arabs and the Christians in Europe. The term "Ishmael" was used in the Middle Ages for Islam (because the Arabs are descended from Ishmael) and the term "Edom" for Christendom (because the Edomites were the Biblical rivals of the Israelites).

"And he will set up an ensign for the nations" (verse 12). It is as if God will lift up an ensign for the nations to come hurriedly to the place of the ensign. On that day all the nations will send the Israelites among them to depart in glory.

"The envy also of Ephraim shall depart, and they that harass Judah shall be cut off; Ephraim shall not envy Judah, and Judah shall not vex Ephraim" (verse 13). When the children of Israel will again be gathered in their land the envy which prevailed among them when they were exiled from their land will depart. For at the time of their exile the kingdom was divided because of their envy of David's house. "Judah." This means that in former times there were in Judah those who harassed Ephraim. "Ephraim" means the whole of Israel apart from Judah. Because the whole of Israel were envious of the kingdom of David, the men of Judah harassed them and were their enemies. We see that David's rule was held back for seven years while he reigned only over Judah (II Samuel 2:11 and 5:3). And when David reigned once more, after he had fled from Absalom, it is said: "Why have our brethren the men of Judah stolen . . . " (II Samuel 19:42). And it is said: "And the words of the men of Judah were fiercer than the words of the men of Israel" (II Samuel 19:44). And "Sheba, the son of Bichri . . . blew the horn . . . " (II Samuel 20:1). And so it continued until the kingdom was divided in the days of Rehoboam, who said: "I will add to your yoke" (I Kings 12:11). When the prophet says here "cut off," he means they will no longer be, as in the verse: "And the battle bow shall be cut off" (Zechariah 9:10). In our verse the same idea is repeated in different words.

Kimhi understands the verse to mean not "those who harass Judah" but "those whom Judah harasses." Ephraim was the Biblical name for the Northern Kingdom, Judah the name of the Southern Kingdom. Kimhi gives examples of how the reign of the house of David was repeatedly challenged until eventually the kingdom was divided into two. In the Messianic age there will again be only one kingdom and there will be no rivals to the house of David. "Cut off" does not mean that any Israelites will be destroyed, but that the enmity of one group for another will cease. In support of this Kimhi quotes the verse in Zechariah in which "cut off" can only mean that there will be no more battle bows since war will be no more.

"And they shall fly down upon the shoulder of the Philistines on the west; together they shall spoil the children of the east; they shall put forth their hand upon Edom and Moab; and the children of Ammon shall obey them" (verse 14). "And they shall fly down" means that they will move across to the Philistines to the west of the land of Israel. This is how Jonathan translates it. But we understand the words "fly down" to signify flying in the sense of a very speedy movement. The prophet uses this expression to denote their speedy attack on the Philistines, to destroy them and to despoil them. Others explain the word to mean: "And they shall be weary," namely, they shall wear themselves out when they attack the shoulder of the Philistines. The word *katef* (shoulder) is in apposition to the word "Philistines" (so that the translation should be: "And they shall fly down to the shoulder, to the Philistines on the west"). For if the word were in the construct state (meaning "the shoulder of the Philistines") it would have been pronounced with six vowel points (i.e., *ketef*). Ben Asher writes that it is in this form because of the accent which is on the last syllable, otherwise the letter *peh* at the end of the word might be confused with the *peh* at the beginning of the next word *pilishtim* (Philistines). "Edom and Moab." Nowadays the nations have lost their identity, with the exception of the Israelites who were kept separate from the nations by virtue of their religion and therefore did not become assimilated among the nations. But the majority of the other nations lost their identity and became assimilated. Nowadays, therefore, they are mixed among those who follow the religion of the Ishmaelites (Islam) and those who follow the Christian religion. So that when the prophet refers to Edom and Moab he means their lands and the people who now live there. The same explanation must be given to Daniel's prophecy of the future: "But these shall be delivered out of his hand, Edom, and Moab, and the chief of the children of Ammon" (Daniel 11:41). "They shall put forth their hand," that is Israel will send forth their hands against them to do as they please. "Shall obey them" to do whatever they command. He mentions these places because they are near to the land of Israel, but all the other nations, too, will be under Israel's rule.

First it must be acknowledged that Kimhi's interpretation is certainly narrow and chauvinistic. Israel is to rule over all the nations and so forth. But we must remember that Kimhi was writing at a time when the Jews were persecuted and despised so that what we today call "overcompensation" can be excused. Kimhi makes a grammatical point. There are no vowels, only consonants, in the Biblical text, so that the vowel sounds have to be supplied. Now the traditional reading of the word ktf is katef, with the accent on the last syllable. Kimhi says that this cannot possibly mean "the shoulder of" but simply "the shoulder," hence, according to Kimhi, the verse should be translated (not as the English version): "the shoulder, the Philistines." If, argues Kimhi, the meaning were "the shoulder of" (as in the English version) the word would have to be read as ketef, with the accent on the first syllable. Ketef is spelled with two "eh" sounds and each of these is represented by three

*dots, hence his reference to six points. Ben Asher was a famous
early medieval scholar who helped fix the correct texts and readings
of the Biblical books. Ben Asher gives a reason why the reading is
katéf, not ketef. This is so as to avoid having an unaccented
syllable ending with the same letter as the next word, for then the
letter would tend to drop out. Kimhi's final difficulty is that if the
vision is Messianic, then in that time there will be no Edom and
Moab since these nations no longer existed even in Kimhi's day. His
reply is that the reference is to the people who will be living in the
lands of Edom and Moab.*

"And the Lord will utterly destroy the tongue of the Egyptian sea;
and with His scorching wind will He shake His hand over the River,
and will smite it into seven streams, and cause men to march over
dryshod" (verse 15). The word *veheherim* used here means "to cut,"
for the root meaning of *haram* is to cut and to destroy. So the
meaning here is that of cutting and parting. The same meaning is
used when speaking of the sea in the verse: "To Him who divided
the Sea of Reeds into parts" (Psalms 136:13). "The tongue of the
Egyptian sea." This is the river in Egypt called Shihor (Jeremiah
2:18). By the will of God a path will there be made through which
those who are redeemed can pass. "And He will shake His hand
over the River." This is the Euphrates, as Jonathan translates it. The
meaning of "will shake His hand" is that He will bring a strong
wind to dry its waters, as He did to the Sea of Reeds at the time of
the Exodus (Exodus 14:21), as it is said: "And there shall be a highway for the remnant of His people" (verse 16). *Bayom* means
"strong," with the strength of His wind (not with a "scorching
wind") which He will bring upon the River to dry up its waters. The
meaning of this word, found nowhere else in Scripture, can only be
conjectured from the context. But my teacher, my brother Rabbi
Moses, understands the word *ayom* as connected with "a heap *(I'ee)*
in the field" (Micah 1:6) which means a "heap" (so that *bayom*
means "with an ayom," a "heap"). Therefore he understands the
word to refer to the heaps, namely, the waves of the sea and the
river, against which God will shake His hand and His wind to still
them and dry them (translating: "And He will shake His hand
against the waves of the River with His wind"). "And will smite it
into seven streams." The Holy One, blessed be He, will smite the

River Euphrates and bring His mighty wind upon it until it becomes divided into seven separate streams and there will be a pathway between one stream and the next. "And cause men to march dry-shod." God will cause those who march through these paths to walk with shoes on their feet. The pathway will be so dry that it will be as if there had never been water there and those who walk there will be able to keep their shoes on their feet. The word ve-hidrich ("cause to march") is causative. God is the One who causes them to march and those who pass through are the object of the verb. The reason the number seven is mentioned may be because there will, in fact, be seven pathways and no more. But it is also possible that seven simply means a large number and the meaning may be "many streams." This is the usage in Hebrew, as in the verse: "I will chastise you seven times more for your sins" (Leviticus 26:18), and in the verse: "For a righteous man faileth seven times, and riseth up again" (Proverbs 24:16).

Kimḥi's point about the verb ve-hidrich is that the verb has no object in the text ("men" is added in the English translation but is not in the text). Therefore Kimḥi understands it as causative and, as in the English, the object is to be supplied. His point about "shoes" is that the Hebrew word translated as "dryshod" really means "with shoes." Kimḥi's fine feeling for the Hebrew usage is to be seen in his concluding remarks. "Seven" is not to be taken literally but is a poetic way of saying "many" as in the other passages he quotes.

"And there shall be a highway for the remnant of His people, that shall remain from Assyria; like as there was for Israel in the day that he came up out of the land of Egypt" (verse 16). Through this River there will be a highway for the remnant of His people, that is to say, the way will be so well-mapped that it will be as if there had been a highway there for a long time. We have explained earlier why the word "remnant" is used. The reason he says "from Assyria" is because for those who will be in Assyria the direct way to go to the land of Israel is through the River Euphrates. "Like as there was," namely, just as there was a highway through the Sea of Reeds, so there will be a highway through the River Euphrates.

Thus ends Kimḥi's commentary to the chapter. There are many fanciful elements in it, but then he is commenting on a vision which he interprets in Messianic vein. But note how in spite of this he is still at pains to grasp the meaning of the verses and to interpret them accurately and grammatically.

Naḥmanides

What is the image of God?
How should we interpret stories of angels?
What is implied in the command to be holy?

Moses ben Naḥman (Naḥmanides) was born in Gerona, Spain in 1195 and died at Acre in Palestine around the year 1270. He is known as Ramban, after the initial letters of his name (Rabbi Moshe ben Naḥman). Naḥmanides' Commentary to the Pentateuch is one of the most popular commentaries. It was also the first Biblical Commentary to use the teachings of the Kabbalah. The Commentary is frequently printed together with the text in editions of the Pentateuch. The first edition was published in Italy before the year 1480. The best edition is that of Chavel, Jerusalem, 1959-1960.

A. WHAT IS THE IMAGE OF GOD?

Comment on: "And God said: Let us make man in our image, after our likeness. They shall rule the fish of the sea, the birds of the sky, the cattle, the whole earth, and all the creeping things that creep on earth" (Genesis 1:26). Naḥmanides discusses among other things the old problem of why the plural is used, "Let us make man," since there is only one God—and he also discusses the meaning of man being created in God's image.

A special "saying" of God was reserved for man because of man's lofty estate. Man is different from the beasts and the cattle which God created by the previous "saying." The correct understanding of "Let us make man" is as follows. I have previously shown you that God only created something out of nothing on the first day of creation. He formed and made all other creatures out of the elements He had created out of nothing on that day. God endowed the waters, for instance, with the power to bring forth swarms of living creatures, hence the "saying" applied to the waters: "Let the waters bring forth swarms" (Genesis 1:20). Similarly, the "saying" in connection with animals was: "Let the earth bring forth" (Genesis 1:24). Therefore, when God came to create man He said: "Let us make," meaning: "Let me and the earth just referred to make man." This means that the earth should bring forth man's body from its elements, as it did in connection with the beasts and the cattle, as it is written: "The Lord God formed man from the dust of the earth" (Genesis 2:7) and then God infused into him from on high of His spirit, as it is written: " . . . breathed into his nostrils the breath of life" (Genesis 2:7). It says: "in our image, after our likeness" since man resembles both of them. In the construction of his body man resembles the earth from which his body was taken. And in his spirit he resembles those on high (the angels), for his spirit does not die as does his body. In the next verse (Genesis 1:27) it says: "in the image of God He created him" in order to relate the great marvel, that man is different from all other creatures. This is the plain meaning of the verse. I discovered it in the writings of Rabbi Joseph Kimḥi and it is the most reasonable explanation of the verse of all that have been put forward. The word "image" means "form," as in the verse: "and the form of his visage was changed" (Daniel 3:19), and as in the verse: "Surely man walketh with a form" (Psalms 39:7), and as in the verse: "Thou wilt despise their form in the city" (Psalms 73:20). The word means, then, the form of his appearance. And the word "likeness" means a resemblance in character and deed since of things close to one another in idea it can be said that they resemble one another. Now man resembles both the beings below on earth and the beings above in heaven in character and glory, as it is written: "And hast crowned him with glory, and honour" (Psalms 8:6). This refers to man's spiritual ambition to acquire wisdom and knowledge and to improve his actions. As for "likeness," man's body resembles dust and his soul resembles the beings on high.

Nahmanides' interesting interpretation is that God calls, as it were, on all that He had made to participate with Him in creating man, hence the plural is used. Man is the apex of creation. In his person there is united the properties of all things on earth and all beings in heaven. He has a body created out of dust but he also has a soul which spurs him on to acquire wisdom and perfection. Joseph Kimḥi (died about 1170) was a famous grammarian, poet and Biblical commentator, brother of David Kimḥi.

They shall rule the fish of the sea. **Since they were male and female the plural form: "***They* **shall rule" is used. The Midrash (Genesis Rabbah) comments on the verse: "Let the earth bring forth a living creature" (Genesis 1:24): Rabbi Eleazer said: "A living creature" refers to the spirit of the first man. It cannot have been the intention of Rabbi Eleazer to teach that the spirit of the first man was created from the earth. He alludes rather to the idea we have mentioned, namely, that the formation of that spirit in man that is in the blood was from the earth, just as this spirit in beast and cattle was from the earth. All vital spirits were created together and then God provided bodies for them. First He made the bodies of beast and cattle. Then He made man's body and put this spirit into it. Afterwards He breathed into him the soul from on high, that is the separate soul. Of this a special "saying" is attributed to God who gave it, as it is written: "He breathed into his nostrils the breath of life" (Genesis 2:7).**

Nahmanides believed, like most of his contemporaries, that man has two souls. The first is the simple life force and this is in no way different from the life force which animates all other living creatures. But in addition man has a soul from on high. This is from God Himself, hence the expression "He breathed the breath of life into him."

B. HOW SHOULD WE INTERPRET STORIES OF ANGELS?

Comment on Genesis 18:1-15 which tells of how three "men" (angels) appeared to Abraham to tell him that his wife Sarah would have a son. Abraham and Sarah offered their guests hospitality and eventually the guests conveyed the good tidings that Sarah would bear a son even though Abraham was 100 years old and Sarah 90 years. When Sarah laughed at the thought of such a thing she was rebuked. Nothing is too hard for God to do. Sarah denied that she had laughed because she was afraid. Naḥmanides here takes issue with Maimonides' rationalistic interpretation of the passage and prefers his own more literal and more mystical understanding of what it means. But first, and in order to lead up to his exposition, Naḥmanides offers a few brief comments on the words in his passage: "And the Lord appeared to him" (verse 1); "three men" (verse 2); "as they ate" (verse 8).

And the Lord appeared to him. **Rashi comments as follows: To visit the sick. Rabbi Hama ben Ḥanina said: It was the third day after he had been circumcised, so the Holy One, blessed be He, came to inquire how he was.** Three men. **These are the angels who came to him in the guise of men.** Three. **One to bring the tidings to Sarah, one to heal Abraham, and one to overturn Sodom. Raphael who healed Abraham went from there to save Lot. This is not an instance of one angel performing two missions, since it happened elsewhere and he was commanded so to do at a different time or because they were both missions involving deliverance.** As they ate. **It appeared as if they ate.**

Naḥmanides first quotes from Rashi, the famous French commentator. According to the Rabbis a man is never more God-like than when he performs acts of kindness. So they imagine God Himself, as it were, visiting the sick. The reference to Abraham's circumcision is in the previous chapter. According to the Rabbis the third day after the operation is the day on which the patient feels the worst so that he appreciates a visit especially on that day. Naḥmanides continues that three angels were required because, say the Rabbis, an angel is sent by God to carry out a single mission. Raphael means "God is Healer." This angel also went to save Lot from Sodom (see the next portion, chapter 19). This is not treated as two missions either because they both had the same aim or because God commanded the angel to perform them at different times, and the objection to "two missions" is only when one angel is sent on both at the same time. Naḥmanides takes literally all the Rabbinic references to angels. He follows the Rabbis, too, in stating, however, that angels do not eat, so that when Scripture says that they ate it only means that they pretended to eat because they appeared to Abraham in the guise of humans.

It is written in the book *Guide for the Perplexed* (11, 41) that this portion is written in the form of a general statement followed by its details. First Scripture says that God appeared to him in a prophetic vision. What did he see in this vision? "Looking up" in the vision "he saw three men standing near him." He said in the vision "if it please you." This is the account of what he said in the vision to the greatest of the three. But if in the vision only three men eating meat appeared to him, how can Scripture say that God appeared to him? For God appeared to him neither in the vision nor in his thought. You do not find anything like this in any of the accounts of prophecy. Furthermore, according to him (Maimonides) Sarah did not really bake cakes, neither did Abraham really prepare a calf, nor did Sarah really laugh; but it was all seen in a vision. If that is so, then this dream contained much nonsense just like the false dreams. For of what advantage was it to show him all this? Maimonides also says that the account of "And a man wrestled with him" (Genesis 32:25) was a prophetic vision. But in that case I fail to understand why he (Jacob) limped on his hip when he awoke. And why in that case did he say: "I have seen a divine being face to face, yet my life has been preserved" (Genesis 32:31) since the prophets are never afraid that they will die as a result of their prophetic vision. Jacob himself saw a far greater vision than this, for he saw the Great Name many times in prophetic visions. Now according to Maimonides one would have to say the same thing in connection with the story of Lot (Genesis, chapter 19), that the angels did not really come to his house nor did he really bake unleavened bread for them, but it all took place in a prophetic vision. Even if we accept that Lot was capable of having a prophetic vision, how did the evil and wicked men of Sodom become prophets, for who told them that the three men had come to Lot's house? And if it is argued that all this, too, was in Lot's prophetic vision, then it would mean that the account of how the angels urged Lot to take his wife and escape and the account of the angel saying: "Very well, I will grant you this favor too" (Genesis 19:21), and all that is related in the portion is not factually true but took place in a prophetic vision, which would mean that Lot had remained in Sodom. Maimonides evidently thinks of the various events taking place of their own accord with the various speeches taking place in the vision. But such ideas contradict Scripture. It is forbidden even to listen to them, let alone accept them as true.

Nahmanides is here critical of Maimonides' view in the Guide for the Perplexed. Maimonides' basic idea is that all the Scriptural references to persons seeing angels mean that the angels were seen in a prophetic vision, otherwise how can one "see" an angel? That is why in our portion Scripture begins by saying that the Lord appeared to him, i.e., he had a prophetic vision. Then it goes on to describe what he saw in the vision, i.e., the three men and the rest of the account. Nahmanides finds this hard to accept. Since the vision was not of God, how can Scripture say that the Lord appeared to him? Furthermore, if it all did not really happen but was only seen in a vision, what purpose did all the detailed events in the vision serve? All that was required was for the essential message—that Sarah was to have a child—to be conveyed. According to Maimonides the account of Jacob wrestling with the angel is also not factual but was a vision. In that case, argues Nahmanides, why did Jacob limp? If one dreams of wrestling with someone and of being injured, one does not limp when one awakens. Furthermore, if the account is factual and Jacob really did see the angel, we can understand why he was afraid of dying. He had seen a divine being. But if he only saw the angel in a vision, why was he afraid of dying? All the prophets see a vision of God and yet they are not afraid of dying. Moreover, in a number of Biblical passages it is said that God Himself—the "Great Name"—appeared to Jacob in a vision. If he was not afraid of dying because he had seen God in a vision, how could he have been afraid of dying merely because he saw an angel in a vision? Although Maimonides does not say so explicitly, it follows from his theory that the story of Lot, in which angels are mentioned, also took place in a vision. But then to be consistent one would have to say that none of the events recorded really happened, and this is absurd since Lot did not remain in Sodom. The only solution open to Maimonides is that the detailed events really did happen, but they happened fortuitously and the Scriptural interpretation on them in terms of angels speaking and the like only took place in a vision. This Nahmanides considers to be heretical. Nahmanides now proceeds to give his own account of the matter. Basically he agrees with Maimonides that a human being cannot "see" an angel or "hear" an angel speaking to him, since an angel, as a purely spiritual being, cannot communicate with man through the senses. Consequently, when Scripture uses the word "angel" the reference is to a vision (though not a prophetic vision). But, Nahmanides cleverly notes in this passage, and those others he has considered, Scripture speaks not of "angels" but of "men." This means that the angels adopted the guise of men and in this guise *they can communicate with humans. The events, therefore, really did take place and they are not events seen in a vision.*

Now it is true that whenever Scripture refers to an angel being seen or heard it is a vision or dream, since an angel cannot be comprehended by the senses. But such a vision is not a prophetic vision for the capacity to comprehend an angel does not make a man a prophet. It is not correct to say, as the Rabbi (Maimonides) decrees (*Guide*, 11, 41) that every prophet, apart from Moses, received his prophetic vision through an angel. The Rabbis say of Haggai, Zechariah and Malachi in relation to Daniel that, whereas they were prophets, he was not a prophet. That is why Daniel's book does not belong among the prophets because his experience was through the angel Gabriel, even though the angel appeared to him and spoke to him while he was awake. As it is said in connection with the vision of the second Temple: "Yea, while I was speaking in prayer, the man Gabriel" (Daniel 9:21). And the vision of the redemption (Daniel 10) took place while Daniel was awake, walking with his companions by the riverside. Hagar the Egyptian (Genesis 16:7) was not one of the prophets. It is also clear that her experience was not that of hearing a heavenly voice as the Rabbi suggests. When Scripture distinguishes between the prophecy of Moses our Teacher and that of the patriarchs, it says: "I appeared to Abraham, Isaac and Jacob as El Shaddai" (Exodus 6:3). The reference is to one of the holy names of God, not to an angel. Our Rabbis describe further the difference between Moses and the other prophets when they say: What is the difference between Moses and all the other prophets? The Rabbis reply: All the other prophets saw through a glass that was not polished, as it is written: "And I have multiplied visions and by the ministry of the prophets I have used similitudes" (Hosea 12:11). But Moses saw through a polished glass, as it is written: "And he beholds the likeness of the Lord" (Numbers 12:8). The Rabbis say this in the Midrash Leviticus Rabbah and in other places but nowhere do they associate the prophecy of the other prophets with an angel. Do not be surprised at that which is written: "I am also a prophet as thou art; and an angel spoke unto me by the word of the Lord, saying" (I Kings 13:18). For there the meaning is: "I am also a prophet as thou art; and I know therefore that the angel which spoke unto me was by the word of the Lord." This refers to a stage of prophecy, as the man of God said: "For so it was charged me by the word of the Lord" (I Kings 13:9) and he said: "For it was said to me by the word of the Lord" (I Kings 13:17). Our Rabbis say the same thing about Balaam. Balaam said: "Now therefore, if it displease thee, I will get back" (Numbers 22:34). The Rabbis explain that Balaam said to the angel: I did not go until God told me so to do and now you tell me to go back. This is how God behaves. Did He not tell Abraham to sacrifice his son and then tell an angel to order him to stop? (Genesis 22). It is His habit to say something and then to revoke it through an angel. So you see that the Rabbis call our attention to the fact that the stage of prophecy in the first word, in which God's name is mentioned, cannot be compared with the second word in which it is said that it was through an angel. But it is the way of prophecy that God issues commands by means of prophecy and cancels them by means of an angel, and the prophet knows that this, too, is by the word of the Lord. At the beginning of Leviticus Rabbah the Rabbis say: "And he called unto Moses" (Leviticus 1:1). Not like Abraham. Concerning Abraham it is written: "And the angel of the Lord called unto Abraham a second time out of heaven" (Genesis 22:15); the angel called and the word of God was then spoken. But here the Holy One, blessed be He, says: "I am He who calls and I am He who speaks." This means that Abraham could not comprehend prophecy until he had first prepared his soul to comprehend an angel and from that stage he was able to ascend to the stage of the prophetic word. But Moses was ready for prophecy all the time. In any event the Rabbis call our attention to the fact that the sight of an angel is not prophecy and that those persons who see angels and speak with them are not necessarily prophets, as I have mentioned in connection with Daniel. The sight of angels is a kind of vision that is called an opening of the eyes, as it is written, for instance: "Then the Lord opened the eyes of Balaam, and he saw the angel of the Lord" (Numbers 22:31). And so Elisha prayed: "Lord I pray Thee, open his eyes, that he may see" (II Kings 6:17).

Maimonides argues that every prophetic experience, apart from that of Moses, was by means of an angel. This Naḥmanides denies. Daniel was not a prophet because he had no vision of God, only that of an angel. We see that when the Rabbis do discuss the difference

*between Moses and the other prophets they describe the difference
in various ways but nowhere suggest, as Maimonides says, that
Moses had an experience of God whereas the prophets had an
experience of an angel. Naḥmanides then points to an apparent
contradiction from the book of Kings but, he says, a careful
examination of the passage reveals that the meaning is that there
are two stages: the higher one of prophecy and the lower one
through an angel. This latter is also a stage of prophecy, in that it is
only possible for lofty souls, but it is not the prophetic vision. The
book of Kings means, then, that the prophet is able to discern
whether the voice of the angel is from God, but it is not as high as
the true prophetic vision. Note the interpretation of the Midrash
regarding the "call" of Moses. Abraham had first to be "called" by
an angel, i.e., to reach the lower stage in which he could comprehend
an angel and only then could he have the prophetic vision.
Naḥmanides distinguishes three stages: 1) prophecy, a direct
experience of God, but not as intense and as intimate as that of
Moses; 2) "opening of the eyes," a vision of an angel but not the
physical sight of an angel, belonging to a lower degree of prophecy
and not really true prophecy; 3) the physical sight of an angel only
possible because the angel has become clothed in flesh or, at least,
in the appearance of flesh.*

**But wherever angels are referred to as "men," in this portion, for
instance and in the portion of Lot, and in connection with "And a
man wrestled with him" and in connection with "a man came upon
him" (Genesis 37:15), which, say the Rabbis, refers to an angel, in
all these instances the reference is a special glory created to appear
in the angels. This is called, by those who know, a "garment." It can
be perceived with the eyes of flesh by those pure of soul like the
saints and the disciples of the prophets, but I am not allowed to
explain it in detail. As for those places in Scripture in which you
find a vision of God and a speech by an angel or a vision of an
angel and a speech by God, for example, the instance of Moses at
the beginning of his ministry (Exodus 3:2) and the instance of
Zechariah (1:14 etc.), I shall further reveal the words of the living
God by hint. As for the verse "and they ate," the Rabbis remark that
each dish vanished in turn. The meaning of this "vanishing" you will**

understand from the instance of Manoah (Judges 13:19), if you will have merit.

The idea of a "created glory" goes back to Saadia Gaon. As applied by Nahmanides here it means a kind of subtle light which can be seen by human eyes. Through this the angel appears as a "man," but even in this guise he can only be seen by pure souls who, though they may not have attained to the more elevated stage of prophecy, are still capable of seeing this "garment" in which the angels are clothed. Nahmanides refers to "those who know," that is, to the Kabbalists. The mystics were extremely reluctant to speak of these heavenly matters and that is why Nahmanides, too, is so guarded in his speech, saying that he is not allowed to reveal more of this mystery. He promises to say more about Moses and Zechariah, but if he ever did so his writings on this topic have not come down to us. The Rabbis say that the angels only appeared to eat but, in reality, each dish vanished into thin air as soon as it was placed before the angels. This, too, is a mystery and Nahmanides connects it with the story of Manoah and the angel, but again he is very circumspect so that it is not at all clear what he really means. He now proceeds at last to give his own interpretation of our narrative.

To turn to the interpretation of this portion. After it had been said: "Thus Abraham and his son Ishmael were circumcised on that very day" (Genesis 17:26), it is said that God appeared to him when he was sick after his circumcision and was sitting at the door of his tent because the heat of the day had weakened him. The reason why this is mentioned is to inform us that he had no intention of having a prophetic vision. He neither fell on his face nor did he pray, and this vision came to him. "By the terebinths of Mamre" (Genesis 18:1). This is to inform us of the name of the place in which he was circumcised and that is why the Divine Presence appeared to him, namely, to pay him honor. We find the same thing in connection with the Tabernacle, where it is said: "When they came out, they blessed the people; and the Presence of the Lord appeared to all the people" (Leviticus 9:23). Because they had tried so hard to carry out the command to erect the Sanctuary, they had the merit of seeing the Divine Presence. Neither in the one instance nor in the other was the appearance of the Divine Presence for the purpose of

issuing some command or in order to convey something to them, but it was solely as a reward because they had obeyed the command, a demonstration that God had accepted their work, as it is written: "As for me, I shall behold Thy face in righteousness; I shall be satisfied, when I awake, with Thy likeness" (Psalms 17:15). Of Jacob, too, it is said: "and angels of God encountered him" (Genesis 32:2). No word was conveyed to him at that time and nothing new happened except that he had the merit of seeing the angels on high and so knew that his deeds were acceptable to God. So, too, in the narrative of Abraham, the vision of the Divine Presence was a merit and a promise. The Rabbis say the same thing of those who crossed the Sea of Reeds and said: "This is my God and I will exalt Him" (Exodus 15:2). As they stood by the sea, say the Rabbis, even a maidservant saw a vision greater than that of the prophet Ezekiel. This was a reward at the time of the great miracle when they believed in God and in Moses His servant (Exodus 14:31). It may happen, too, that a vision of the Divine Presence is given at a time of Divine wrath. "As the whole community threatened to pelt them with stones, the Presence of the Lord appeared in the Tent of Meeting to all the Israelites" (Numbers 14:10). This was to protect His servants the righteous (Moses and Aaron) and was also in their honor. Do not be concerned that there is a division of sections (between that of circumcision and this one) since the two portions are connected. That is why it says: "And the Lord appeared to him" not "And the Lord appeared to Abraham" (since Abraham is the person spoken about in the previous portion). In the previous portion there is a description of what transpired at the time of his circumcision and now it is said that the Divine Presence appeared to him and sent His angel to bring the tidings to Sarah and also to save Lot for his sake. As far as Abraham was concerned, he had already been told by the Divine Presence that he was to have a son (Genesis 17:19), but now Sarah heard it from the angel who spoke to Abraham that Sarah might hear, as it said "Sarah was listening" (Genesis 18:10). This is what the Rabbis mean when they say that God appeared to him to visit the sick. They mean that it was not to convey any message but simply to pay him honor. The Rabbis say further on the verse: "Make for Me an altar of earth" (Exodus 20:21). "If I appear," says God, "to the one who only builds an altar for My sake and I bless him then, how much more should I appear to Abraham who circumcised himself for My sake." It is also possible that the very appearance of the Divine Presence brought healing to the sickness caused by the circumcision, for so it is proper, as it is written: "In the light of the king's countenance is life" (Proverbs 16:15).

Thus for Naḥmanides, the Lord appeared to Abraham and not only to the angels. (Unlike Maimonides, who takes the words "And the Lord appeared to him" to be a description of the vision he had of the three angels.) But what was the purpose of this vision? Naḥmanides replies that it had no other purpose than to reward Abraham for having carried out his duty, and he gives other instances of such reward. Therefore, it is no refutation of Naḥmanides thesis to ask, if God appeared to him, what did He say?

C.   WHAT IS IMPLIED IN THE COMMAND TO BE HOLY?

Comment on: "Speak to the whole Israelite community and say to them: You shall be holy, for I, the Lord your God, am holy" (Leviticus 19:2). This is a command issued not to a few "holy men" but to "the whole Israelite community." Consequently, it must refer not to a remote ideal but to something that can and ought to be attained by every Jew. Naḥmanides here considers what this can be. What are we being asked to do or to be when we are commanded to be holy?

You shall be holy. **Rashi comments as follows:**

"Separate yourselves from forbidden sexual relationships and from sin for wherever you find an injunction to fence yourself in against such relationships you find holiness." But I have seen in the Midrash known as *Torat Kohanim* **simply "separate yourselves" (without referring to forbidden sexual relationships). The passage there reads as follows: " 'You shall sanctify yourselves and be holy, for I am holy' (Leviticus 11:44). Just as I am holy so shall you be holy. Just as I am separate (from the world), so shall you separate yourselves." It seems to me that the "separation" referred to here does not mean from forbidden sexual relationships, as the Rabbi (Rashi) would have it. Rather this "separation" is that which is mentioned everywhere in the Talmud and whose practitioners are called Pharisees (Separatists). The meaning of it is this. The Torah warns against forbidden sexual relationships and against forbidden foods, but it**

permits a man and his wife to live together and it permits a man to eat meat and to drink wine. A lustful fellow would therefore have the opportunity of engaging in uncontrolled passion with his wife or with his many wives and he could indulge in winebibbing and the gluttonous eating of flesh (Proverbs 23:20). He could also speak as much loose talk as he desired, since there is no explicit prohibition of this in the Torah. Such a man could be a scoundrel with the full permission of the Torah. Therefore, after the Torah had stated in detail those things it had forbidden categorically, it issues a general command that we should separate ourselves from those things which are permitted but which we can do without. For instance, a man should not cohabit overmuch. As the Rabbis say, scholars should not be with their wives as frequently as cocks in a barnyard. He should only cohabit when it is necessary to fulfill his obligation. He should sanctify himself in the matter of wine, only drinking a little, just as the Torah calls a Nazirite "holy" (Numbers 6:5), and he should be aware of the evils that are mentioned in connection with winebibbing in the account of Noah (Genesis 9:21) and Lot (Genesis 19:33). He should also separate himself from impurity, even where there is no prohibition against it in the Torah. As the Rabbis say, the garments of the ignorant (who do not observe the laws against impurity) are a major source of impurity to the Pharisees, and the Nazirite is called "holy" because he also keeps himself separate from contamination by a corpse (Numbers 6:6). A man should also guard his mouth and his tongue from becoming abominable in overeating and in uttering obscene talk, as Scripture says: "And every mouth speaketh wantonness" (Isaiah 9:16). He should be careful in this matter until he attains to the stage of separation like that of Rabbi Ḥiya of whom it was said that he never uttered anything unnecessary. It is in connection with matters such as these that the command is issued, after the detailed things that are categorically forbidden, so that the command even embraces the cleanliness of hands and body. As the Rabbis say: "'You shall sanctify yourselves'—this refers to washing the hands before meals. 'And be holy'—this refers to washing the hands after meals. 'For I am holy'—this refers to anointing the hands with fragrant oils after meals." Although such rules are of Rabbinic origin, yet the main idea of Scripture is to command us to observe

such things that we should be clean, pure and separate from the masses of people who soil themselves by doing unnecessary and ugly things.

According to Naḥmanides, Judaism is not only a matter of doing certain things, but of being a certain kind of person. The aim of the Torah is to produce persons of the noblest character. Consequently, over and above the detailed rules and regulations there is a general command to be holy, that is, for Naḥmanides, to keep oneself apart from too much indulgence even in permitted things. Of course, one man's luxury is another man's necessity. Each person must decide for himself, say, how many drinks he may have. He may drink a little, since drinking is not forbidden by the Torah. But he must have his limits and when he sees that he is in danger of overdoing, he must learn how to stop. Note especially Naḥmanides' very remarkable expression: "A scoundrel with the full permission of the Torah." Naḥmanides now proceeds to give further examples of how his principle can be applied.

It is the way of the Torah to give detailed rules and then to state a general principle, as it does here. For instance, after the Torah had stated in detail the laws governing business dealings such as "Thou shalt not wrong another," it goes on to give a general principle: "And thou shalt do that which is right and good" (Deuteronomy 6:18). This means that a man should be prepared always to do the right thing and to be ready to compromise and to please his fellows by going beyond the strict limits of what the law demands, as I shall explain with God's help in my comments to this verse. Also with regard to the Sabbath, certain classes of work were forbidden by a negative command and this is followed by a positive injunction to rest (Exodus 23:12). I shall explain this further, with God's help. The reason Scripture states here: "For I, the Lord thy God, am holy" is to teach that if we are holy, then we shall have the merit of cleaving to Him.

Everyone knows how easy it is to take an unfair advantage of another person without actually infringing the law. A dishonest person can always find sufficient loopholes in the law if he so wishes. It is also possible for a man to keep all the Sabbath laws and yet not really keep the Sabbath, i.e., if his Sabbath has nothing in it of the special sacred Sabbath atmosphere. So, in all these ways, the Torah demands something more of the Jew than a mere mechanical observance of the rules. Naḥmanides does not, of course, deny the value of the rules, but he wishes at the same time to call our attention to the refinement of character which is the aim of these rules.

Daat Zekenim

What lessons are to be derived from the Ark?
What is the true meaning of the Shema?
How did Moses die?

The work Daat Zekenim Mi-Baale Ha-Tosafot (The Opinion of the Elders—Of the Authors of the Tosafot), *usually abbreviated to* Daat Zekenim, *was compiled by an unknown author at the end of the thirteenth century. The* Tosafot *(Additions) are the work of French and German scholars of the twelfth and thirteenth centuries. They are extended notes to the Talmud, frequently taking Rashi's commentary to the Talmud as their launching-off point. The* Daat Zekenim *purports to give the opinions of these same scholars on the Pentateuch, and in more or less the same style. The* Daat Zekenim *was first printed in Livorno as late as the year 1783, but since then its popularity ensured it a place in many editions of the Pentateuch. As it is an anthology, its contents are varied, as the following examples show.*

A. WHAT LESSONS ARE TO BE DERIVED FROM THE ARK?

Comment on the command to fashion an ark to contain the two tablets of stone on which the Ten Commandments were engraved, Exodus 25:10-16. The numbers are those of the verses on which Daat Zekenim *comments.*

10. "And they shall make an ark." In connection with all the other furniture for the Tabernacle it is written: "And thou shalt make" (Exodus 25:18, 23, 25, 26, 28, 29 etc.) but here it is written: "And they shall make" because everyone had to have a hand in arranging for the ark to be made, out of respect for the Torah it was to contain. How much more should the inhabitants of a city be obliged to work on behalf of the scholars in their midst in order to pay them honor. As the Rabbis say in tractate Yoma: "And they shall make an ark." From this it is derived that the inhabitants of his city are obliged to do the work of a scholar for him. "Within and without shalt thou overlay it" (Exodus 25:11). Raba said: Any scholar who is not the same inside as out is no scholar. Furthermore, the Holy One, blessed be He, commanded all of them to occupy themselves with the ark so that all should share in the reward of the Torah which rests therein.

A typical Rabbinic idea holds that the Torah does not only belong to the scholars but to all Israel. Even those incapable of studying the Torah can have a share in it by supporting scholars and enabling them to have leisure for their studies. The reference to the scholar's "inside" being the same as his "outside" is that the ark is the symbol of the scholar, since he too, is a "container" for the Torah. The ark had to be overlayed with gold both inside and out. Scholars naturally present a "golden" exterior to the world, but they must not be hypocrites. They must really mean what they say; their inner life must not be a lie, they must be gold within as well as without.

11. "And thou shalt overlay it." The ark should ideally have been made entirely of gold (not of wood with a golden overlay), but since it was carried on the shoulder (Numbers 4:1-20 and 7:9) it would have been too heavy if made entirely of gold. Although the Rabbis say that those who carried the ark were borne aloft by it, this happened only occasionally. But I find this hard to understand for, if so, why was Uzzah (II Samuel 6:6, 7) punished? It is necessary to give further thought to this matter. Of the golden altar, too, we find that the Holy One, blessed be He, commanded that it be made of acacia wood covered with gold (Exodus 30:1-3) and the same applies to the altar of brass (Exodus 27:1, 2), because these, too, were carried on the shoulder and if they had been made of solid gold or solid brass, they would have been too heavy. "And thou shalt make

upon it a crown of gold." It would seem that this crown-like addition was purely decorative, but there is a hint in it of the crown of the Torah. As it appears from the comment of the Rabbis in tractate Yoma: There are three ornamental crowns on the three vessels of the Tabernacle: the crown of the ark, symbolizing the crown of the Torah; the crown on the table (Exodus 25:24), symbolizing the kingly crown; and the crown on the altar (Exodus 30:3), symbolizing the priestly crown. So far as the crown of priesthood is concerned, Aaron came and took it himself. So far as the kingly crown is concerned, David came and took it himself. But the crown of the Torah is there all the time. Anyone who so wishes may come and take it for himself.

The Rabbis comment that Uzzah was punished because he tried to save the ark when it toppled and so touched it, without realizing that there was no need for him to attempt to save the ark. The ark had the miraculous property of carrying aloft those who carried it and it certainly did not need any human hands to keep it from falling. Now Daat Zekenim has heard a suggestion that the reason why the ark was not made of solid gold was that it would then have been too heavy to carry. But what of the Rabbinic saying that in reality, it carried those who carried it? The reply is that this miracle only happened occasionally, but normally the ark needed its carriers. But why then was Uzzah punished, since he could not have anticipated a miracle? Daat Zekenim gives no answer, declaring that further thought is required; a formula, incidentally, that is frequently found in the Tosafot to the Talmud. Note the fine idea at the end. Only a king can wear the kingly crown and only a priest the priestly crown. Both are a matter of privilege by birth. But the Torah is there for anyone to make it his own. The Rabbis substituted the aristocracy of learning for those of royal and priestly birth.

15. "They shall not be taken from it." Because of the ark's high degree of sanctity, the Holy One, blessed be He, did not want it to be moved about when the Levites placed the staves in the rings and removed them from the rings. Consequently, when they came to carry it, all they had to do was to grasp the ends of the staves and lift them and when they set it down, all they had to do was to let go, because of the dread that resulted from the high degree of the ark's sanctity. Our verse means: "The staves shall be in the rings of the

ark"—when Moses puts them there and fixes them (as it is stated later in Exodus 40:20) and once they are there—"they shall not be taken from it."

16. "And they shall put into the ark." This is not where the main command to place the testimony in the ark occurs, since this is recorded later (verse 21). It is mentioned here to state the reason why the staves must not be removed from the ark. This is so that the Levites should not move it about, since the testimony will be placed in it and it will be so holy.

Holy things must not be approached in a familiar way. Therefore the staves must always remain in the ark once Moses had put them there and the Levites would thus avoid any unnecessary moving of the ark.

B.   WHAT IS THE TRUE MEANING OF THE SHEMA?

Comment on the Shema: "Hear, O Israel: The Lord, our God, the Lord is One" (Deuteronomy 6:4). Daat Zekenim lived in an age of fierce polemics between Jews and Christians on the meaning of the Bible. Some Christians argued that since there are three divine names in the Shema, it proves that the doctrine of the Trinity is correct. Daat Zekenim turns the tables on them by arguing that, on the contrary, the Shema specifically refutes the doctrine.

It would have been impossible to have written this verse without the three divine names. If it had simply said: "Hear, O Israel: The Lord is One," each nation would have said that it is their god who is the One. Now that it says "our God," it clearly speaks of the God of Israel. And if it had said: "The Lord our God is One," it might have been taken to mean our God is one of the gods; how much more if it had simply said: "Our God is One." But now that the divine name is repeated thrice, it means: "The Lord who is our Lord is the only Lord and there is no other apart from Him."

Naturally, Daat Zekenim had to be circumspect, but it is clear that he is referring to the Christian doctrine. In an age of religious persecution, he did not dare to give expression to his rejection in an offensive way, so he speaks of the "nations" and their God, knowing that his readers would understand his reference.

It is necessary to recite the words *El Melech Neeman* ("God, Faithful King") before reciting: "Hear, O Israel." These three words added to the words *Baruch Shem* ("Blessed be His name, whose glorious kingdom is for ever and ever"), and these added to the words of the *Shema*, you will find, make a total of 248. These correspond to the 248 limbs of the human body. Whoever recites the *Shema* properly will be protected by God in all the 248 limbs of his body. This is why Scripture says: "Keep My commandments, and live" (Proverbs 4:4). God says: If you keep that which is Mine, I shall keep that which is yours. Rabbi Simeon ben Halafta said: This can be compared to a king who resided in Galilee and had a vineyard in Judah. Another man resided in Judah and had a vineyard in Galilee. Year by year this one had to go all the way from Judah to Galilee to attend to his vineyard and this one all the way from Galilee to Judah. One day they met and one said to the other: Why do we go to all this bother. I shall look after your vineyard that is in my city and in return, you look after my vineyard that is in your city. Take care to look after it properly and I shall do the same for you.

The full Shema *consists of three portions: Deuteronomy 6:4-9; Deuteronomy 11:13-21; and Numbers 15:37:41. From Rabbinic times it has been customary to recite too, "Blessed be His name," which contains six Hebrew words (for all this see Singer's Prayer Book, pp. 41-44). Now the total number of words here is 245 and with the three words* El Melech Neeman, *there is a total of 248. The Rabbis say that the human body contains 248 parts or "limbs." Hence the idea that the Torah embraces all of man's life and that, as Daat Zekenim says, one who keeps the Torah is protected by God in all his limbs. The parable of the vineyard is that God dwells in Heaven but his vineyard, the Torah, is on earth, while man dwells on earth but his vineyard, the soul, is of Heaven.*

C. HOW DID MOSES DIE?

Comment on: "So Moses the servant of the Lord died there" (Deuteronomy 34:5). Daat Zekenim quotes a Midrash on the death of Moses and concludes with a note about reading the Torah.

"So Moses the servant of the Lord died there." At the time of his death, Moses pleaded with the Holy One, blessed be He: "I shall not die, but live" (Psalms 118:17). The Holy One, blessed be He, replied:

"This cannot be, for all men must die." Moses then said: "I ask of Thee only one thing, that all the gates of heaven and of the abyss open that all may see that there is none apart of Thee", as it is said: "Know this day, and lay it to thy heart, that the Lord, He is God in heaven above and upon the earth beneath" (Deuteronomy 4:39). Moses immediately declared: "There is none else." Then the Holy One, blessed be He, said: "Thou hast said 'there is none else' (od), therefore I shall say of thee: 'And there has not risen a prophet since (od) in Israel like Moses' (Deuteronomy 34:10)." There and then the Holy One, blessed be He, descended together with three of His angels, Michael, Gabriel and **Zagzagel.** Michael spread out Moses' couch. Gabriel spread a cloth of purple over it. Zagzagel placed at his head a cushion of fine wool. Then the Holy One, blessed be He, stationed Himself over Moses' head, with Gabriel at the foot of the couch and Michael and Zagzagel at either side. The Holy One, blessed be He, said to Moses: "Stretch out thy legs," and he did so. "Close thine eyes," and he did so. There and then the Holy One, blessed be He, called out to the soul of Moses, saying: "My daughter! I had set aside one hundred and twenty years for thee to inhabit Moses' body. Come out now and do not delay, for the time has come for thee to depart." The soul replied: "I know that Thou art the God of all souls and spirits and every living thing is in Thine hand. Thou didst create me and put me in Moses' body. Hast Thou any purer body in which to put me than that of Moses, a body over which worms and maggots will not prevail forever, a body over which no flies were ever seen? And Moses was so generous a man. I do not wish to leave it." The Holy One, blessed be He, said to her once again: "Do not delay, for the time has come for thee to depart. I shall elevate thee to the highest of the high heavens and let thee dwell under the Throne of Glory, near the *Serafim, Ofanim* and the angels." She replied: "Sovereign of the universe! I would rather remain in the body of Moses than be among the *Cherubim* and the angels. For two of the angels, Azza and Azazel, descended from heaven to earth to love the daughters of men and to cohabit with them. They became corrupt, so that as a punishment Thou didst suspend them between heaven and earth. But Moses did not return to his own wife from the day Thou didst reveal Thyself to him in the burning bush. Leave me be, I pray Thee, where I am." When the

Holy One, blessed be He, saw this, He kissed Moses and took his soul with a kiss, as it is said: "By the mouth of the Lord" (Deuteronomy 34:5). Then the Holy One, blessed be He, wept over Moses, saying: "'Who will rise up for Me against the evil-doers' (Psalms 94:16), who will pray for My sons?" The ministering angels wept, saying: "Where will wisdom be found?" (Job 28:12). "It will be hidden from all the living" (Job 28:21). The heavens wept, saying: "The godly man is perished out of the earth" (Micah 7:2). The earth wept, saying: "The upright man is no more" (Ibid.). All the orders of creation wept, saying: "The righteous hath perished, and no man layeth it to heart" (Isaiah 57:1). The sun and moon wept, saying: "Give heed, ye brutish among the people" (Psalms 94:8). And all the planets wept, saying: "And ye fools, when will ye be wise?" (Psalms 94:8). The holy spirit wept, saying: "And there hath not arisen a prophet since in Israel like unto Moses" (Deuteronomy 34:10). When Joshua looked for Moses but could not find him, he wept, saying: "Help, Lord; for the godly man has ceased; for the faithful failed from among the children of men" (Psalms 12:2). All Israel wept, saying: "And there came the heads of the people, he executed the righteousness of the Lord, and His ordinances with Israel" (Deuteronomy 33:21).

There are a number of Midrashim dealing with the death of Moses. One of them is called Petirat Mosheh, *"The Death of Moses." It is a version of this that Daat Zekenim quotes here. The Midrash is a poetic reconstruction of what took place when Moses died. There are many legends about fallen angels. Details of these and other legends mentioned in this passage can be found in Ginzberg's* Legends of the Jews. *Daat Zekenim concludes with a short note on the reading of the Torah.*

Our Rabbis, of blessed memory, say that these last eight verses of the Pentateuch should be read by only one person. This is a strange ruling, since it is said in tractate Megillah concerning all the portions of the Torah, that only one person and not two should read them. The fact that nowadays two do read, namely, the Reader and the *Hazzan* (Cantor), is because we rely on the passage in tractate Bikkurim which states that at first it was the practice that whoever could read would do so and whoever could not would have the portion read for him. But when this was seen to cause embarrassment to those who could not read, it was ordained that everyone should have his portion read for him. As for these eight verses, the Deputy of the Congregation (the Cantor) alone should read them.

Daat Zekenim is puzzled by the ruling that only one person should read these eight verses. This is surely true of all verses? He does not give a solution. The Tosafot to the Talmud also occasionally raise a difficult question without providing the answer. Daat Zekenim notes that nowadays we do have someone to read for us, but the reason is as he states.

Ḥazzekuni

What lessons can be derived from the story of Adam?
Why is it forbidden to plow with two different animals?

The Commentary to the Pentateuch by the thirteenth century French scholar Hezekiah ben Manoah is called Ḥazzekuni, "Strengthen Me" (a play on his name). The work was first printed in Venice in 1524 and has since been printed together with the text in some editions of the Pentateuch. The Ḥazzekuni relies on Rashi and other commentators and quotes various Midrashim. But, of course, he has many original ideas especially of a mystical nature. In his introduction, the author dedicates his book to his father Manoah, "who offered up his right arm as a burnt offering to the God of the Hebrews," evidently a reference to some act of martyrdom of which we have no details.

A. WHAT LESSONS CAN BE DERIVED FROM THE STORY OF ADAM?

Comment on: "And the Lord God commanded the man, saying: 'Of every tree of the garden, thou mayest freely eat; but of the tree of knowledge of good and evil, thou shalt not eat of it; for in the day that thou eatest thereof thou shalt surely die'" (Genesis 2:16, 17).

God did not put Adam to the test for His sake, since all that has happened in the past and that will happen in the future is revealed

to Him. It was rather to persuade the ministering angels, who prayed too much for mercy on Adam's behalf, that Adam would not emerge successfully from the test.

God told Adam not to eat of the fruit of the tree in order to put him to the test. But surely God knew how he could behave? Hazzekuni quotes a Midrashic explanation that the test was for the benefit of the ministering angels who were too biased in Adam's favor. A very curious idea. Perhaps the notion behind it all is that man is not an angel and too much should not be expected of him. Hazzekuni now quotes a famous passage in the Talmud. According to the Rabbis, there is a Torah, a law, for all men, not only for Jews. Non-Jews also have to obey seven basic rules and, if they do, they are called the "righteous of the nations." These are known as "the seven laws of the sons of Noah" because, after the flood, Noah became the father of the whole human race. But since these rules are so basic, they are ascribed to Adam. They are derived in the Talmudic passage based on our verse, but in all probability the Rabbis were using the verse as a kind of peg on which to hang these laws, as if to say, these laws are essential rules of human conduct. They are hinted at in this verse, the first command issued to Adam, the first man. The seven laws are:
1) not to murder; 2) not to worship idols; 3) not to commit adultery or incest; 4) not to rob; 5) not to blaspheme; 6) not to eat a limb torn from an animal while it is still alive (prohibiting gross cruelty); 7) to have an adequate system of law to regulate human society.

Our Rabbis derive from this verse by the Midrashic method the seven laws of the sons of Noah: "And the Lord God commanded." This refers to men having an adequate system of law, as it is said: "For I know him, that he will command his children and his household after him, and they shall keep the way of the Lord, to do justice and judgment" (Genesis 18:19). "The Lord." This refers to the honor of the Holy One, blessed be He, as it is said: "And he that blasphemes the name of the Lord, he shall surely be put to death" (Leviticus 24:16). "God." This refers to idolatry, as it is said: "Thou shalt have no other gods before Me" (Exodus 20:3). "The man." This refers to murder, as it is said: "Whoso sheddeth man's blood" (Genesis 9:6). "Saying." This refers to adultery, as it is said: "Saying, if a man put away his wife" (Jeremiah 3:1). "Of every tree

of the garden." But not of robbery. "Thou mayest freely eat." But not a limb torn from a living animal. Abraham came and the command of circumcision was added (Genesis 17:10-14). Jacob came and the command regarding the sinew of the thigh was added (Genesis 32:33). Judah came and the command of levirate marriage was added (Genesis, chapter 38, and Deuteronomy 25:5-10). Israel came and there were added the commands regarding the sabbath and honoring parents. "Commanded on the man." This means on him and on his seed were these commands placed, therefore, it does not say "the man" but "on the man."

The point to this midrash is that certain key words occur in our verse and in the verse quoted, e.g., "command." Levirate marriage means the duty of a member of the family (levir = "brother-in-law") to marry the widow if a member of the family dies without issue. Hazzekuni speaks of "honoring the Lord" because he does not wish to use the word "blaspheme." He really means "dishonoring the Lord," but uses a euphemism. The reference to the sabbath and honoring parents is that according to the Rabbis, Israel was commanded to obey these even before they were given the Torah as a whole. Hazzekuni's final point is that the Hebrew does not say et ha-adam (which means simply "the man), but al ha-adam (which means literally "on the man). Hazzekuni understands this to mean that the commands were not only issued for Adam but they were placed "on" him, i.e., as commands for his descendants.

"Of every tree of the garden thou mayest freely eat." You may say that this leaves the way open for someone to object that Adam ate of the tree of life. If that is so, how could he have been punished with death even though he did eat of the tree of knowledge? One can reply that he did not, in fact, eat of the tree of life, for he only remained in the Garden of Eden for three hours. But if you wish to say that he did eat of it, it is possible that the tree of knowledge was poison to whomever had eaten of the tree of life, but the tree of life was an antidote to whomever had eaten of the tree of knowledge. Consequently, after he had eaten of the tree of knowledge, the Holy One, blessed be He, said (Genesis 3:22): "Behold, the man is become as one of us, to know good and evil; and now, lest he put forth his hand, and take also of the tree of life"—once again—"and eat, and live for ever," and then people will be misled by him. But since he will not be allowed to eat of the tree of life after he has eaten of the tree of knowledge, he will surely die. Another explanation: "Of every tree of the garden thou mayest freely eat" does not include the tree of life. To prohibit this, no special warning was necessary, because when the verse says: "the tree of life also in the midst of the garden" (Genesis 2:9), it means in the center of the garden. The proof is that the *Targum* translates it, in fact, as "in the center of the garden." The tree of knowledge surrounded the tree of life on every side. They were both placed in the center of the garden in such a way that the tree of life was protected by the tree of knowledge and Adam could not have reached the tree of life without first disobeying the command not to eat of the tree of knowledge. That is why Adam was only warned regarding the tree of knowledge. But when he had transgressed and had eaten of it, then the Holy One, blessed be He, said: "Behold, the man is become as one of us," etc. Another explanation: Adam was indeed permitted to eat of all the trees in the garden, except the tree of knowledge, as it is written: "But of the tree of knowledge thou shalt not eat." For as long as you do not eat of it, you will have neither the knowledge nor the inclination to distinguish between good and evil. I shall then only judge you as an unintentional sinner and not as a real sinner so that, since you will not have sinned, it does not matter if you live forever. But if you do eat of it, I shall judge you on the spot and punish you with death, otherwise you would live as a sinner forever. Another explanation: The reason Adam was not warned regarding the tree of life was because he was to transgress the command. Better, then, that he should eat of the tree of knowledge than that he should eat of the tree of life.

Ḥazzekuni's problem is that evidently Adam was not forbidden to eat of the tree of life. Perhaps he did eat of it and since, according to the narrative, this makes man immortal, why did he eventually die? Ḥazzekuni gives a number of possible solutions. First, he calls attention to a saying of the Rabbis that it all took place in only three hours and in that short time Adam had no time to eat of the tree of life, even though this was not forbidden to him. Secondly, it can be argued that he did eat of the tree of life, but the tree of knowledge counteracted the effects of the tree of life. The tree of life could then, in turn, have counteracted the effects of the tree of knowledge, but Adam was driven out of Eden before he could eat of the tree of life a second time. (The reading in the printed editions of the Ḥazzekuni is peculiar at this point, but as the note in some editions remarks, the rendering we have given here is the only one that makes sense). Thirdly, Ḥazzekuni suggests, Adam was only permitted to eat of the trees "in" the garden, not of those in the "center" of the garden. The Aramaic translation known as the Targum renders the words "in the midst of the garden" as "in the center of the garden." It was unnecessary, therefore, to have a special prohibition of the tree of life since Adam could not get at the tree of life without first eating of the tree of knowledge which surrounded it, and this he was forbidden to do. Fourthly, Ḥazzekuni suggests, even though Adam had eaten of the tree of life, the immortality it conferred on him was conditional on his not sinning. Once he had eaten of the tree of knowledge, any sins he committed would be intentional. He would be a real sinner and a real sinner cannot enjoy immortality. The meaning, then, of God saying that he might eat of the tree of life, after he had eaten of the tree of knowledge, was not intended to suggest that if he did this he would become immortal, but to state why, as a sinner, he could not be allowed to live forever. Finally, Ḥazzekuni suggests, the whole test could only have been given on the tree of knowledge. It would have been far worse if the sin, which he did eventually commit, had concerned the tree of life. All this is very ingenious, but is there anything more to it than a play with ideas? It is possible that Ḥazzekuni is asking us to read something more significant out of this fanciful exegesis. For instance, Professor Louis Ginzberg, in a lecture at the Hebrew University, used Ḥazzekuni's idea of the tree of life being contained within the tree of knowledge to yield the thought that there can be no worthwhile life without knowledge. One has to eat of the tree of knowledge before one can taste the fruit of the tree of life!

B. WHY IS IT FORBIDDEN TO PLOW WITH TWO DIFFERENT ANIMALS?

Comment on the prohibition of plowing with an ox and an ass together (Deuteronomy 22:10), and of wearing a garment made of wool and linen (Deuteronomy 22:11). Various reasons have been given for these prohibitions. Here are Ḥazzekuni's.

"Thou shalt not plow with an ox and an ass." The cow chews the cud all the time, while the ass does not chew the cud. This means

that while one animal eats, the other fasts and this is cruelty to animals. Another explanation: Because the ox is a king among beasts and its image is on the throne of glory (Ezekiel 1:10). The ass, on the other hand, is a miserable beast, so that it is unfitting for the two to be yoked together. Another explanation: The Holy One, blessed be He, has compassion on all His creatures and the strength of the ass cannot compete with the strength of the ox. "Together." Only if they are yoked together, not if they plow side by side without being compelled to go in the same direction. Our Rabbis declare that the law applies to any two different animals, because we derive it from the sabbath law where there is also a reference to an ox (Deuteronomy 5:14). But a man may plow together with any animal.

Since the ox appears to be eating all the time, the ass, seeing this, will suffer. The rest of Hazzekuni's commentary is self-explanatory, except for the reference to the sabbath. The point here is that with regard to the sabbath laws, all animals are included, even though only an ox and an ass are specified (because these are the animals generally used). The Rabbis conclude, therefore, that here, too, the prohibition covers any two different animals. This does not fit in too well with Hazzekuni's reasons, but he would probably say that his reasons are according to the "plain meaning," though he would not, of course, reject the Rabbinic Midrash.

"Wool and linen together." Since catastrophe resulted from both of these, it is forbidden to wear a garment made of both of them. Abel brought his offering of the firstlings of his flock and Cain brought his offering from seedlings of flax (Genesis 4:3-4). Another explanation: Since the priestly garments (Exodus 28:1-5) were made up of both of these, it is prohibited to wear them together for any secular purpose. They are reserved for God's servants when they minister to Him. That is why you find that the law of plagues in garments only applies to garments of wool and linen (Leviticus 13:47), to demonstrate that there is sinfulness when these are mixed. Scripture repeats it here to show that the term "a mingled stuff" means one of wool and linen.

According to an ancient tradition, Cain's offering was from flax. Thus the first murder came about through these two and it is forbidden to wear a mixture of wool and linen to express our abhorrence of murder. According to the Rabbinic interpretation of the relevant Scriptural verses, the priestly garments were made of wool and linen. Hence the prohibition is not (as in the first interpretation) because of any abhorrence but, on the contrary, because this mixture is reserved for the most sacred purposes.

Baḥya ibn Asher

Why is sheepherding an ideal occupation?
Why is the slave's ear pierced?
Why is Moses called the servant of the Lord?

The Spanish teacher Baḥya ibn Asher (died 1340) wrote a Commentary to the whole of the Pentateuch. In this he relies on the teachings of the Talmudic Rabbis, the commentators who preceded him, the works of the philosophers, and, especially, the doctrines of the Kabbalists. So popular did his Commentary become that the author is generally referred to as "Rabbenu Baḥya" (or, as others have it, "Beḥai"), i.e., "Our teacher Baḥya." Baḥya is particularly concerned with discovering the deeper meaning of Scripture, its permanent values, its significance for Jewish life. The Commentary was first printed at Naples in 1492. Other editions are those of Pesaro, 1507, 1514, 1517; Constantinople, 1517; Rimini, 1524; Venice, 1544, 1546, 1559, 1566. The best edition is that of Chavel, Jerusalem, 1966. Various scholars wrote commentaries to Baḥya's Commentary. No fewer than ten of these are known.

A. WHY IS SHEEPHERDING AN IDEAL OCCUPATION?

Comment on Genesis 46:32: "The men are shepherds; they have always been breeders of livestock, and they have brought with them their flocks and their herds and all that is theirs." In this verse, the occupation of the sons of Jacob who had come to live in Egypt is described as that of shepherd. Baḥya here considers why they chose that profession.

There are two reasons why the tribes chose this profession, which was, in fact, the profession of their ancestors. The first is because there is much profit to be obtained from this occupation in terms of the shearings of the wool, the milk and the young. Moreover, it is an occupation which does not demand heavy labor and great effort and nothing sinful is involved in it. Solomon in his wisdom advised men to follow this occupation when he said: "Be thou diligent to know the state of thy flocks, and look well to thy herds" (Proverbs 27:23). The second reason is that the tribes knew that they and their offspring would be exiled in Egypt. The Egyptians worshipped sheep and so the tribes chose this occupation in order that their offspring would be thoroughly familiar with it and the result would be that the worship of sheep would become very remote for them.

Bahya follows the Rabbis in calling the sons of Jacob "the tribes," because they were the progenitors of the twelve tribes of Israel, Reuben, Simeon, Levi and so forth. Their "ancestors," Abraham, Isaac and Jacob, were also cultivators of sheep and herds, as we find it stated in the book of Genesis (e.g., chapters 12-13; 26; 14; 29-31). The first reason Bahya gives is that this method of earning a living is admirable in itself. There is profit in it without overmuch effort and, unlike many other occupations, there are few opportunities for committing any dishonest acts. The quotation from the book of Proverbs is said to be the advice of Solomon, in the Rabbinic tradition the author of the book. Bahya's second reason is that a shepherd who becomes thoroughly accustomed to his sheep will always see them as sheep and as no more than sheep. He will never be tempted to worship them as gods. The Rabbis believed that the Egyptians worshipped sheep much as nowadays in some parts of the world there are "sacred cows." Thus, for Bahya, the occupation of shepherd was both profitable and innocent in itself and served at the same time as a campaign in the battle of the tribes against idolatry in the form of animal worship.

You will also find that the majority of the righteous men and the prophets were shepherds. Thus you find it said of Abel: "Abel became a keeper of sheep" (Genesis 4:2). Of Moses, too, it is said: "Now Moses, tending the flock" (Exodus 3:1). Of Samuel the prophet, of Saul (I Samuel 11:5), and of David (I Samuel 16:11), it is said that they were shepherds (or tended herds). They chose this occupation because it kept them far from the haunts of men. Numerous sins are caused by life in society, for example, talebearing, slander, false oaths, adultery, theft and robbery. The more a man keeps himself away from social intercourse, the more he is spared from sin; the more remote he is from human habitation, the more remote he is from iniquity, from theft and robbery and from other sins.

This passage seems extremely antisocial, but it must be remembered that Bahya is not holding up an ideal for his own day (Bahya himself was not a shepherd and he lived a social life.) He is rather trying to explain why the great leaders of old engaged in this occupation as a preparation for their true task. The prophets, of course, once they had had a communication from God, brought a message of justice and righteousness to their people with the strongest possible social content. Chavel remarks that he has been unable to discover anywhere a reference to Samuel as a shepherd or a herdsman. Perhaps Bahya is thinking of I Samuel 12:3: "Whose ox have I taken? or whose ass have I taken?." Bahya evidently gives this third reason for adopting the profession of shepherd because the first two he gives do not apply to the prophets. They would not be interested primarily in profit, nor would they need to be trained to protest against animal worship.

The proof of this is from Lot, of whom it is written: "Lot went up from Zoar and settled in the hill country" (Genesis 19:30). He was obliged to leave Sodom in order to escape destruction because of their sins. After he had left Sodom, he made his way to Zoar, as it is said: "Look, that town there is near enough to flee to it; it is such a little one" (Genesis 19:20). He went there because its inhabitants had only settled it a short while previously and its sins were therefore few in number. In spite of this, Lot was still apprehensive while he remained in Zoar because of his fear of the sins that are so frequent in an inhabited place. That was why he eventually was obliged to leave even that place for the hill country.

We have here a series of puns, based on a passage in the Talmud (Shabbat 10b). The name "Zoar" is associated with the word for "little." The word for "near" is connected with the idea of "nearness" in time, i.e., the town had only recently been inhabited. The "near" (= more recently inhabited) town is "little" (= small in sinfulness). Since the townsfolk had not been there very long, they had had no

*time to become grasping and cynical. Thus the ideal state for man
is to live far away from civilization, especially if, like Lot, he had
lived in a sinful society. At first, Lot thought he would escape from
sin in Zoar whose sins were few. But even there temptations were
to be found, so that eventually he left Zoar to dwell in the hills
away from all traces of civilization. This passage in Baḥya is one of
the very few in Jewish literature to hold up for admiration
something like the hermit ideal. But, again, Baḥya is thinking of
the prophet and the rare soul, not an ideal for all men.*

**Furthermore, there (away from the haunts of men) is the place
where the solitude necessary for prophecy can be attained. There
a man cannot see anything to distract him from having all his
thoughts on God. You know that the great prophets used to depart
far from civilization to find solitude in the wilderness, even without
the need to go there with their flocks. These are Elijah and Elisha.
Of Elisha it is said: "With twelve yoke of oxen before him" (I Kings
19:19). But he gave up this occupation in order to follow Elijah.
Therefore it is written: "Let me, I pray thee, kiss my father and my
mother, and then I will follow thee" (1 Kings 19:20). And it is
written: "Then he arose, and went after Elijah, and ministered unto
him." Without doubt, this was the custom of the sons of the prophets
in that and in the previous generation. They would leave the
business of the world behind them, relinquishing all care for
material things, going out into the wilderness to be there in
solitude, with their heart attached to God.**

*The "sons of the prophets" are the disciples of the prophets, as
Elisha was the disciple of Elijah. According to Baḥya, an important
part of their training was to leave aside all worldly things in order
to be alone with God. Some of these men even gave up the occupation of shepherd or herdsman, as Elisha did to go after Elijah.*

B. WHY IS THE SLAVE'S EAR PIERCED?

*Comment on Exodus 21:6: "He shall be brought to the door or the
doorpost, and his master shall pierce his ear with the awl; and he
shall then remain his slave forever." This is the law of a Hebrew
slave who is entitled to go free after he has served for six years.
But if, at the end of six years, the slave does not want to go free
and wishes to remain a slave, the master has to take his slave to*

the door (according to the Rabbis, the door of the courthouse) and
bore a hole in the slave's ear and then the slave remains his
"forever." Bahya first quotes some Rabbinic interpretations of the
details of the law and then he proceeds to explain the meaning of
this strange ceremony.

"He shall be brought to the door." I might have thought that it
makes no difference whether the door is fixed or not fixed. Therefore Scripture goes on to say **"the doorpost,"** to teach you that
just as the doorpost is fixed, so, too, the door must be fixed. **"And
his master shall pierce,"** and not the master's son or the master's
deputy or the deputy of the court. **"His ear"** and not **"her ear,"**
since the law of boring the ear does not apply to a female slave.
"With the awl," not **"with an awl,"** so that the meaning is with a
special awl. **"And he shall then remain his slave,"** and not the
slave of his son. From which it can be derived that when the master
dies, the slave goes free. **"Forever,"** this means **"forever until the
Jubilee year."** Thus do our Sages interpret it in tractate Kiddushin
(21b).

Bahya quotes a number of typical examples of how the Rabbis
examined every word of the legal passages in Scripture to discover
the exact application of the law. These passages were seen as
having been written with the care and precision of a legal document
in which every word counts. If the verse had only spoken of the
door, it might have been argued that any door will do, even a door
that has been taken off its hinges. But since, in fact, Scripture
speaks of both the door and the doorpost, then it clearly means a
door fixed in the wall, just as the doorpost is only so called when it
is fixed in the wall to stand upright. Scripture speaks of the "master"
performing the act of boring the ear, from which it follows that it
cannot be done by the master's son, or by a deputy the master
appoints for the purpose or by someone appointed by the court of
law, such as a policeman. Since the verse speaks of the master
boring "his" ear, it is implied that the law does not apply if it is
"her" ear, that is to say, a female slave who does not wish to go
free when her time comes is not subjected to the ordeal. The
Hebrew is ba-martzea, "with the awl," not be-martzea, "with an
awl." The definite article is used to teach that it cannot be done
with any sharp instrument, but with the special instrument that is

known as "the awl." The verse states that he remains his slave for life. This means that when the master dies, his son does not inherit the slave as he does the rest of his father's estate. Finally, although the term "forever" is used, it means, say the Rabbis, until the Jubilee year comes round. The Jubilee year fell once every fifty years, so that if, for instance, the ordeal of boring the ear took place ten years before the Jubilee year, the slave would only serve for a further ten years and not all his life. (For the Jubilee year, see Leviticus 25:8-24). Bahya now proceeds to explain the meaning of the law and in the course of his exposition it will also become clear why these details are mentioned and how they fit into the total picture.

It is well known that, according to the custom of the world, it belongs to the nature of a slave owned by a master to loathe himself and to be sick of his life in bondage because he longs to be free. This person who wishes to remain a slave and to have over him a master, other than God, behaves in a very unusual way. Consequently, the law demands here that the master himself, whom the slave has chosen and whom he loves, must bring his slave to the court and bore his ear at the door of the court. Thus that very organ which sinned is smitten. For it was the ear which heard at Sinai: "Thou shalt not steal" (Exodus 20:13), and yet this slave did steal. Or it was the ear which heard that which is written: "For it is to Me that the Israelites are servants" (Leviticus 25:55), implying that they should not become the servants of servants, and yet this slave did go and acquire a master for himself. For whatever reason, it is treated as a sin. For the slave has become estranged from the Supreme Master, blessed be He, who warned us when we received the Torah against serving any but Him, and this slave now casts off the yoke of God's service. It seems to me that this is why Scripture says here: "When you acquire a Hebrew slave," or "When you acquire a Hebrew as a slave." This is because "Israel" is the honored name that was given to us after the giving of the Torah. But this person, who acts in contradiction to that which he had heard at Sinai, does not deserve to be called by the name "Israel." Therefore, Scripture calls him a "Hebrew," a name older and less honored than the name "Israelite."

To understand Baḥya's comment, it is necessary to know that according to the Rabbis there are two ways in which a Hebrew can become a slave. One is when he had stolen some money which he is unable to repay. He can be sold as a slave so as to be able to repay his victim with the purchase money. The second instance is when a man freely sells himself for gain. Now it is wrong for a man to become a slave to others. A man is God's servant. It is God's will for him to be free. The man who sells himself thus offends against God's law and the man sold for theft is similarly to blame, since if he had not stolen, he would not have been sold as a slave. Strictly speaking, the ear should have been pierced right at the beginning of his period of bondage, but then an opportunity is given to him to taste the evils of a life of slavery and to feel remorse. But if the slave wishes to remain a slave, even when he has the opportunity of going free, this demonstrates that he has experienced no remorse. Very well then, let his ear be bored. Why the ear? Because it was the ear that heard at Sinai that a man should not steal or become a slave. Baḥya explains the previously stated law that the master himself and not his son or deputy must bore the slave's ear. This is because the slave wishes this man to be his master instead of God. Baḥya continues that the passage in which this law occurs begins with a reference to buying a "Hebrew" slave. "Israel" is the name of honor which was earned at Sinai. Consequently, one who disregards the Torah, as this slave does, forfeits thereby his right to the honored name, at least when he commits that which is forbidden. He can only be called a "Hebrew," the name the Israelites had before the Torah was given. The man who wishes to be a slave is a "Hebrew," a Jew without the Torah. He is not an "Israelite," a Jew who keeps the Torah.

Consequently, the Torah commanded that the organ which sinned should be smitten, for that organ heard the command and yet the slave disregarded it. Moreover, the wound must be inflicted by the master the slave has chosen in order to demonstrate that both the slave and his master are obliged to serve the Supreme Master, blessed be He, to whom alone belong lordship and dominion, not to flesh and blood. This is why the verse says: "His master shall take him before God" (Exodus 21:6). This refers to the place where the court sits, the place of justice, "for judgment is God's" (Deuteronomy 1:17). Scripture states this because the slave rejects God's dominion, that is, he rejects the quality of judgment which slew the firstborn of Egypt in order to save Israel from bondage. And the verse goes on to say: "He shall be brought to the door or the doorpost," corresponding to the rejection of the sign of the blood on the doors, on the lintel and on the two doorposts (Exodus 12:22), as a result of which Israel emerged from slavery to freedom. Therefore "his master shall pierce his ear with the awl," that blood might come from it, and it is all a question of measure for measure. Although it is not essential for the master to make the ear bleed, since the ordeal is valid even if it is performed with an acid, nonetheless in the majority of cases it is not done with an acid and the ear does bleed. The instrument generally used is called *martzea*, which has the numerical value of 400. This is because the slave wishes to add to the 400 years of Egyptian bondage (see Genesis 15: 13). The Midrash comments on the verse: "He shall be brought to the door" as follows: God says: "I opened a door through which he can go free and yet he closed that door to remain a slave, therefore let him be smitten at the door."

Bahya here draws a number of parallels, some of them rather farfetched, to demonstrate that the ordeal is carried out in obedience to the principle of measure for measure. The slave is brought before God in His attribute of judgment. This is a reminder of God's sternness in slaying the Egyptian firstborn. At the Exodus, various events took place as a prelude to Israel's freedom. Among them were: the slaying of the firstborn and the blood on the doorposts. Both of these are given symbolic expression in the ordeal, says Bahya, because so far as this slave is concerned, they might just as well not have happened since he totally disregards the basic message of the Exodus that God wishes man to be free, not a slave. Bahya's point about the acid is that, according to the Talmud, if the perforation of the ear is carried out in this way instead of with an awl, the ordeal is still valid, but usually it is performed with an awl and then the ear bleeds. Bahya then uses the curious method known as gematria (from the Greek meaning "to measure," as in our words "metric" and "geometry"). Since each Hebrew letter is also a number, it is possible to make one word represent a different word if their total letters have the same numerical value and it is also possible to make a word represent a number. Now the Hebrew for "awl" is martzea. The letters of this are: mem = 40; resh = 200;

tzaddi = 90; ayin = 70, the total of which is 400. The Israelites were
destined to serve as slaves in Egypt for 400 years, then to be freed
by God. So far as our slave is concerned, they might as well have
remained slaves in Egypt, so little does he value freedom. Let his
ear be pierced then with a martzea. The Midrash Baḥya finally
quotes is not found in any of our Midrash collections, but on a
number of occasions Baḥya quotes Midrashim known in his day
which have been lost.

One should understand further that a secret is conveyed by the word
delet **("door"), and this is why the definite article is used, "He shall**
be brought to *the* **door." We find, too, in the book of Deuteronomy:**
"And put it through his ear into the door" (Deuteronomy 15:17). Now
the door is the place through which one enters the house. It is
impossible to enter the house unless one goes through the door.
The word *delet* **refers to the letter** *dalet* **in the verse of the Shema.**
The house is the Community of Israel and this is the Gate through
which the righteous enter. And when it says "to the doorpost," it
refers to the numerical value of God's name and is clear. The
Hebrew slave failed to know or understand this. He substituted the
lordship of the profane for the lordship of the holy. Therefore the
command is issued that he must serve his master until the time will
come when all lords and masters above and below will bow before
the Lord of lords and all will recognize that "The earth is the Lord's,
and the fullness thereof" (Psalms 24:1).

Here Baḥya introduces a Kabbalistic interpretation which he calls
a "secret" or "mystery" and very mysterious it is. The point he
appears to be making is this. Each of the divine names represents
an aspect of God in His manifestation in the universe. One of the
divine names is Adonai, and this is connected with the word adon,
"master," used in our passage for the master of the slave. This
name of God is also represented by the letter dalet in the Shema,
Israel's declaration of faith: "Hear, O Israel: The Lord our God,
the Lord is One" (Deuteronomy 6:4). Tradition has it that the letter
dalet of the word eḥad ("One") has to be written large. The word
dalet, moreover, resembles the word delet, "door." God's dominion
or lordship is thus represented by the door. (Actually, in Kabbalistic
terminology this represents what is known as the Shechinah, the
Divine Presence. Through this aspect of the Deity His grace flows

through all creation, and it is thus the "door" of the divine realm). This is, in fact, called in the Kabbala, "The Community of Israel" because it is the counterpart on high of Israel down below on earth. Another pun is here intended, because this can also mean "The Entrance of Israel"—Israel being here construed as still higher manifestations which come down through the "door." The slave denies God's lordship by accepting the lordship of another. He thereby offends against the "door" principle and so his ear must be bored at the door. Furthermore, he offends against the "doorpost" principle, which is the same thing. The letters of the word for "doorpost" (mezuzah) total 65 (mem = 40; zayin = 7; vav = 6; zayin = 7; he = 5) and this is the numerical value of Adonai (alef = 1; dalet = 4; nun = 50; yod = 10). The slave must serve his master "forever," which can mean "until eternity," i.e., until time is at an end and eternity dawns (i.e., in the Messianic age). At that time all men will acknowledge God as their Master and there shall be no more masters and slaves.

"And he shall remain his slave forever." Our Rabbis had a tradition that "forever" means "until the Jubilee year." This is the fiftieth year for a timespan of fifty years is called (loosely) "forever." We find this in connection with Samuel: "And there abide forever" (I Samuel 1:22). This refers to the "forever" period of the Levites, as it is said: "From twenty-five years old and upwards" (Numbers 8: 24) "until fifty years" (Numbers 4:3). Samuel only lived fifty-two years and he was at that time two years old. This law that the slave goes free in the Jubilee year applies whether that year is near or distant.

The Rabbis say that the slave does not necessarily remain a slave for the rest of his life. He does go free on the Jubilee year, so that the term "forever" is used loosely to represent an epoch. Why is this called "forever"? Because the Jubilee year comes at the end of fifty years and a fifty year span is loosely called "forever." This can be seen from the case of Samuel. His mother Hannah promised that she would bring him to serve in the Sanctuary and he would stay there "forever." But, according to tradition, Samuel only lived fifty-two years and he was two years old when his mother brought him to the Sanctuary. Although he only served there for fifty years, it was still called "forever." Moreover, Samuel was a Levite and in the book of Numbers it is stated that Levites served in the Sanctuary until their age of retirement at fifty. Fifty years can consequently be termed "forever" so far as Levites are concerned. Baḥya adds that whether the Jubilee year came soon or late after the ordeal, the slave would then go free. Baḥya now adds another Kabbalistic comment, another "secret" or "mystery." "Fifty years" is called "forever" to hint at the idea that the total span of all time is fifty thousand years, as he goes on to say.

Or is it possible that the reason why the term "forever" is used for the fifty year period is because this is the period that the world will endure. For the slave who serves for fifty years serves as many years as the number of years that the world will endure. Hinted at here is the idea that all the days of the world form one great Jubilee. This is contained in the verse: "The word which He commanded to a thousand generations" (Psalms 105:8). For a generation covers fifty years, the number, too, of the timespan of the world. King Solomon, on whom be peace, hinted at this: "And the earth abideth *forever*" (Ecclesiastes 1:4). This refers to "forever" in the sense of "until the Jubilee of the world." Understand this.

This curious passage can better be understood when we recall that the Hebrew word olam, which means "forever", can also mean "world." Thus the term olam can mean an epoch. Now according to a very ancient theory (rejected, incidentally, by many of the later Kabbalists), popular in Baḥya's day, the world will endure for six thousand years, followed by a "sabbath" of one thousand years. After this epoch, the whole creation will begin again, as it were, and will last for another six thousand years, followed by a "sabbath." This process is repeated seven times and then the world comes to a complete end. This is the great Jubilee at the end of forty-nine thousand years, i.e., the fiftieth thousandth year. This is why, according to Baḥya, the Jubilee year is called olam, meaning both "forever" and "the world," because fifty is the number of thousands that the world will endure. Ecclesiastes is traditionally attributed to King Solomon. He says: "And the earth abideth le-olam"—"forever" or "for the time of the duration of the world" = fifty (thousand) years. There can only be masters and slaves during these recurring epochs. Hence it is appropriate that the number fifty should occur in connection with these laws about the slave remaining in bondage. Of course, all this belongs to a "prescientific" age and, in any event, as we have noted, many Jewish scholars of the past rejected the whole notion, especially since in some versions of the theory there is a different Torah for each epoch! The later teachers viewed with horror the idea that the Torah was only for a particular period and was not eternal.

C. WHY IS MOSES CALLED THE SERVANT OF THE LORD?

Comment on: "So Moses the servant of the Lord died there in the land of Moab, by the mouth of the Lord" (Deuteronomy 34:5). Bahya wishes to examine why Moses is referred to as "the servant of the Lord" only here, when Scripture is describing his death. Bahya's reply is most interesting. While a man, even a great man like Moses, is alive he may become a sinner and so cancel out all the good he has done. Only when a man has died and we can look back on his life of goodness, can it be said that he was God's servant.

"So Moses the servant of the Lord died there." He was not called "servant" until he died. During his lifetime he was called, at the beginning of this portion (Deuteronomy 33:1), "the man of God." Now, at the end of the portion he is called "the servant of the Lord," a title given him nowhere else in the Pentateuch. The meaning of this title is that Moses was elevated and his comprehension of the divine great, for a servant is always near to his master, having the right to enter with him into the most private rooms and to serve him constantly. The Rabbis state explicitly that the righteous are greater in death than in life. We find, too, that no man is called "holy" until he has died. This is why Scripture says: "As for the holy that are in the earth" (Psalms 16:3), which the Rabbis say refers to the dead patriarchs. For thus say the Rabbis in the Midrash to Psalms: "The Holy One, blessed be He, does not call the righteous holy until they are interred in the earth. Because the evil inclination torments a man in this world, the Holy One, blessed be He, does not trust him until he has died. And even the patriarchs were not called holy until they were interred in the earth." Thus far the Midrash. This is why the Rabbis ordained that we should say in our prayers: "And the holy ones praise Thee every day. Selah." It is the soul of the righteous which utters praise, as it is said: "Let every soul praise the Lord" (Psalms 150:6).

*This passage is self-explanatory. Note the homiletical interpretation
of "in the earth," which really means "on earth," but which the
Midrash interprets as "buried in the earth."*

**Many people ask, how is it that of Moses, through whom the Torah
was given, it is recorded that he died and yet we find that Enoch
(see Genesis 5:24) and Elijah (II Kings 2:11), who did not reach the
elevated stage of Moses, lived on forever? But the matter has to be
understood as follows. Moses, because he sinned by the water of
Meribah (Numbers 20:12,13), was condemned to die and was included in the decree of death pronounced against Adam (see
Genesis 3:19). But Enoch and Elijah who did not sin were not included in the decree pronounced against Adam and live in eternal
life.**

*Moses, argues Baḥya, was undoubtedly greater than Enoch (who
was believed to have gone to Heaven while still alive) and Elijah.
But, on the other hand, he had sinned and they had not. When
Adam, the father of the human race, sinned, death was decreed for
him and for all his descendants who would sin. According to this
view, if a man never sinned he would never die. Note Baḥya's idea
that a man may live all his life without sin and yet may be a lesser
man than one who did sin but also achieved great things.*

**"By the mouth of the Lord." The plain meaning is that God had
said to him: "You shall die on the mountain" (Deuteronomy 32:50).
But the Midrashic interpretation is that it means death by a divine
kiss. This means that Moses' intellect arose to cleave to the Glorious
Name.**

*Like many other commentators, Baḥya distinguishes between the
"plain meaning" of Scripture and the Midrashic interpretations
read into it. He remarks here that the plain meaning of the verse is
that Moses died "at the mouth of"—"at the command of God." But
he then quotes a beautiful Rabbinic homily which takes "mouth"
literally. God kissed Moses and his soul departed. But, of course,
this is poetry. God does not have a "mouth." And so Baḥya goes on
to explain "death by a divine kiss" to mean that Moses' intellect
soared at his death to attach itself to God.*

Gersonides

What lessons are to be derived from the story of Hannah?
Did the sun really stop for Joshua?

*Levi ben Gershon (1288-1344), French philosopher, Talmudist and
mathematician, also wrote commentaries to various Biblical books.
He is known as Gersonides and as Ralbag (after the initial letters
of his name Rabbi Levi ben Gershon). His major philosophical work
is Milḥamot Adonai, The Wars of the Lord, of which a selection is
given in Volume II of this series. Gersonides' Commentary to the
Pentateuch was first published in Mantua (1476-1480); his
Commentary to the Earlier Prophets in Leiria (1494). These
Commentaries have frequently been published together with the
text in editions of the Bible. A unique feature of Gersonides' method
is to state at length at the conclusion of each Biblical section the
moral and philosophical lessons to be derived from it. He is
convinced that the Biblical narratives are not simply records of
ancient events, but contain guidance for the Jew in his daily life.
He calls these lessons Toaliyyot ("advantages," i.e., to be gained
from a study of the text).*

*The following is Gersonides' comment on the first chapters of the
first book of Samuel in which he describes the lessons to be derived
from the narrative. No comment on this selection from Gersonides
is necessary, since the material is self-explanatory.*

A. WHAT LESSONS ARE TO BE DERIVED FROM THE STORY OF HANNAH?

The following are the lessons to be derived from this narrative. [1] To inform us, in order to pay honor to Samuel, that he came from a good family. The rock from which he was hewn was an honorable one both on his father's side and on his mother's, for, as we can tell from what the narrative says about her, she was a prophetess. Consequently, Samuel was deserving of the high stage to which he attained since from his birth he was dedicated and devoted to God. [2] To inform us that God's special care is for the lowly. Hannah, whom Elkanah loved, had no children, whereas God gave Peninnah children (I Samuel 1:2). The same thing is related in the Torah of Rachel and Leah (Genesis 29:31). [3] To inform us that although neither women nor children have an obligation to go on pilgrimage to the Sanctuary (the obligation only devolves on an adult who is able to walk on his own feet once a year from Jerusalem to the Temple mount), yet it is proper for the perfect man to go there together with his wives and little children. There are two reasons for this. The first is to train them in the true Beliefs which they will see for themselves when they visit the Temple. The second is that a man's real joy is not complete unless he shares it with his wife and children. It would seem that this total pilgrimage should take place in the feast of Tabernacles, the feast of rejoicing. That is why Scripture records (I Samuel 1:3) that Elkanah went up out of his city from year to year to worship and to sacrifice to the Lord. This means that he left none of his household behind in the city. Once a year his wives and all his daughters were with him at the Sanctuary. [4] To inform us that it is proper to show favor to those who suffer and to cheer them up as much as one possibly can. This is why Scripture relates that because Hannah was distressed when she saw the numerous gifts given to Peninnah, her sons and daughters, and she was left out of it, therefore Elkanah cheered up Hannah to the best of his ability (I Samuel 1:4-5). He gave her the portion he had set his eyes on, setting it directly in front of Hannah, whereas he distributed the other portions in an offhand manner. And so he comforted her for the vexation her rival caused her (I Samuel 1:6), saying to her that he was better to her than ten sons (I Samuel 1:8). [5] To inform us that it is not right to be proud because one has attained so much and to look down on those who suffer. You see that Peninnah boasted of her many sons and daughters and she taunted Hannah with being barren. God saw Hannah's affliction and gave her sons and daughters, while Peninnah's children died young. As Hannah said: "While the barren hath borne seven, she that had many children hath languished" (I Samuel 2:5). [6] To inform us that it is improper to pray soon after eating or drinking, for in that state one cannot concentrate adequately in prayer. That is why Scripture relates (I Samuel 1:13-15) that since Hannah rose to pray to God just after mealtime, Eli could not imagine that she was saying her prayers but thought she was drunk. He could not imagine that she would do such an improper thing as to pray immediately after eating and drinking. But Hannah's reply was that she had drunk neither wine nor strong drink and therefore there was no objection to her offering prayers at that time. [7] To inform us that it assists concentration when one prays long and with tears. This is why the Rabbis say that the gates of tears are not closed. Lengthy prayer strengthens the bond between the worshiper and God. For this reason Scripture records that Hannah's prayer was heard because she prayed long (I Samuel 1:12) and because she wept (I Samuel 1:10), to testify that by means of these things an impression was made and her prayer was answered. It appears that this is why God gave her that which she requested. [8] To inform us that it is not necessary for the voice of the one who prays to be heard. God knows man's thoughts, although it is necessary to utter the words of the prayers verbally. This is why of Hannah's prayer it is said: "only her lips moved, but her voice could not be heard" (I Samuel 1:13). [9] To inform us that whoever asks God for something he has no right to demand should make a vow that he will fulfil when his prayer is granted. As a result he will come to have faith that the goodness he receives is from God for whose sake he carried out his promise. The fulfilment of the vow is then the means of recording gratitude for the kindness done to him. This is why you find so many examples in Scripture that vows made were of this nature, for example, the vow of Jacob (Genesis 28:20-22) and the vow of Jephthah (Judges 11:30-31). That is why we find Hannah making her vow at this juncture (I Samuel 1:11). Even though according to the law a woman cannot impose a Nazirite vow on her son, nor, for that matter, can a man in the case recorded, since Samuel was not even conceived when the vow was made, yet it would seem that Samuel felt obliged to fulfil the vow in order to publish abroad the miracle and wonder God had wrought for her. [10] To inform us that it is proper for the perfect man to take note of men's deeds and to rebuke them if they do something unworthy. Therefore Scripture relates (I Samuel 1:12) that Eli watched her mouth to see what she was doing, even though it was hardly the habit of that perfect man to gaze at women. When Eli saw that she continued to do this thing, he imagined that she was drunk and he rebuked her for it. [11] To inform us that it is proper for every man to save himself from false suspicion as far as he is able. That is why Hannah told Eli the truth (I Samuel 1:15-16). Even though she must have suffered embarrassment to speak to Eli, who, after all, was born the High Priest and a prophet, yet she did not fail to present him with her defence. [12] To inform us that the prayer of a prophet is more likely to be heard than the prayer of anyone else. That is why Hannah rejoiced when Eli prayed to God to grant her her request and why she asked him to pray on her behalf (I Samuel 1:17-18). And that is why she was so sure that her prayer would be answered that she ate and her vexation was no more (I Samuel 1:18).

Gersonides continues to give more lessons, no fewer than thirty-six, but enough has been quoted to give the general thrust of his thought.

B. DID THE SUN REALLY STOP FOR JOSHUA?

In this passage Gersonides comments on the account in the book of Joshua 10:12-14, in which it is told that Joshua prayed to God to make the sun stand still while he conquered the Amorites and the sun stayed in the midst of the heaven. The passage has always been puzzling to commentators. Can it mean that the sun really did stand still? A similar puzzle, on which Gersonides also comments here, is the account in the second book of Kings 20:11 that as a sign for King Hezekiah, the shadow on the sundial went ten degrees backward. Gersonides, as a rationalist philosopher, cannot accept these accounts as literal. His general attitude, expressed frequently in his writings, is that the Jewish religion does not demand of its adherents that they accept as true that which is contrary to reason.

"Then spoke Joshua" (Joshua 10:12). In this portion there are many problems which have to be investigated. The first is that if the sun really did stand still and stop its movement, it would have been an infinitely greater miracle than any of those performed through Moses. The miracles performed through Moses involved only a change in the nature of lowly things. But it is infinitely more marvelous that such change should take place in the heavenly bodies, that these should depart from their function of ruling over the lowly things and change the whole order. For in that case the fault would be in the heavenly bodies themselves and such a thing would be irrevocable. Generally speaking, no proof is required for this to anyone who has studied these deep matters. I have explained this in a comprehensive manner in the sixth part of my book *The Wars of the Lord.*

To understand what Gersonides is saying here, we must sketch his views on the way things are ordered by God. The regularity of nature is, for Gersonides, evidence of God's marvelous order. The fact that normally nature does not change is more wonderful than the fact that miracles occasionally happen. Indeed, miracles only happen when there is a pressing need to demonstrate to men God's tremendous power. But miracles are a suspension of the natural order and they cannot, therefore, be irrevocable. As soon as possible, things must revert to the natural order. Furthermore, Gersonides relies on the Greek notion, popular in the Middle Ages, of Intelligences. These are, for him, the way in which God produces the natural order. Now the lowest of these is known as the Active Intellect. The Active Intellect operates on the sublunar world, i.e., the world of "lowly" things, things beneath the heavenly bodies. These heavenly bodies represent God's controlled order. They never suffer change any more than God does. All miracles are the result of the Active Intellect operating on things beneath the heavenly bodies. (These ideas obviously depend on the medieval view that the earth is at the center of the universe and influenced by the sun, moon and stars, a view which, needless to say, has been exploded by modern astronomy). So there is the ordered universe and the heavenly bodies in it representing order and there is the sublunar world in which the order can be interrupted in the form of miracles. Once a miracle has happened, the order inherent in the heavenly bodies brings about a return to the natural order. When, for example, Moses throws down his staff before Pharaoh and it changes into a snake, the Active Intellect is at work. But the snake changes back eventually into a staff, because here the order of the heavenly bodies prevents any permanent change. It follows that there cannot possibly be a miracle which changes the order of the heavenly bodies. First, the Active Intellect, which is the cause of miracles, does not operate there. Secondly, if a miracle of change were to operate there, it could not be revoked, since the revoking power of a miracle resides in the heavenly bodies themselves, representing God's permanent order. That is why Gersonides finds our passage so difficult.

If it were to have happened (that the sun stood still), then it would contradict that which the Torah records that no prophet ever arose like Moses in all the signs and wonders which Moses wrought in the sight of all Israel (Deuteronomy 34:10-12). Even if it be suggested, as some of the Rabbis would have it, though there is no reference to this in the Torah, that the same miracle was, in fact, performed by Moses, the problem remains, since Joshua would then be Moses' equal in the greatest of all the miracles performed through him. Moreover, if it were really so (that Moses, too, had caused the sun to stand still), it would have been proper for the Torah to have related this wondrous miracle. For we see that the Torah intends to publish the miracles and wonders as an aid to belief in God. We find this idea mentioned in the Torah in connection with the miracles done to Pharaoh: "And that thou mayest tell in the ears of thy son, and thy son's son, what I have wrought upon Egypt, and My signs which I have done among them; that ye may know that I am the Lord" (Exodus 10:2). Furthermore, from the plain meaning of the text, it appears that the sun did not stop moving, nor did the moon. This is clear from the fact that it says: "and hasted not to go down" (verse 13), that is to say, it did not set speedily. This suggests only a negation of speedy movement, not of all movement. This verse implies that it did move, as do the other verses which tell of what happened. For example, it says (verse 12): "Sun, stand thou still upon Gibeon; and thou, Moon, in the valley of Aijalon." It does not say simply: "Sun stand thou still, and thou, Moon," but refers their absence of movement to a large area of sky which could be seen from that place. Now everyone knows that to negate movement from a large area is not to negate it absolutely since there can still be movement within that area, so that this verse and the other verses really say that the sun and the moon did move. To illustrate this, take the case of someone who says that "A" has stayed in his land for so many days. The only deduction we are entitled to make is that he did not leave his land, but no conclusion can be drawn as to whether or not he moved about in that land. If the intention were to say that "A" had not moved at all, the way of doing it would be to say that he had not moved, not that he had not left his land. This is obvious to anyone who is familiar with the rules of logic. A further proof is provided by the verse (14): "And there was no day like that before it or after it, that the Lord had hearkened unto the voice of man; for the Lord fought for Israel." This shows that the miracle had to do with the battle itself. If the miracle had involved a cessation of the sun's movement, it would have had no connection at all with the battle. Another proof is that it is clear from Scripture that God only performs miracles where they are necessary or where they encourage men to hold true beliefs, but there is no mention of these in the account of this miracle. Furthermore, we have explained in the book *The Wars of the Lord* that no miracle performed by a prophet can affect the beings on high, namely, the heavenly bodies. Consequently, it is obvious that, contrary to what appears on the surface, the miracle was not of this nature.

Gersonides gives a number of proofs from logic and from an examination of Scripture that it is quite impossible that our narrative intends to imply that the sun's movement actually stopped. Later on, he will explain what, in that case, the narrative does mean. But first he has to deal with the Hezekiah narrative. This seems to contradict his basic supposition that the order of the heavenly bodies cannot be interrupted.

But someone may object to our whole position, arguing that we can see that a miracle through a prophet which involved a change in the whole order of the heavenly bodies did take place. This is when Isiah said to Hezekiah, when the latter asked him for a sign that God would heal him and allow him to go up to the house of the Lord (II Kings 20:8): "shall the shadow go forward ten degrees, or go back ten degrees?" (verse 9). Now it is obvious that the shadow can only move if the sun moves, so that this passage states that there was a change in the sun's movement. To such an objector, I reply that if one examines carefully the statements made in this account it must follow that the miracle did not involve any change in the order of the sun's movement. If it did, what can Hezekiah have meant when he said that it is a light thing for the shadow to decline ten degrees? (verse 10). If the miracle involved a change in the order of the sun's movement, it would have been the same tremendous marvel whether the movement was forward or backward. Consequently, it is essential that these things be explained accurately, so that the nature of the miracle which did take place will become clear. It would seem, so far as we can tell, that Isaiah gave Hezekiah the choice in this matter, saying to him that the miracle could take place in one of two ways. Either the shadow would move ten degrees more than it would normally have done or the shadow would move ten degrees backward. From what we have said, it follows that the miracle of Joshua was in connection with the battle (not with the sun) and from this it follows further that the miracle of Hezekiah could not have been in the movement of the sun. I shall now explain it all. Our experience tells us that when clouds move across the sun and the sun's rays shine on them, the passing clouds cause us to imagine that the sun is not really where it is in the sky. The clouds produce a great movement of shadow in only a small space of time, whether to the east or the west, the north or the south, according to the position of the clouds and the direction in which they are moving. There is no doubt that this is so, for we notice the phenomenon all the time. Now since Hezekiah noticed that according to the way the clouds were moving at that time it would have been easy for the shadow to move ten degrees forward, he requested that the shadow move in the opposite direction from that which seemed feasible by the movement of those clouds. That is why he asked for the shadow to move ten degrees backward. In the parallel passage in the book of Isaiah (38:1-8), it is said (verse 8): "So the sun returned ten degrees, by which degrees it was gone down." This means that, judging by our normal experience something miraculous took place, as it is said there: "Behold, I will cause the shadow of the dial to return backward." So this problem has been solved. But if, in spite of this, anyone wishes to hold that these two miracles did involve a change in the order of the sun's movement, I have no objection. If no greater mistake were ever made than this, it would be no bad thing. One who holds this opinion does so, after all, because, in his view, this increases God's power and might.

Gersonides' interpretation of the Hezekiah narrative is that it was only the shadow which moved, not the sun. This is quite possible, since clouds moving across the sun frequently produce shadows. There was indeed something of the miraculous there, since the shadow moved in the opposite direction from that demanded by the movement of the clouds. A "sign" there was to be sure, but no miracle involving what, for Gersonides, is impossible, a change in the order of the sun's movement. Note how at the end Gersonides quietly holds fast to his own view, but is at the same time tolerant of those who, out of motives of piety, see the thing differently. Gersonides now turns to his own understanding of the Joshua narrative. His basic view is that the passage does not mean that the sun actually stood still, but that God so helped Israel to win the battle in only a short time that it seemed as if the sun had not moved at all from the beginning of the battle until it was all over. The miracle was, in fact, in the speed in which the battle was won!

Now that this problem has been resolved, we can return to our explanation of our passage. Joshua said that before the sun had moved from being seen over Aijalon, the nation will have avenged themselves of their enemies. Scripture does state this briefly, but it is indicated in the next verse (Joshua 10:13): "And the sun stood still, and the moon stayed, until the nation had avenged themselves of their enemies." The meaning is that while the sun still stayed over Gibeon and the moon over Aijalon, the work of vengeance was completed. This was a marvelous thing, for not only does it testify to the fact that Israel avenged themselves on those who had attacked them, but that the vengeance was achieved in such a short span of time. That is why it continues (verse 14): "And there was no day like that before it or after it, that the Lord hearkened unto the voice of a man; for the Lord fought for Israel." The reason is here given why they were able to win the battle in so short a span of time, since the Lord's power is not limited. The verse refers to "the voice of a man" since God had not decreed that the battle be concluded so speedily, but God still hearkened to the voice of Joshua. This follows the same idea as that continued in the verse: "That confirmeth the word of His servant, and performeth the counsel of His messengers" (Isaiah 44:26). As for the reference to the "book of Jashar" (Joshua 10:13), I surmise that this was the title of a book that was lost during the period of the exile. But the Rabbis, of blessed memory, have many explanations of what it means. You should know that the day is renewed by the sun. That is why we say when the sun is near to setting that the day has greatly decreased, for at that time of the day the sun's light is faint. The sun's light is at its strongest when the sun is in the middle of the sky. We observe this from our experience. This is the meaning of: "But the path of the righteous is as the light of dawn, that shineth more and more unto the perfect day" (Proverbs 4:18). That is to say, just as the sun's light increases as the day draws on, so does the path of the righteous lead straight onwards to increase in perfection. It is well-known that when the sun is in the middle of the sky, it takes a long time before one notices its descent. This is perfectly obvious to anyone with the slightest acquaintance with the science of astronomy. It can be seen, too, by observing such astronomical instruments as the astrolabe and the quadrant. For when the sun is at its zenith, no descent can be detected in these instruments for about half an hour. It would seem that at that time the sun was in the middle of the sky, for they were near Gibeon and they saw the sun over Gibeon. And the sun did not go down, just as on a perfect day when the sun does not go down quickly.

Gersonides' final remarks here are an explanation of verse 13: "and hasted not to go down about a whole day" (English translation). Gersonides understands the Hebrew ke-yom tamim to mean not "about a whole day" but to mean "as on a perfect day." We refer to a bright and sunny day as a perfect day. On such a day the sun seems to remain long in the sky.

I surmise that the length of the city of Gibeon lay from east to west, so that in the middle of the day the movement of the sun over Gibeon was hardly discernible. So that the verse states that, so far as appearances went, the sun did not go down away from Gibeon, even though the area was small; for the sun, as is its wont, does not descend speedily in the middle of the day. Here is concluded our

exposition of this portion and all the problems connected with it have been resolved.

Note again how Gersonides stresses that nothing untoward happened to the sun. At midday the sun always appears to stand still. The miracle was in the swiftness with which the battle was won.

Jacob ben Asher

Hints at various truths in the words and letters of the Torah

Rabbi Jacob ben Asher (died in Toledo, Spain, before 1340) was the author of a great and authoritative Code of Jewish law (see the section on Codes in the first volume in this series). This Code is known as the Tur ("Row"), but more specifically as the Turim ("Rows," because it consists of four sections or "rows," a title suggested by the "four rows of stones" on the breastplate of the High Priest, see Exodus 28:17). Jacob ben Asher is consequently known by the name Baal Ha-Turim, "The Author of the Turim." His Commentary to the Pentateuch, first printed at Constantinople in 1500, is called: Rimze Baal Ha-Turim, The Hints of the Baal Ha-Turim, *but is generally known simply as* Baal Ha-Turim. *It is actually part of a larger work, but the "hints" part was so popular that it was printed by itself. The Commentary is printed together with the text in most editions of the Pentateuch. It differs from all other commentaries in a curious way. Baal Ha-Turim believed, as did, indeed, most of his contemporaries, that beneath the text of the Bible there are numerous "hints" to further deep meanings. These hints are conveyed by such methods as the use of letters to represent whole words, but chiefly by the method known as Gematria (see the section on Baḥya ibn Asher in this book). Each Hebrew letter has a numerical value, e.g., alef (the first letter of the* alphabet) = 1; bet *(the second letter)* = 2; and so on. *(The eleventh letter* kaf = 20 *and so on to the letter* kof = 100 *and so on). Consequently, one Hebrew word can have the same numerical value (i.e., the total of its letters in numbers) as another Hebrew word. This opens up all kinds of possibilities in demonstrating that one word refers to an idea expressed by a different word. Few today would take this method at all seriously, but we cannot help admiring the skill amounting to genius with which Baal Ha-Turim obtains his effects. We give here Baal Ha-Turim's comment to the first verse of Genesis.*

A. HINTS AT VARIOUS TRUTHS IN THE WORDS AND LETTERS OF THE TORAH

There is a Midrash which says that the reason the Torah begins with the letter *bet* **and not with the letter** *alef* **is that** *bet* **stands for** *berachah* **("blessing"), whereas** *alef* **stands for** *arirah* **("curse"). God said: "I shall begin with blessing and would that the world should endure."**

Another reason: *bet* **(=2) represents the two worlds God created, this world and the next.**

Another reason: *bet* **(=2) represents the two** *torot,* **the Written Torah and the Oral Torah, to teach you that God created the world in the merit of the Torah and His people.**

The comment of the Midrash is a curious fancy. It is as if to say, the world needs all the help it can get, so God used the word bereshit *("In the beginning") at the beginning of creation (the first word of the Pentateuch) to suggest, too, the word* berachah, *"blessing." (See the section in this book on Ibn Ezra who ridicules this method of exegesis, with especial reference to this Midrash). Bet has the numerical value of two. Hence, by beginning with this letter the Torah teaches us that God did not create only this world, but the next world (the Hereafter) as well. Furthermore, there are two Torahs. The Written Torah is the Bible itself. The Oral Torah is the traditional interpretation of the Written Torah handed down from generation to generation and recorded in the Rabbinic literature.*

The letters of *bereshit* **("In the beginning") form the word** *bet rosh* **("the first house"), namely, the First Temple, as it is said: "Thou**

throne of glory, on high from the beginning, thou place of our sanctuary" (Jeremiah 17:12).

Another explanation: these letters form the words a be-tishri ("the first of Tishri"), for that is when the world was created.

Another explanation: these letters form the words bara shete ("He created two"), because God created two torot.

Another explanation: these letters form the words: yare' shabbat ("fear the sabbath"), to tell you that the world was created in the merit of the sabbath.

Another explanation: these letters form the words berit esh ("covenant of fire"), for in the merit of the covenant of circumcision and in the merit of the Torah, which is fire (Deuteronomy 33:2), they are saved from the punishment of Hell.

Another explanation: these letters form the words barata yesh ("Thou hast created yesh (=310)." God created 310 worlds for each righteous man.

Baal Ha-Turim now offers a number of anagrams.
The interpretation of the verse in Jeremiah is that, from the
"beginning" the Temple was, as it were, in God's mind. The letters
of the word bereshit *are: bet, resh, alef, shin, yod, tav. These can*
be rearranged in a different order to form other words. The second
interpretation is: a (=alef = 1) be-tishri. There is a Rabbinic view
that the first of Tishri (the day of Rosh Ha-Shanah, *"The New Year")*
is the birthday of the world and there are references to this in the
Rosh Ha-Shanah liturgy. Baal Ha-Turim *and his contemporaries*
believed in Hell, but he says here that the fire of Hell has no power
to cause pain to those who are circumcised and who keep the
Torah. The final comment is that the letters of bereshit *can be*
rearranged to form the words meaning "Thou hast created yesh."
Now the numerical value of yesh (yod = 10, shin = 300) is 310. The
reference is to the idea found in the Rabbinic literature that God
will provide every good man, as a reward for his righteousness,
with 310 worlds over which he will have control. This saying,
incidentally, has been interpreted in mystical fashion to mean not
physical "worlds," but as representing tremendous spiritual
experience in the Hereafter.

The numerical value of *bereshit bara* ("In the beginning He created," the first two words of the Pentateuch) is the same as that of *be-rosh ha-shana nivra* ("On Rosh Ha-Shanah it was created").

Another explanation: the numerical value of *bereshit* is the same as that of *be-torah yatzar* ("He formed because of the Torah"), because of the Torah, which is called *reshit* ("the beginning"), God created the world.

Another explanation: It has the same numerical value as that of *shesh sedarim* ("six orders").

Another explanation: It has the same numerical value as that of *yisrael bahar ba-ammim* ("He chose Israel from among the nations") and as that of *taryag yatzar* ("He created 613"). God created the world so that His people would keep the 613 precepts.

The letters of bereshit bara *are:* bet = 2; resh = 200; alef = 1; shin = 300; yod = 10; tav = 400 (total 913); bet = 2; resh = 200; alef = 1 (total 203); total 1,116. The letters of be-rosh ha-shanah nivra are: bet = 2; resh = 200; alef = 1; shin = 300; he = 5; shin = 300; nun = 50; he = 5; nun = 50; bet = 2; resh = 200; alef = 1 (total 1,116). The reference is, as above, to God creating the world on the first of Tishri (Rosh Ha-Shanah). In the next comment there is a double wordplay on bereshit. This can mean "because of reshit," and the Torah is called reshit in the verse: "The Lord made me as the beginning (reshit) of His way" (Proverbs 8:22). This is a Midrashic interpretation quoted by Rashi in his comment to our text. But Baal Ha-Turim notes that bereshit (numerical value 913, as above) has the same numerical value as be-torah yatzar, i.e., bet = 2; tav = 400; vav = 6; resh = 200; he = 5; yod = 10; tzadi = 90; resh = 200 (total 913). Baal Ha-Turim refers to shesh sedarim. Since the word seder is masculine, it ought to be shishah, but this would make it a he (=5) too many, so Baal Ha-Turim is not too concerned with his grammar. The letters of shesh sedarim are: shin = 300; shin = 300; samech = 60; dalet = 4; resh = 200; yod = 10; mem = 40 (total 914). This is one too many (bereshit = 913), but such a small discrepancy is not going to worry those fond of gematria. The way out is to count the word (bereshit) itself as 1, so that we obtain 913 + 1 = 914. The "six orders" are the six sections or divisions of the Mishnah (see the section on the Mishnah in the first volume of this series).

Bereshit means "with *reshit*," standing for: *rakia* (**firmament**");
eretz ("**earth**"); *Shamayim* ("**heavens**"); *yam* ("**sea**"); *tehomot*
("**deep**"). **Another explanation: the letters of *bereshit* stand for:**
barishonah raah elohim she-yikabbelu yisrael torah (**"God saw at
the beginning that Israel would accept the Torah"**).

Bereshit. **The word occurs in Scripture at the beginning of three
verses: the one above; "In the beginning** *(bereshit)* **of the reign of
Jehoiakim" (Jeremiah 26:1); "In the beginning** *(bereshit)* **of the
reign of Zedekiah." That is why the Rabbis say in tractate Arakin:
"The Holy One, blessed be He, wanted to reduce the world to
formlessness and emptiness because of Jehoiakim, but when He
considered his generation, His anger was abated. The Holy One,
blessed be He, wanted to reduce the world to formlessness and
emptiness because of the generation of Zedekiah but when He
considered Zedekiah, his anger was abated."** *Bereshit bara elohim.*
**("In the beginning God created"). The final letters of these three
words form the word** *emet ("truth"). This teaches that God created
the world with truth, as it is said: "The beginning of Thy word is
truth" (Psalms 119:160).*

Bara elohim et (**"God created," Genesis 1:1). The final letters of
these three words form the word** *emet.*

Va-yar elohim et (**"And God saw," Genesis 1:4). The final letters of
these three words from the word** *emet.*

Va-yivra elohim et (**"And God created," Genesis 1:21). The final
letters of these three words form the word** *emet.*

Va-yar elohim et (**"And God saw," Genesis 1:31). The final letters of
these three words form the word** *emet.*

Bara elohim laasot (**"Which God in creating had made," Genesis
2:3). The final letters of these three words form the word** *emet.*

This is why the Rabbis introduced the word *emet* **six times in the
hymn** *emet ve-yatziv.*

Emet me-eretz titzmah (**"Truth springeth out of the earth," Psalms
85:12). The initial letters of these three words form the word** *emet.*

Itti me-levanon tavoi (**"Come with me from Lebanon,"** Song of **Songs 4:8). The initial letters of these three words form the word** *emet.*

But where the truth is absent and where the truth is cast down to the ground, then: *tashuri me-rosh amanah* (**"Look from the top of Amana,"** Song of Songs 4:8). **The initial letters of these three words form the word** *emet,* **but in reverse order, therefore: "From the lions' dens"** (Song of Songs 4:8).

Baal Ha-Turim's first comment here is that each letter of the word reshit *stands for one of the things created at the beginning. Thus the letter resh is the first letter of the word* rakia, *and so on. The things referred to are mentioned in the opening verses of Genesis. The second comment similarly takes each letter of the word* bereshit *as standing for a word beginning with that letter. The third comment is in the form of a different wordplay. The Rabbinic passage quoted means that sometimes a good generation has a bad leader and sometimes a bad generation a good leader. In each generation, God, as it were, is tempted to undo the whole work of creation, but in the end He decides not to do so, in the one case for the sake of the generation, in the other for the sake of the leader. By a coincidence, the word* bereshit *occurs at the beginning of the creation narrative, in the verse about Jehoiakim, and in the verse about Zedekiah. But Baal Ha-Turim will not allow that it is a mere coincidence; rather it intentionally hints at the Rabbinic teaching he records. Six verses are then quoted in which the letters of the word for "truth"* (emet) *occur. (Actually the word* et *is a sign of the accusative in Hebrew and is not translated). The hymn* emet ve-yatziv *is recited each morning (see Singer's Prayer Book, p.44.) The final comment is that in the words* tashuri me-rosh amanah *the initial letters are in the order* tav, mem, alef, *which is the word* emet *spelled backwards. This represents a perversion of the truth (spelled backwards) and where there is a perversion of the truth, only harm follows. Hence: "From the lions' dens."*

"God created." These two words come together here and in one other verse: "Since the day God created man upon the earth" (Deuteronomy 4:32). For from the beginning, God foresaw Abraham, who is called "the greatest man among the Anakim" (Joshua 14:15), and He created the world.

Elohim ("God") has the same numerical value as *ha-kissé* ("The Throne"). God first created the Throne.

There are seven words in the first verse of Genesis. These correspond to: the seven days of the week; the seven years in the cycle ending with the year of release (Leviticus 25:3-7); the seven cycles in the Jubilee (Leviticus 25:8-13); the seven heavens; the seven lands; the seven seas; and the seven planets, Saturn, Jupiter, Mars, Sun, Venus, Mercury and Moon. Corresponding to these David said: "Seven times a day do I praise Thee" (Psalms 119:164). This is why the Rabbis introduced the response: *yehé shemé rabba mevarach le-olam u-le-olemé alemaya* ("Let His great name be blessed forever and to all eternity"). This has seven words and it is recited seven times daily. Our verse has twenty-eight letters and there are twenty-eight letters in *yehé shemé rabba*. Consequently, to correspond to these Solomon recited seven verses, from "A time to be born" to "a time for peace" (Ecclesiastes 3:2-8), containing twenty-eight "times." For in each day there are four changing "times." The first time is from dawn to midday; the second from midday to nightfall; the third from nightfall to midnight; and the fourth from midnight to dawn. There are also seven words and twenty-eight letters in the verse: "And God spoke all these words saying" (Exodus 20:1). This is why the Rabbis say that whoever utters the response *yehé shemé rabba* with all his might, it is as though he becomes a copartner with God in the work of creation.

The reference to the "great man" being Abraham is Rabbinic. God created the world because He foresaw that one day an Abraham would live who would, as it were, make the whole of creation worthwhile. The "Throne" referred to is the Throne of Glory. The letters of elohim are: alef = 1; lamed = 30; he = 5; yod = 10; mem = 40 (total 86). The letters of ha-kissé are: he = 5; kaf = 20; samech = 60; alef = 1 (total 86). In the first verse of Genesis there are seven Hebrew words and these contain twenty-eight letters. The response yehé shemé rabba is the response in the Kaddish prayer. The verse: "And the Lord spoke" introduces the Ten Commandments. The connection between the response and our verse is on the basis of the Rabbinic saying, that one who utters this response with all his might becomes a copartner with God in the work of creation, i.e., he helps God, as it were, to fulfill the purpose for which man was created. This is a sublime idea, typical of Rabbinic Judaism that, in a sense God needs man, just as man needs God. The fact that Baal Ha-Turim pegs it onto the verse in a very fanciful way does not affect the significance of the idea. Indeed, many of the ideas recorded here by Baal Ha-Turim are significant in themselves and no great harm is done if he prefers to employ ingenious but farfetched methods of deriving them from Scripture.

Isaac Arama

What is the purpose of animal sacrifices?

Isaac ben Moses Arama was born in Spain about the year 1420. He died at Naples in 1494. Most of his life was spent as a Rabbi in various Spanish communities, but toward the end of his life when the Jews were expelled from Spain (in 1492), he fled to Naples. Arama's commentary to the Pentateuch is called Akedat Yitzhak, "The Binding of Isaac." This very popular Commentary is in the form of extended expositions of important Pentateuchal themes. Each of these is called a "Gate" and there are 105 "Gates" in the work. The best edition is that of Ḥaim Joseph Pollak, published in Pressburg in 1849. The first edition was published in Salonika in 1522. Arama's method is first to quote a passage from the Rabbinic Midrash relevant to his theme, which he then proceeds to develop using the teachings of the Talmud, the Kabbalah, and especially the works of the philosophers in order to present a coherent and comprehensive picture. The best method of studying Arama is to examine a whole "Gate" of the Akedat Yitzhak. It occurs at the beginning of the book of Leviticus which deals in the main with animal sacrifices. Arama, as a philosophical thinker, finds it hard to understand at first glance what purpose there can be in man offering animal sacrifices to God. How can God be said to need these sacrifices?

A. WHAT IS THE PURPOSE OF ANIMAL SACRIFICE?

Gate Fifty-Five. In it is explained the need for the various sacrifices, their advantage and their meaning. The Midrash (Leviticus Rabbah section 7) states: "When any of you presents an offering of cattle to the Lord" (Leviticus 1:2). Rabbi Berahiah in the name of Rabbi Ezra of the village of Hatia said: A king had two cooks. One of them prepared a dish that was pleasing to the king and the other prepared a dish that was pleasing to the king. It was not known, however, which of the two was more pleasing to the king. But when the king ordered the second cook to prepare for him another dish of the same kind, it was known that the dish of the second cook was the more pleasant to him. So, too, Noah offered a sacrifice and it was pleasant to God, as it is said: "The Lord smelled the pleasing odor" (Genesis 8:21). And Israel offered a sacrifice, as it is said: "Be careful in presenting to Me at stated times the offering" (Numbers 28:2). We do not know which of the two was more pleasing to God. But when God commanded Moses: "This is the ritual of the burnt offering" (Leviticus 6:2), we know that Israel's sacrifice was the more pleasant. Therefore Scripture says: "Then shall the offering of Judah and Jerusalem be pleasant unto the Lord, as in the days of old, and as in ancient years (Malachi 3:4). "As in days of old" means as in the days of Moses. "And as in ancient years" means as in the days of Solomon. Another explanation is: "As in the days of old" means as in the days of Noah, as it is written: "For this is as the waters of Noah unto Me" (Isaiah 54:9). "And as in ancient years" means as in the days of Abel, when there was no idolatry in the world.

Arama quotes a Midrash in which, he holds, the essential ideas he is about to expound are contained. Both Noah and the Israelites offered sacrifices, but God is better pleased with Israel's sacrifices. Two explanations are given in the Midrash of the verse in Malachi in which it is declared that Israel's sacrifices in the future will be as pleasant to God as those of the days of old and of ancient times. According to the first explanation, these two periods are those of Moses and Solomon. But according to the second interpretation, the two periods are those of Noah and Abel. In the days of Abel, sacrifices were especially regarded because there was no idolatry in the world. Thus the Midrash clearly sees a connection between sacrifices and idolatry and Arama will pursue the implications of this in the course of his exposition.

There is a tremendous puzzle in the matter of animal sacrifices, one that is neither unreal nor remote, for the following powerful objection is perfectly evident. Sacrifices offered to God are either a kind of recompense or bribe to God in payment for the distress caused to Him by the sinner's actions and their aim is propitiation or appeasement, just as kings are propitiated by gifts. Or they are a fine and punishment for the sin, a means of paying off the score, though of no benefit to God, in which case they can be compared to corporal punishment in a legal system. Or they are for the benefit of the priests who serve at the altar and who eat the meat of the sacrifices. Or they are for the purpose of destroying the animals that are offered.

Now the first reason is obviously nonsense. For it can only make sense if we postulate that God lacks something, so that He can be appeased when it is offered to Him. God forbid that any such notion be put forward. As the Psalmist says: "I will take no bullock out of thy house . . . For every beast of the forest is Mine . . . " (Psalms 50:9-10). This will be explained further on. The prophet Isaiah spoke of this explicitly when he said: "Yet thou hast not called upon Me, O Jacob . . . Thou hast not brought Me the small cattle . . . Thou hast bought Me no sweet cane with money . . . But thou hast burdened Me with thy sins . . . " and finally he states: "I, even I, am He that blotteth out thy transgressions for Mine own sake" (Isaiah 43:22-25). The meaning is that God had no benefit whatsoever from all their sacrifices, for He benefited naught from them. One might argue that they deserved to be pardoned for their sins for having given to God their sacrifices and gifts. All that God had received from them was the weariness caused Him by their sins, without having received from them any benefit or pleasure. If you will say, in that case, how can they find atonement? To this he replies: "I, even I, am He that blotteth out thy transgressions for Mine own sake." Consider how excellent is the repetition of the Divine Name. It is as if to say, I and only I have done this, not for any other thing associated with me. If My pardon had been given in payment for something, then both of us would have been responsible for the pardon. As it is, since there has been no exchange, the thing was only done because of My righteousness. As for your sins, to which I have referred, I shall not now mention them in detail so as not to put you to shame. But if you wish it, "put Me in remembrance" and "let us plead together." You confess as many of your sins as you wish: "declare thou, that thou mayest be justified" (Isaiah 43:25-26). So it is clear that the prophet seeks to eradicate this absurd notion entertained only by stupid minds. This is why the expression "service" is never used of sacrifices of this type in the Torah. Moses only said: "And we know not with what we must serve the Lord" (Exodus 10:26), because he could only speak to him (to Pharaoh) in a language he could understand and it is the habit of the idolators to bring their sacrifices as a service (they perform for their gods). As it is said: "Let us go after other gods, which thou hast known, and let us serve them" (Deuteronomy 13:3). This is why Scripture warns: "Take heed to thyself that thou be not ensnared to follow them, after that they are destroyed from before thee; and that thou inquire not after their gods, saying: 'How used those nations to serve their gods? even so will I do likewise.' Thou shalt not do so unto the Lord thy God; for every abomination to the Lord, which He hateth, have they done unto their gods" (Deuteronomy 12:30-31). This means that the sacrifices commanded in the divine Torah are not in the way of service as the idolators serve their gods. The proof is that the idolators burn their sons and daughters before their gods, imagining that by doing this they are serving their gods and giving them pleasure. The divine Torah, on the other hand, has no other purpose for you than that you should keep that which the Lord commands you, neither adding to it nor taking away from it. Of this the Torah has no scruples about using the word "service": "Thou shalt fear the Lord thy God; Him shalt thou serve" (Deuteronomy 10:20); "And ye shall serve the Lord your God" (Exodus 23:25). For whenever the service is that of the heart and by the improvement of man's deeds, it is obvious that the purpose is for the advantage of the one who serves, not for the one who is served. As it is said: "To walk in all His ways, and to love Him, and to serve the Lord thy God with all thy heart and with all thy soul; to keep for thy good the commandments of the Lord and His statutes, which I command thee this day" (Deuteronomy 10: 12-13). This is why the Rabbis attribute the question "What mean ye by this service?" (Exodus 12:26) to the wicked son of the four sons. For it is he alone who imagines that the sacrifice (of the paschal lamb) is a form of service by means of which the one who offers it expresses his intention to buy off God. So that this opinion has clearly been demonstrated to be null and void.

Note how skillfully Arama plays on the word "service." The "four sons" are, of course, the four sons of the Passover Haggadah, to each of whom is attributed a Biblical verse. The offence of the wicked son is, according to Arama, that he has a quid pro quo attitude to religion. He looks upon the commandments as a payment God demands. Arama comes down heavily against such a perverse notion and hence against the first reason for sacrifice, that they are in form of a payment or bribe. No, says Arama, the term "service" can only be used about man's worship of God when it is clear that God does not need it, but man needs it in order to move towards perfection. Arama now proceeds to refute the other possible reasons he stated at the beginning.

As for the second suggested reason, though it is not so farfetched as the first, our human intellect prevents us from accepting it as adequate. This is because it is impossible to place a ransom on the sinner, unless such a ransom is proportionate to his offence against the One before Whom he has sinned. Since nothing whatever can be compared to God, it is impossible to place any assessment on a sin against God. This is the meaning of Eli's complaint to his sons: "Nay, my sons; for it is no good report which I hear the Lord's people do spread abroad. If one man sin against another, God shall judge him; but if a man sin against the Lord who shall judge him?" (I Samuel 2:24-25). That is to say: My sons, the report circulating about you among God's people is not good. And I do not know on whom you can rely when you sin against the Lord your God. For if a man offends his neighbor the case comes before the judges who impose a fine proportionate to the one who committed the offence and to his victim, and when he pays the fine he can be pardoned. But if a man sins against God, who is to be the judge and to declare that he has paid that which he is obliged to pay for having committed the offence? It is in connection with this that the prophet says: "Will the Lord be pleased with thousands of rams . . . Shall I give my first-born for my transgression? (Micah 6:7). So this is no adequate reason; surely it is extremely unworthy that the priests should eat the meat of their people's sin-offerings and rejoice therein. Can such a thing be pleasing to the Lord? Furthermore, there are many kinds of sin-offerings and burnt-offerings in which the priests have no share at all, for the whole of them is burned on the altar or outside the camp. And there is no need to say that the fourth suggested reason is tasteless. God forbid that it should be said that God wishes wantonly to destroy.

The first possible reason for animal sacrifices—that they are a kind of payment to God—has been utterly rejected by Arama. The second reason, that the sacrifice is a fine, i.e., the sinner gives up one of his animals as a penance, is similarly rejected because a fine has to be in proportion to the offence and how can anyone assess the heinousness of an offence against God? The third reason—that the purpose of the sacrifices is to provide the priests with food—falls down because this would be a very cumbersome way of making provisions for the priests and it would mean, moreover, that the priests could only enjoy their food at the expense of the sins of others. As for the fourth reason—that God wishes to have animals destroyed—Arama treats it as beneath contempt. God would never wish wantonly to destroy any of His creatures. Having demolished all four reasons Arama proceeds to give his own reason, actually it is an extension of the second reason he has rejected. But before so doing and in order to lead up to it, he states another difficulty in connection with the whole institution of the sin-offering.

There is a further tremendous problem in that the Torah only commands the sinner to offer a sacrifice if he has sinned unintentionally. But on the face of it, there are two reasons why a sacrifice should rather be for an intentional sin than an unintentional sin. First, far more people sin intentionally than unintentionally, refusing to exercise self-control, so that the majority need should be catered to. Secondly, the unintentional sinner is not really a sinner at all. He does not need to repent, because he experiences neither remorse nor penitence. What is the purpose of a sacrifice where there is no repentance? The intentional sinner, on the other hand, is a real sinner. Since the Torah demands that such a sinner should repent and commands him so to do, it would surely have been proper to impose on him a sacrifice when he repents and feels remorse to atone for his sin that he might find pardon.

Arama now raises further difficulty. The law has it that a sin-offering is never brought to atone for a sin a man commits intentionally, only for one he commits unintentionally. This does not seem to be reasonable. The very opposite should have been demanded. Arama will offer the solution to this further difficulty in the course of his subsequent discussion of the whole meaning of animal sacrifices.

However, with regard to this type of sacrifice which the Torah imposes on a sinner, we can say that its purpose is for the sake of the sinner, namely, to remonstrate with him and to rebuke him for his sin. True, there is no comparison between him and His God, but this is no reason for him to get off scot-free. Rather by divine mercy his punishment was limited and a compromise made for the benefit of society, so that no door is kept closed in the face of those who repent of their sins. This is one of the instances where God gives up for the sake of His people some of the greatness that is His, as we have explained in the section on the Tabernacle, Gate 48. As the prophet declares: "I, even I, am He that blotteth out thy transgression for Mine own sake" (Isaiah 43:25) and as we have explained.

Arama now reverts to his second reason, that sacrifices are a fine or punishment for the sinner. Earlier he had declared this reason inadequate because no such punishment can be proportionate to the offence against God. Agreed, now says Arama, but since the sinner has a powerful desire to find atonement, God in His mercy imposes a kind of token fine in order to encourage the sinner to repent. This is beneficial to society, since it is an unhealthy society in which people who wish to give up their evil ways are prevented from so doing.

The following passage occurs in the Midrash (Yalkut Ezekiel 358): They asked of Wisdom: What is the punishment of the sinner? Wisdom replied: "Evil pursueth sinners" (Proverbs 13:21). They asked of Prophecy: What is the punishment of the sinner? Prophecy replied: "The soul that sinneth, it shall die" (Ezekiel 18:4). They asked of the Torah: What is the punishment of the sinner? The Torah replied: "Let him bring a sacrifice and he will find atonement." They asked of the Holy One, blessed be He: What is the punishment of the sinner? The Holy One, blessed be He, replied: Let him repent of his sins and confess them and he will find atonement, as it is written: "Take with you words, and return unto the Lord" (Hosea 14:3). Therefore it is written: "Good and upright is the Lord: therefore does He instruct sinners in the way (Psalms 25:8). Now you see that here the Rabbis set forth the different views on this topic and describe how these change according to circumstances. They saw that human wisdom, having analysed the degradation of the sinner and the greatness of the One he has offended, Who is infinite and without peer or comparison, cannot admit that the sinner has any means at all of putting right the wrong he has done. Wisdom therefore decrees that evil pursueth sinners until they are utterly destroyed, as it is said of the house of Eli, to which attention has been called earlier: "I will cut off thine arm, and the arm of thy father's house, that there shall not be an old man in thy house" (I Samuel 2:31).

However, when they asked the same question of Prophecy, a stage higher than Wisdom, a different answer was forthcoming. Prophecy discerns the nature of souls and their true essence. It knows that each is unique and it refuses to associate the soul of a father with that of his son or of any other member of his family to demand that one should be destroyed with the other (as Wisdom does). As the wise King Solomon said in his inspired words regarding the perfect part of man (his soul): "There is one that is alone, and he hath not a second; yea he hath neither son nor brother" (Ecclesiastes 4:8), as he explains there fully. Consequently, Prophecy declares: "The soul that sinneth, it shall die; the son shall not bear the iniquity of the father with him, neither shall the father bear the iniquity of the son with him; the righteousness of the righteous shall be upon him, and the wickedness of the wicked shall be upon him" (Ezekiel 18:20). The meaning of this is that Prophecy rejects the opinion of human wisdom that evil pursueth sinners from father to son. For prophecy declares that each soul is separate from others and none is punished for the sins of another. The prophet explains the reason for this fully when earlier on he declares: "Behold, all souls are Mine; as the soul of the father, so also the soul of the son is Mine; the soul that sinneth, it shall die" (Ezekiel 18:4). He declares: How can souls be associated with fathers and sons? In that they are souls they have neither father nor son, but are all equally Mine. As it is said: "Ye are children of the Lord your God: ye shall not gash yourselves" (Deuteronomy 14:1). This means: Let not a son gash himself with knives (in anguish at his father's death) for "Ye are children of the Lord your God" and your Father is still alive. And let not a father gash himself, for his sons are God's sons, may He be exalted. All this is from the point of view of the soul. It follows that the sinner and the sinner alone must bear his sin, as we shall explain with God's help in Gate 99. This is the reply of Prophecy, in that Prophecy is a form of perfection which flows only into the person of the prophet.

However, since the Prophetic nature of the Torah is more comprehensive, in that the purpose of the Torah is to provide laws for the benefit of society as a whole, the Torah replies: Let him bring a sacrifice and he will find atonement.

Note how skillfully Arama reads his ideas into the Midrash. Wisdom is, for him, plain commonsense which is frequently quite ruthless in declaring that the whole family of a wicked man deserves to suffer. The very memory of such a man should be blotted out, even if this means that his children will be destroyed. But the prophet knows the much deeper truth, that each individual is responsible to God as an individual, not merely as a member of a family or a group. Consequently, only the sinner must die, not his children or his parents. Note, too, the remarkable interpretation of the son gashing himself with knives when his father dies. His earthly father has died, but his Father in Heaven lives. Finally, the reply of the Torah, while accepting the principle stated by Prophecy, ordains that a sacrifice be offered not only for the sake of the sinner, but as a powerful means of preventing sin and thus benefiting society. This Arama now proceeds to explain. In our terminology Arama has referred to three kinds of responsibility: 1) collective responsibility; 2) individual responsibility; 3) social responsibility.

It is perfectly right and proper that for the benefit of society there should be a law that one who sins against one of the laws of the Torah should bring a sacrifice and thus find atonement. As all the earlier teachers of blessed memory say, it is a marvelous method of bringing home to sinners what they have done. For when the sinner observes the sacrifice offered for his sin being slaughtered, skinned, cut up into pieces and burned on the altar in fire, he will reflect that all this he deserves to have done to him and so it would have been were it not that God in His mercy allows him to substitute a guilt-offering or some other animal sacrifice for his own person. In this way the sinner will come to fear Heaven in a proper manner. This is a marvelous way of bringing home to him the heinousness of his sin, for generally speaking, a sinner does not acknowledge how great his sin is until he has suffered the punishment for it. Observe what is said of Cain. When God said to him: "The voice of thy brother's blood . . And now cursed art thou from the ground . . When thou tillest the ground, it shall not henceforth yield unto thee her strength; a fugitive and a wanderer shalt thou be in the earth" (Genesis 4:10-12), then, and only then, did he realize how great was his sin so that he said: "My sin is greater than I can bear. Behold, Thou hast driven me out . . . "(Genesis 4:13-14). Then he realized that since the punishment was so great, his sin was so great, something he had not hitherto appreciated.

Cain and his ilk can be compared to the drunkard who enters a tavern and drinks heavily, but fails to realize how much wine he has imbibed until he is asked to foot the bill. As the Sage says: "When a man sets his eye on the money-bag he will walk uprightly" (Proverbs 23:31). The verse as written reads ba-kis ("on the money-bag") and we can derive a lesson from this word, both from the way it is written and from the way it is traditionally pronounced. The meaning of the text in the way it is written is that when a man sets his eye on how much he can afford to pay for the wine and does not drink as much as he wants but only as much as he can afford, then he will walk uprightly. The meaning of the text as pronounced (ba-kos, "on the cup") is that when he sets his eye on the cup of wine and considers the harm that may result from it, he will know when he has had enough and will stop drinking. It is not because he cannot afford more. Be that as it may, the punishment demonstrates to the sinner how great is his sin.

Arama's little excursus on wine is based on an interpretation at variance with the conventional English rendering of the verse in Proverbs. His point is that the traditional way of writing the word is ba-kis, "on the money-bag," while the traditional way of reading the word is ba-kos, "on the cup." We can learn a lesson from both ways of reading the text. The first advises the potential drunkard to think of his money and he will not spend much on drink. The second advises him to think of the harm drunkenness will cause and he will not drink too much even if he can afford it. In any event, Arama has made his point about the purpose of sacrifices. When the sinner sees what happens to the animal and is moved to consider that, were it not for God's mercy, the bloodletting would have happened to him (a bit gruesome this), he will experience remorse. Thus, for Arama, the sin-offering is a kind of dramatic enactment of the severest punishment and has the psychological effect of bringing home to the sinner how great is his sin. This explains both difficulties Arama has mentioned. We now see the power of animal sacrifices (or, at least, of sin-offerings) and we can also see why they are brought only for unintentional sins. As Arama continues later in his exposition, there are two reasons why this expiation cannot apply to intentional sins. First, if sacrifices were to be offered for inten-tional sins, it would give some kind of official recognition that there are people who sin intentionally and would lead to a lowering of standards. The official system refuses to acknowledge openly that men sin intentionally. Secondly, the intentional sinner cannot find atonement through the token sacrifice of an animal, but must suffer in his own person by fasting and the like. Arama concludes that this is the meaning of God's reply in the Midrash: Let him repent and he will find atonement. Note how throughout Arama's exposition the psychological value of the sin-offering is stressed and how Arama rejects any suggestion that the sacrifice can influence or coerce God, unlike the idolators who said that their sacrifices could influence or coerce their gods. Considerations of space prevent us from giving any more of Arama's lengthy exposition, but it should be said that he gives a reason, too, for other sacrifices apart from sin-offerings, i.e., animal sacrifices brought voluntarily as gifts to God. Briefly, his idea is that man has a body as well as a soul and he is consequently influenced by material things which alone make a lasting impression on him. All the detailed rules regarding the sacrifices, their order and their regulations, have as their aim the calling of man's attention to God and His commandments. Thus it is not the mere act of bringing the sacrifice that God wants, but the awakening of man's soul when he brings it. Does the soul need food? Yes, in a sense, says Arama, since without food the body would die. In similar fashion the soul needs the concrete physical reminders

provided by the sacrifices that God is Lord of all. Thus there are two
kinds of sacrifices: 1) the sin-offering; 2) the freewill offering.
The latter is more elevated in that its sole purpose is to encourage
man to rise to higher moral and spiritual levels. Arama concludes
that this is the meaning of the Midrash with which he began his
exposition. Noah's sacrifice was a sin-offering. God is pleased with
this, too, but He is more pleased, as it were, with the freewill
offerings Israel brought. Of course, Arama's view is only one among
many. Maimonides has a quite different exposition of the sacrificial
system—it is, for him, a kind of concession to human weakness in
order to wean men away from idolatry—but Arama takes issue in
this passage with Maimonides.

Abravanel

What is the meaning of the Tower of Babel?
Did Lot's wife really turn into a pillar of salt?
Why must a kid not be seethed in its mother's milk?

Don Isaac (ben Judah) Abravanel was born in Lisbon in 1437 and died in Venice in 1508. His Commentary to the Pentateuch was first published in Venice in 1579. He also wrote Commentaries to the Prophetic books. Abravanel is frequently considered to be a forerunner of modern Biblical scholarship in his critical sense, his breadth of knowledge, and his comparative method. His Commentaries are not as popular as most of the others mentioned in this book, probably because he treats his topics at great length. But his style is clear and his thought well ordered so that his influence on the few, at least, was very considerable.

A. WHAT IS THE MEANING OF THE TOWER OF BABEL?

Comment on the tower of Babel narrative, Genesis 11:1-9. Abravanel discusses the various theories that have been advanced to explain this puzzling episode. The chief difficulty is to determine how the people sinned in building the city and the great tower and how the punishment of scattering them and confusing their tongues fit the crime. In the Rabbinic literature the term for the men who built the tower is "the generation of the dispersion," because they were "scattered abroad" (verse 8 and 10:25). This is the name Abravenel uses here.

Both recent and earlier commentators have been puzzled by this topic of the generation of the dispersion. What was their sin and what their iniquity that they should have been punished by a confusion of language and by being scattered among the various lands? There are Midrashim which seek to answer these questions, but their explanations do not fit the plain meaning of the verses. One of these Midrashim suggests that their sin consisted in a plan to ascend to heaven in order to wage war with God who dwells there. But such a view is extremely hard to accept. How could the whole of mankind agree to embark on such a stupid, impossible project? Among that generation were Noah, Shem and Eber, and Abraham, men of the highest intelligence, the wisest of the wise. If they really were all so stupid, they would not have deserved any more punishment than that God in heaven would laugh at them. Moreover, God testified to the possibility of their carrying out their plan, as it is written: "And now nothing will be withholden from them, which they purpose to do" (verse 6). Another Midrashic interpretation is that they denied the root principle and lopped off the branches. But this is hard to understand for if that were their sin, how could the punishment of language confusion and of scattering have been sufficient? They would have deserved to have been utterly destroyed, with fire and brimstone and the wind of terror as their portion. Without doubt these Rabbinic homilies have a different meaning and they hint at something other than they seem to say.

Abravanel first dismisses the Midrashic explanations. According to one of these the punishment would have been too severe. God does not punish the merely stupid, only the consciously wicked. According to the other Midrashic view, the punishment would have been too light. The expression "lopping off the branches" is Rabbinic and denotes severe heresy, lopping off the branches of the King's orchard or the tree of faith. "Denying the root principle" means a complete denial of God, out and out atheism. Note that Abravanel cannot bring himself to reject completely the Rabbinic Midrashim, so he suggests that these Midrashim must not be taken literally and hint at something else. But since we do not know what this is, these Midrashim are of no help to us in our attempt to understand the passage.

Some commentators suggest that their aim in building the tower was that it be a refuge for them in the event of another flood. But Rabbi Abraham ibn Ezra has already refuted such an interpretation on the grounds that Noah and his sons, who were alive at that time, were the family patriarchs and their words were heeded. How could it have been possible, then, for these patriarchs not to have informed them that God had sworn by His right hand that He would never again bring a flood upon the earth (Genesis 9:8-17), and that He had made a covenant with mankind on this matter, one that He had promised never to change? In further refutation of such a view, I argue that if this had been their aim they would hardly have built their tower in a plain, the lowest of spots, where a flood of water would have swept it away. Our Rabbis, of blessed memory, say that the reason that place was called "Shinar" (11:2) is because all the waters of the flood were poured out there. They should rather have erected their tower on a high and lofty mountain of the mountains of Ararat from whence they came (8:4-19). Furthermore, on a mountain they would have found huge and valuable stones for use in their building and they would have had no need to make bricks as they had to do in the plain (11:3) because there were no stones there.

Abravanel refutes the view that the purpose of the tower was to serve as a refuge from the waters of another flood if it ever came. Ibn Ezra rejects this on the grounds that Noah and his sons would surely have told them that their fears were unfounded since God had promised never to bring such a flood again. Furthermore, Abravanel adds, if this had been their aim, why did they build their tower in such an exposed place as the plain and not on the mountains? The Rabbinic passage he quotes contains a pun on the word "Shinar" to read she-ninaaru ("that were poured out there"), i.e., that plain was much lower than the surrounding lands so that all the waters of the flood were eventually emptied into that basin. This shows that if it had been their aim to escape from another flood, that plain would have been the very worst spot they could have chosen, the place which received the full force of the flood waters.

Abraham ibn Ezra and Ralbag (Gersonides) hold that the builders of the tower did not, in fact, sin against God at all. Their sole intention was to keep their society intact and dwell together, as they said (11:4): "Lest we be scattered abroad upon the face of the whole earth." The reason why God scattered them was, on this view, for their own good. It was either, as Ibn Ezra suggests, in order for the whole earth to become populated, or because if they had remained in one place an earthquake or a great fire might have broken out, or a flood of water or some other natural calamity which would have caused an upheaval with a consequent lack of the means of sustenance, and the human race would have perished. But this view, too, seems to me to be far from what the Torah intended. For they had formed themselves into a social group before this time while they were in the ark and yet they were not scattered throughout the earth. There, too, the destiny of which Ralbag speaks awaited them, and yet God did not scatter them or confuse their tongues until they began to build the tower. This view becomes even more implausible when we consider that to this very day nothing dangerous has happened in the plain of Shinar. To be sure the city of Babylon was overthrown for its sins, as were Sodom and Gomorrah, but the plain itself is still inhabited by human beings. And even though it was the will of God for the whole earth to be populated, since He did not create it to be empty but to be inhabited, in the course of time and with the natural increase of mankind His purpose would have been fulfilled automatically. Men would naturally have spread westward, eastward, to the north and to the south, without there being any need for a confusion of tongues or for all this alarm. You can see that when they were at Ararat and they began to increase, they journeyed from there because it could not contain them all. Why, then, could this not have happened in the plain? Moreover, the simple meaning of the verses demonstrates that there was something here of punishment and sin and a need to prevent further sin, as it is said (11:6): "and this is what they begin to do; and now nothing will be withholden from them, which they purpose to do."

Abravanel demolishes the theory held both by Ibn Ezra and Gersonides that there is no suggestion of any sin or punishment in the narrative. They wanted to remain in one place but God scattered them, not as punishment, but because He wished mankind to spread over all the earth, not to remain settled in only one spot on earth. Abravanel considers this unlikely. Natural increase would have determined a movement of population. Moreover, no great natural disaster has ever happened in that part of the world, i.e., so any fear was really unfounded. Finally, Abravanel points out that a plain reading of the text does not give the impression that the people were completely innocent in wishing to build the tower.

The Ran explains that their sin in building the city and the tower was not because they wanted to dwell together, but because they wished to appoint over them one ruler, one king who would rule over all of earth's inhabitants wherever they would be, from that city and from that tower. Now in itself this was no sin. Had they been followers of a true faith their unified society would have been a very good thing. But since they were idolators, with a desire to reign over all, it would have resulted in the spread of their beliefs all over the world. The God-fearing man would then have had no means of escape, as Abraham escaped when he fled to Canaan which was not under Nimrod's rule. That is why God scattered them; not because of what they had done, but because of what could have resulted from it. This view is in my opinion the most unlikely of all. Nothing is said in the text of a single king ruling over all. Furthermore, differences of language do not involve different kings. It frequently happens that one king rules over peoples speaking different tongues, as we can see from the case of Ahasuerus (Esther 1:1; 3:12). Moreover, even if they had appointed one king over all, there was nothing to prevent God saving his servants without confusing their tongues. For what was there to prevent God from inspiring a mighty warrior to reign over one of those provinces and to rebel against the king in his tower in order to save the chosen of the Lord, just as He inspired Cyrus the Persian King, even though he was a vassal of the Babylonian King, to rebel against Belshazzar in order to give refuge in his dominion to the God-fearing and those who thought on God's name? Apart from this there are many ways open to God. For in the days of Nimrod, Shem and Eber and many other righteous men were under his sway and yet God protected them from harm. How much more when all the kings of that time were idolators, so that whatever danger existed for the righteous from the reign of a single, idolatrous tyrant ruling over all the earth would still have been present when there were many evil kings and great sinners against the Lord.

Finally, of what use was this device of God's in confusing their tongues and scattering them in order to prevent the rise of an idolatrous tyrant to rule over them? Eventually, the exile of Israel and Judah took place under evil kings and yet God saved them even though at that time there was one single idolatrous leader reigning over the whole world. All this demonstrates that the Ran's view is also incorrect. Consequently, I have to look for another view in order to explain it all adequately. I shall not now bother to raise questions on individual verses because I fear prolixity and in any event each matter will be explained in due course.

The Ran is Rabbi Nissim of Gerondi (14th century), so called after the initial letters of his name. According to the Ran, the sin consisted in their desire to have one king reigning over the whole world. But a tyrant who has absolute power can successfully persecute the God-fearing. Consequently, God has to scatter them and confuse their tongues. The Rabbis believed that Abraham had to fly to Canaan because Nimrod had designs on his life. Abravanel proceeds to demolish the Ran's theory and what he says is self-explanatory. Abravanel has now considered a number of interpretations, all of which he believes to be incorrect. Note how he does this by examining closely what the text really says. He now proceeds to give his own interpretation. His reference to "raising questions" is to the method he frequently adopts in his commentaries of first raising a number of difficulties in the text, and then proceeding to give an explanation which removes them one by one. But he avoids doing this here since he fears he has already been too wordy and he still has much to say.

In my opinion the following is the most plausible explanation of the sin of the generation of the dispersion. They committed, in fact, the same sin as our first father (Adam) and his son Cain and his offspring. God created man in His image, endowing him with intelligence, so that he could perfect himself in the recognition of his Creator and the knowledge of His works. God prepared for Adam all of life's necessities, food and drink in the fruit of the garden and the waters of its rivers. All was provided naturally without the need for any human effort whatsoever. Adam had no need to spend any time on acquiring his basic needs and he was able to devote himself entirely to the purpose for which he had been created, the knowledge of the divine. Adam's sin consisted in this, that he became discontented with the natural goods God had provided for him and he allowed himself to be distracted by the lure of desires and of deeds of fame. His punishment was to be driven out of Eden, the place of repose, to become sated with shame. The earth was cursed because of him and its natural goods were no longer enough for him. Since he chose a life of luxury, he was doomed to labor hard to attain it, as the *Guide for the Perplexed* declares. Cain also chose to become concerned with artificial things. That is why he became a tiller of the ground (Genesis 4:2), laboring all day at plowing, sowing and tending his lands. His intellect became subordinate to the animal part of his nature which it began to serve. He became a "servant of the ground" (*oved* = "to serve" as well as "to till"). Abel, on the other hand, became a keeper of sheep (Genesis 4:2), attracted to natural things and content with them, for tending sheep involves neither labor nor effort. All that is required is to lead the flock and to follow nature. That is why our ancestors, Abraham, Isaac and Jacob, the sons of Jacob, Moses and David were all shepherds and not tillers of the ground. Even Noah, though he sinned in his attraction for wine (Genesis 9:20), is not called by Scripture "a servant (*oved*) of the ground," but "a man (*ish*) of the ground," namely, a ruler over the soil. Cain, however, was called "a servant of the ground," in that he made his intellect subordinate to the animal part of his nature in his work on the soil. Cain, therefore, built a city (Genesis 4:17) which he called Enoch (*hanoch* = "training") for he trained his sons and taught them to do those works required in the building of cities and for advanced social life. The sons of Cain, too, followed in their father's footsteps, attracted by luxury occupations. Thus Jubal was the father of all such as handle the harp and the pipe, and Tubal-cain the forger of every cutting instrument of brass and iron (Genesis 4:21,22). Even Jabal, who was a shepherd, became an innovator in such artificial matters as constructing elaborate tents which were previously unknown. Therefore Scripture says of him that "he was the father of such as dwell in tents and have cattle" (Genesis 4:20). All the sons of Cain, in their pursuit of luxury, employed robbery and violence to achieve their ends. Their punishment was to be blotted out from the earth in the days of the flood. The sin of the generation of the dispersion was similar to that of Cain and his sons. All of life's necessities were provided for them by God from heaven. They had no need for hard toil and could have devoted themselves entirely to the attainment of perfection for their souls. But they were discontented with that which God's gift had provided in nature's abundance. They sought instead to have a different aim, to build a city in which all kinds of work would have their place. There would be a tower in that city in which they could hold meetings. Instead of being country folk, they would become urbanised. They saw as their destiny the promotion of urban life, working together for the good of society. This they saw as man's true end. But arising out of this kind of life are the struggles for fame, titles and power, for illusionary honors and the accumulation of possessions, leading eventually to violence and robbery and even murder, all of which were unknown when they were country dwellers, each living on his own. As King Solomon said: "God made men upright; but they have sought out many inventions" (Ecclesiastes 7:29). Since all this is really superfluous and unnatural, preventing men from attaining their true perfection, that of the soul, therefore, these sinners against the soul were punished in that God confused their tongues and scattered them on the face of the earth, just as He drove Adam out of Eden and Cain out of the place where he lived and Cain's sons out of the world itself at the time of the flood. The sin of all these was basically the same sin, namely, they made the tree of knowledge their ultimate aim and neglected the tree of life, the true purpose of man. Consequently, the punishment for them all was of a similar nature.

Abravanel's interpretation is both interesting and provocative. There have always been religious thinkers who have had a romantic longing for the simple life of contemplation, seeing in urban society the source of all mischief. The sin of the generation of the dispersion, according to Abravanel, consisted in their preference for over-sophistication instead of the life of nature represented by the shepherd. (This passage should be compared with the section in this book on Baḥya Ibn Asher who similarly describes the life of the shepherd as the ideal life.) The rest of Abravanel's comment on the tower of Babel is an elaboration of the theme of which two further points must be mentioned. First, he goes on to understand the confusion of tongues as a natural result of the new "technological" society they sought to create. In their previous more simple life the language used by Adam was entirely adequate. Communication between men was easy. But with the increase of new devices and inventions, new terms had to be coined and various "jargons" created. Each trade and each profession coined its own terms and eventually there was a total loss of communication. Secondly, Abravanel deals with the obvious question. Does the story mean to tell us that God does not want men to live in cities? Abravanel replies that once mankind had chosen this way, its prohibition would have been contrary to human nature. Therefore, the Torah accepts urban society but seeks to improve it. It urges men not to succumb to the temptations to which they are especially prone in the city, intrigues, violence, cheating, dishonesty, seeking for power. They may and should live in a city, but they should try to make it a just city. This whole topic has been very widely discussed in our day. What has religion to say to the claims of the "secular city"? It is fascinating to see Abravanel grappling with the problem, influenced no doubt by his experiences in the cities in which he had lived. Abravanel, it should not be forgotten, lived in the late Renaissance, when precisely this kind of topic exercised the minds of thoughtful men.

B. DID LOT'S WIFE REALLY TURN INTO A PILLAR OF SALT?

Comment on: "But his wife looked back from behind him, and she became a pillar of salt" (Genesis 19:26). The verse has usually been taken to mean that Lot's wife looked back at Sodom, although they had been ordered not to do so (verse 17), and so she was turned into a pillar of salt. In other words this was a miracle and was understood as such by the Rabbis. While Abravanel generally accepts the Biblical miracles as real supernatural events, here he is in a more rationalistic mood, though he is not prepared to go as far as Gersonides. (Compare this with Gersonides' understanding of the sun standing still for Joshua, in the section on Gersonides in this book.)

"But his wife looked back from behind him, and she became a pillar of salt." Ralbag (Gersonides) is in error when he supposes that the words "and she became a pillar of salt" refer not to Lot's wife but to Sodom, which became a pillar of salt. Lot's wife, he suggests, died a natural death. He is wrong as can be seen from the story of Lot's daughters (verses 30-38). What caused Ralbag to adopt such an opinion was that he found it difficult to understand why God

should have performed this kind of miracle for Lot's wife. This view is false, for it was not a miracle for anyone's benefit but it was an affliction. Naturally, if fire and brimstone rained down on her, she died. If we were to argue otherwise, why does Scripture say: "his wife looked from behind him"? It should have stated that she died and then recorded separately that Sodom became a pillar of salt. It is not, therefore, as Ralbag says, but the matter has to be understood as follows. Lot's wife looked back from behind him, that is, from behind her husband, Lot. When Lot was about to leave Sodom the angel warned him: "Escape for thy life; look not behind thee" (verse 17). As I have explained earlier, "looking behind" means here that Lot should have no regard for his wealth and property which remained in Sodom. But Lot's wife paid no heed to this admonition. She did look behind him, that is to say, she busied herself in trying to save their herds and sheep and the rest of their property, exactly the opposite of what they had been commanded to do. Since she was so preoccupied in saving their wealth, she did not leave together with her husband. The result was that the catastrophe overtook her and, together with the rest of the doomed city, she became a pillar of salt.

Salt was rained down on Sodom (see Deuteronomy 29:22). Consequently, Gersonides suggests that the words "and she became a pillar of salt" refer to the city ("city" is in the feminine gender in Hebrew). Gersonides understands the verse to mean that when Lot's wife looked backward she saw that the city had become a pillar of salt. But, objects Abravanel, this means that Lot's wife lived on and only died later. In that case, why does the narrative of Lot's daughters clearly imply that only Lot and his daughters were left and that Lot's wife had died? Moreover, Abravanel finds puzzling Gersonides' objection that God would not have performed a miracle for her, as if it were for her benefit. Finally, Abravanel objects, if the reference is to the city being turned into a pillar of salt, what has this to do with Lot's wife? Abravanel's interpretation is that "looking behind" means going back to save the property which remained there. The angel warned Lot precisely of this because, though eager to escape, Lot might have been tempted to look behind him nostalgically at the wealth he was forced to relinquish and he might actually have gone back again to be trapped there. This is what Lot's wife did. When the city was destroyed, she was caught there and became a pillar of salt. Thus, there was no *special miracle in connection with Lot's wife. Abravanel's interpretation is certainly ingenious, but is hardly what the verse states.*

C.   WHY MUST A KID NOT BE SEETHED IN ITS MOTHER'S MILK?

Comment on: "Thou shalt not seethe a kid in its mother's milk" (Exodus 23:19). The prohibition occurs, too, in Exodus 34:26 and Deuteronomy 14:21. In the Rabbinic tradition, the prohibition embraces the boiling or cooking together of any meat and milk and the eating of such a mixture or the enjoyment of any benefit from it. Abravanel offers his explanation of what seems to be a mysterious law.

"Thou shalt not seethe a kid in its mother's milk." You will find this precept mentioned three times in the Torah: once here; the second time at the end of the portion *Ki Tissa;* **and the third time in the portion** *Re-eh.* **Our Rabbis explain the threefold reference: one is to show that it is forbidden to eat the mixture, one to show that it is forbidden to have any benefit from it, and one to show that it is forbidden to boil the two together. The main reason for this law is to eradicate cruel traits. In this it resembles the prohibition of slaughtering an animal and its young on the same day (Leviticus 22:28), and the command to send away the mother bird (Deuteronomy 22:6,7). But the prohibition was extended to include any meat with any milk. The Rabbi (Maimonides), author of the** *Guide for the Perplexed,* **explains that the reason for this rule is because it is gross food since the milk is speedily boiled, not so the meat. Rabbi Ibn Ezra writes that the reason the Torah mentions a kid of goats rather than any other meat is because the meat of the kid is more easily cooked than any other meat and, moreover, this meat provides a nicely balanced meal. To this day the Arabs cook goat's meat in milk. In reality, any meat is covered by the prohibition, but Scripture gives an illustration from the way these things are generally done. Since the kid is close to its mother, it is more likely that the mother's milk will be used when cooking it. But it seems most plausible to suggest that it was the practice of the idolators at their gatherings to do this, namely, to seethe a kid in milk at harvest time, believing that by so doing they would appease their god and draw near to him and he would send his blessing on the work of**

their hands, as it is said: "And they shall no more sacrifice their sacrifices unto the satyrs" (Leviticus 17:7). Shepherds especially used to do this at the time when they had their gathering to draw up rules of conduct. Their food has always been kids cooked in milk and every kind of dish in which there is milk and meat. To this very day this is the custom in Spain, that twice a year all the shepherds gather together for the purpose of taking counsel with one another and in order to draw up rules concerning the rights of the shepherds and their flocks. In their tongue they call this gathering *miesta (fiesta?)*. At such gatherings, as we have investigated, their food is, indeed, composed of meat and milk and the meat of goats is considered to be a special delicacy when used in this kind of dish. I have made enquiries and have investigated it to the full and have been correctly informed that in the isle at the end of the earth, known as Angleterre ("end of the earth" = England), where there is a greater abundance of sheep than in any other land, this is their constant practice. I surmise that, in reality, this is why God instructed the Israelites that when they come together on the feast of Tabernacles (Exodus 23:16), they should not do as the heathens do and seethe a kid in its mother's milk. And in order to keep them as far as possible from the way of the idolators, God prohibited the eating, the enjoyment of any benefit, and the cooking together of these two, as the Rabbis say, and they prohibited every mixture of meat and milk in order that sinners who wish to find an excuse should not argue, what difference is there between this and that? For this reason they even prohibited the meat of poultry cooked in milk according to a majority of the Rabbis, with the exception of Rabbi José the Galilean, who had a tradition that the prohibition does not apply to a species (birds) which has no milk. He, therefore, permitted the cooking together of poultry and milk. But where an individual disagrees in matters of law with a majority, the opinion of the majority is law. They also prohibited the eating of milk dishes after one has eaten meat in case some of the meat, still attached to the teeth and still tasty, becomes mixed with the milk. It is necessary to wait before drinking milk after having eaten meat until any meat still in the teeth will have lost its pungency and become tasteless. But the Rabbis did permit meat to be eaten after milk. All this is set forth in the works of the Rabbis, blessed be their memory.

First Abravanel suggests that the reason for the law is that it is an especially cruel act and the Torah wishes to eradicate cruel traits of character. However, if this is so, it should only have applied to the case stated, not to any meat cooked in milk. Abravanel says that it was a matter of the law being extended. Maimonides is then quoted. He gives as the reason that the mixture is unhygienic. Actually, Maimonides also gives another reason, close to that of Abravanel, and it is strange that Abravanel overlooks it. Maimonides says that he surmised that the idolators did this act. It might be mentioned that in material discovered at Ras Shamara in Syria, dating from about the time of Moses, there is, according to some scholars, a reference to this practice in idolatrous worship. Ibn Ezra is then quoted by Abravanel. He holds that for some reason the prohibition includes, as the Rabbis say, the cooking of any meat together with any milk. Why, in that case, does the Torah mention the kid's meat in its mother's milk? This is simply because the two being normally together, it is this meat that will normally be cooked in this milk and the Torah simply gives it as an illustration. Abravanel then proceeds to give his own explanation. Shepherds have large quantities of goatsmeat and they cook it in milk. He surmises that at their gatherings they would do this in idolatrous worship, i.e., as a special gift to the gods (or, possibly, as a kind of sympathetic magic to influence the increase of the flock and herds and the crops). Thus, according to Abravanel the law is really a protest against idolatry. The rest of the passage simply records some of the laws regarding this rule. Abravanel then concludes with a homiletical interpretation which he had heard.

Now we find in the works of the Rabbis that God said: "Do not cause Me to seethe (i.e., to make ripe too soon) the kids of the produce (i.e., the corn) while they are still in the mother's womb." Basing himself on this idea, one of the sages of our generation suggested the following. God commanded them to celebrate Passover, because at that time they went out of Egypt and it was therefore fitting that they give thanks to Him. And He commanded them to give thanks for the blessing of their crops on Pentecost and on Tabernacles and not be ungrateful to Him. In order to warn them of all this He said: "Do not seethe a kid in its mother's milk." This is an appropriate parable. For a kid that kicks the mother that gives it milk deserves to be seethed in that milk. Similarly, whoever fails to show gratitude for God's providence which has carefully watched over him for his own good, deserves that providence should do him evil. It is then as if He had said: Do not be ungrateful for the good and blessing I have given you, so as not to cause the providence and the good to be seethed in its mother's milk, the blessing turning into a curse, the good into evil. This, too, is a pleasant, figurative interpretation of our verse.

The Rabbinic homily Abravanel quotes says that the verse means: Do not sin, because if you do you will cause Me to seethe (i.e., to spoil) the young crops. Seething a kid in its mother's milk is a symbolic way of expressing concern at ingratitude. Milk is the symbol of good. God's providence is therefore compared to milk. If man is grateful all is well, but if not, then the milk is used for the opposite purpose. Abravanel praises this but, of course, only as a homily. He now concludes with the Karaite interpretation of our verse, with which he naturally disagrees.

The Karaite sages explain the reason for "Thou shalt not seethe a kid" is that the flower should not mix with the stem. And, according to them, the meaning is that the firstborn kid should not continue to be suckled by its mother after seven days (Leviticus 22:27), but on the eighth day you are obliged to bring it as a sacrifice. In their opinion, the meaning of seething *(bishul)* is ripening, as in the verse: "brought forth ripe *(hivshilu)* grapes" (Genesis 40:10). According to this explanation, the precept only applies to the firstborn. But since we see that the precept has been repeated three times, it is more reasonable to accept the tradition of the Rabbis, of blessed memory, as being completely true. On this tradition alone should one rely and all other ideas are childish nonsense.

For the Karaites, see the section in this book on Ibn Ezra. The Karaite explanation of the verse is: Do not let the kid ripen in its mother's milk, i.e., do not let the firstborn stay with its mother for more than seven days. Naturally, Abravanel takes issue with the Karaites.

Sforno

What is the meaning of the binding of Isaac?
How are the Ten Commandments to be understood?

*Obadiah ben Jacob Sforno (died Bologna, Italy, in 1550), philosopher,
Talmudist and physician, wrote a Commentary to the Pentateuch
and to other books of the Bible. His Commentary to the Pentateuch
was first printed in Venice in 1567 and has since been reprinted
frequently together with the text in editions of the Pentateuch.
Sforno relies on earlier commentators, but he also gives original
interpretations of the text based on his wide knowledge of life
and literature.*

A. WHAT IS THE MEANING OF THE BINDING OF ISAAC?

*Comment on the binding of Isaac, Genesis 22:1-19. The numbers are
those of the verses on which Sforno comments.*

**1. "Did prove Abraham." God intended Abraham to express his love
for Him and his fear of Him in actuality just as hitherto he had
possessed these qualities in potentiality. In this way he would come
to resemble his Creator more closely since the Creator is good to
the world in actuality. The purpose for which man was created was
that he should resemble his Creator as far as it is humanly possible,
as God testified when He said: "Let us make man in our image,
after our likeness" (Genesis 1:26).**

3. "And went unto the place." To the land of Moriah.

4. "And saw the place." That is, the place where the sacrifice was to take place on Mount Moriah. "Afar off." By the will of God his eye was given the power to see a distant place, just as it is said: "And the Lord showed him all the land" (Deuteronomy 34:1), and he understood that the place of the sacrifice was to be in that spot.

5. "Abide ye here with the ass." So that they should not protest and thus disturb him when he came to perform the sacrifice.

12. "Now I know." I, the angel, now know that it is only right that God has made you greater than His angels. As the Rabbis, of blessed memory, say: "The righteous are greater than the ministering angels." "Than me." You are more God-fearing than I am, for I am an angel, and you are therefore deserving of a greater elevation than I am, as the Rabbis say: "The righteous are greater", etc. For you feared God in actuality just as God knew beforehand that you were God-fearing in potentiality. Now his actual knowledge can encompass that which enjoys actuality.

13. "And behold behind him a ram caught in the thicket." He understood, therefore, that God had provided him with this ram so that there could be no reason to fear that he was guilty of theft by taking it, since he saw that there was no ram beforehand and yet immediately afterwards he saw this ram caught in the thicket. "In the stead of his son." "Instead of the intention he had had of offering up his son, as it is said: "And speaketh truth in his heart" (Psalms 15:2).

14. "As it is said to this day." The place of which Israel said, when the Torah was given, that God would appear on it, as He said: "Then it shall come to pass that the place which the Lord your God shall choose" (Deuteronomy 12:11). This took place at the time of David. That place was called by Abraham "The Lord shall appear" (verse 14).

16. "Saith the Lord, because thou hast done." I, the Lord, say that because you have done this, I shall bless you. "By Myself I have sworn." That I shall bless you.

18. "And in thy seed shall all the nations of the earth be blessed." When they will all call on God's name to serve Him with one ac-

cord, they will all find blessing in your seed and try to emulate them. "Because thou hast hearkened to My voice." The reward of a good deed is another good deed. You have the merit that your descendants will be an ensign to the people, teaching the nations how to serve God, and the merit of it will be yours.

1. Sforno is bothered by the idea of God "proving" or "testing" Abraham. Surely, God knew how Abraham would behave? Sforno understands it to mean that the "proof" or "test" was not in order to provide God with information He did not already possess, but in order to give Abraham the opportunity of expressing in actuality the love and fear of God he already had in potentiality. Potential love and fear are very fine things, but when a man actualizes them he becomes closer in the process to his Creator and resembles Him the more closely since God is not only potentially good but has given actual expression to His goodness when He created the world and when He sustains it.

3. Sforno's difficulty here is that in the next verse it is implied that he did not know where the place was. Sforno's reply is that here the "place" is the district as a whole, whereas in the next verse it is the actual spot at which the sacrifice was to take place.

4. If the reference is to the site of the sacrifice, how could he possibly see it from a distance? Sforno quotes the example of Moses who was endowed by God with special powers of vision, otherwise how could he have seen "all the land"?

5. Abraham did not take the lads with him because he feared that when they would see what he intended to do they would try to stop him.

12. The difficulty here is obvious. How could God have said: "Now I know"? Did He not know it beforehand? Sforno replies that it was the angel (verse 11), not God, who was speaking and, moreover, the meaning is not: "Now I know that you are God-fearing" but: "Now I know why you humans are greater than we angels." Sforno translates the word mimmeni not as "from Me" (as in the English translation), but as "more than me", i.e., than the angel who was speaking. Note Sforno's final remark here. God would have had an actual knowledge of Abraham's potential love and fear. Now that these have been actualized, God has an actual knowledge of the actual.

13. Sforno evidently takes the Hebrew word aḥar (rendered by the English translation as "behind") to mean "immediately afterwards." Sforno's remarks about "speaking the truth in the heart" mean that since Abraham had resolved to bring a sacrifice he had to bring one, even though the resolve was only in his heart, i.e., even though he had made no verbal promise. The Rabbis use the verse, in fact, to teach that if a man promises himself to do a good deed he should keep his promise, even though it was only made "in the heart."

14. Sforno understands the "day" of the verse to be the day when the Torah was given. (See the section in this book on Ibn Ezra that this verse, if it means the day when the Temple stood, is anachronistic). On that day God had told the people that He would choose a place for His Temple and David did eventually choose one. According to the Rabbis, the spot chosen was where Abraham had intended to make the sacrifice. Indeed, legend has it that the rock within the Dome of the Rock on Mount Moriah, in Jerusalem, is the selfsame rock upon which Abraham bound Isaac.

16. The Hebrew is a little difficult, hence Sforno's paraphrase. Also he has understood the earlier verses as being spoken by the angel, so he now says that this was obviously spoken by God, not by the angel.

18. The nations being "blessed" by Abraham's seed means that in the Messianic age they will all wish to serve God and Abraham's seed will show them the way.

B. HOW ARE THE TEN COMMANDMENTS TO BE UNDERSTOOD?

Comment on the Ten Commandments, Exodus 20:1-14. The numbers are those of the verses on which Sforno comments.

2. **"I" alone "am the Lord." The Cause of all being, the Eternal, known to you by tradition and by rational demonstration. "Thy God." And I will fulfil that which you have accepted, namely, that I will be your God without any intermediary. Consequently, pray to Me alone and worship Me alone without any intermediary. "Who brought thee out of the land of Egypt" through acts that were completely opposed to the acts of all intermediaries, namely, nature and its order. This is what you agreed to when you said: "This is my God, and I will glorify Him" (Exodus 15:2). "Out of the house of**

bondage." To remove from you any kind of coercion which can have no place if one is to carry out a good deed adequately.

3. "Thou shalt have no other gods." Even though you have accepted My sovereignty, do not imagine that you can serve any other at the same time, as one serves the servant of a king, after the fashion of those of whom it is said: "They feared the Lord, and served their own gods" (II Kings 17:33). "Before Me." Since one does not pay honor to the king's servants in the presence of the king, and I am always present.

4. "Thou shalt not make thee a graven image." Even if you have no intention of worshiping it.

5. "Thou shalt not bow down unto them." To the creatures themselves which are in the heavens or the earth. "A jealous God." I do not want those who serve Me to serve others as well, for there is no resemblance whatsoever between Me and others and it is therefore right for Me to be zealous for My honor if it is given to another who has no right to it. "Visiting the iniquity of the fathers upon the children." The reason I am so long-suffering with some of the wicked in this world is because I wait until their measure of sin is full, so that they can perish even in this world. This is because I visit the iniquity of the fathers upon the children if those children follow in the footsteps of their parents and add their own evil intentions to those of their parents, proceeding from one evil to another in each generation, as happened to Jeroboam (I Kings 12: 25-33). "Unto the third generation." If they add to the evil done by their ancestors, as happened to the seed of Zimri (I Kings 16:9-20). "And the fourth generation." As happened to the seed of Jehu (II Kings, chapters 9 and 10). If they do not turn aside from the evil deeds of their ancestors, but instead reach such a stage of corruption that for a particular generation it becomes a permanent acquisition without hope of repentance, then they deserve to perish, as it is said: "for the iniquity of the Amorite is not yet full" (Genesis 15:16).

6. "And showing mercy unto the thousandth generation." Occasionally, the reason for My long suffering is that I show mercy unto the thousandth generation because of the merit of some ancestor who loved Me and in his merit I show mercy to be patient with his descendants for many generations.

7. "Thou shalt not take the name of the Lord thy God." In an oath, as it is said: "And an oath be exacted of him to cause him to swear" (I Kings 8:31). "In vain." Falsely. For there is no doubt that when such a thing is done, the curse of the oath will fall upon the one who takes it. "For the Lord will not hold him guiltless that taketh his name in vain." Pointlessly, without cause. Even if he swears truthfully God will not hold him guiltless, how much more so when he swears falsely. For it is not to pay honor to God when a man takes His name in an oath, unless it be for the purpose of establishing some truth that could not otherwise be established. But when a man swears falsely in God's name, saying that what I swear is true as God is true, he denies and profanes God's name. It is as if he said that God, blessed be He, is not true. As it is said: "And ye shall not swear by My name falsely, so that thou profane the name of thy God" (Leviticus 19:12).

8. "Remember the sabbath day." Remember the sabbath day at all times, when you engage in your weekday pursuits. This has the same force as: "Remember what Amalek did to thee" (Deuteronomy 25:17) and: "Observe the month of Abib" (Deuteronomy 16:1). "To keep it holy." Do this in order to keep holy the sabbath day. A man should do his utmost to arrange his weekday affairs so that he can forget all about them on the sabbath day.

9. "Six days shalt thou labor." In temporal occupations which, without doubt, are slave labor, for in most of them a man is anxious about a world that is not really his. "And do all thy work." That is essential for thy needs.

10. "A sabbath unto the Lord thy God." That is to say, to study and to teach, to observe and to keep, and to take delight in sufficient worship for God's honor. As one of the Rabbis said: "Wine and odorous spices made me wise." "Thou, nor thy son, nor thy daughter." This refers to little children who do what their father tells them to do.

11. "For in six days the Lord made." And the purpose of creation was for man to resemble his Creator, as far as is humanly possible, by studying and by engaging in contemplation and by choosing freely to carry out deeds acceptable to Him. "And rested on the seventh day." On this day He had completed all that was necessary for His purpose and rest was therefore complete. "Wherefore the

Lord blessed the sabbath day." With an extra soul that is, with a special capacity of serving God. "And hallowed it." That it should be entirely devoted to God.

12. "That thy days may be long." By keeping these five commandments, your days will be long. They will cause you to enjoy infinite days which have length but no breadth, as the Rabbis, of blessed memory, say: "In the world where there is only length." For these five commandments are all concerned with God's honor, as a result of which the one who pays such honor inherits eternal life. These commandments involve: that we should acknowledge Him as Creator out of nothing; that we should acknowledge only Him as our God; that we should worship no other; that we should rebel against Him neither in thought, speech nor deed; and that we should honor Him who is our Father who has acquired us. "Upon the land." By keeping them you will have this reward, that you will attain to this length of days, of which I have spoken, on the land, for you will not be exiled from it. But as for the other five commandments, which involve that no man should harm another's person, his property and his honor, neither by deed, word nor thought, these are rules which protect a man from punishment both in the world to come and in this world.

13. "Thou shalt not commit adultery." This refers mainly to adultery with a married woman, which is the most frequent form it takes among those who sin, but it includes, too, every type of forbidden sexual relationship. "Thou shalt not steal." This embraces every kind of theft, kidnapping, stealing another's property and misleading others, even though, as the Rabbis, of blessed memory, teach us the commandment refers chiefly to kidnapping, as can be seen from the context. "Thou shalt not bear false witness against thy neighbour." Even though the commandment chiefly refers to one who testifies in a court of law, it embraces talebearing and slander.

14. "Thou shalt not covet." The thing should be an utter impossibility so far as you are concerned. For nature does not covet at all that which is impossible of attainment. As it is said: "neither shall any man covet thy land" (Exodus 34:24). For covetousness leads to robbery, as it is said of Achan: "then I coveted them, and took them" (Joshua 7:21).

2. Sforno understands the first commandment chiefly as a warning that God should be worshipped directly and not through an intermediary. God intervened directly in Egypt and He brought Israel out of Egypt to worship Him directly. It is quite possible that there is an anti-Christian polemic in this comment of Sforno. Note Sforno's concluding remark regarding coercion. Since God made Israel free, it is not proper for them to serve God because they are in some way forced to do so, but only because they freely respond to His love.

3. Sforno understands the second commandment as forbidding the worship of any other than God, even when God is also worshipped. God demands our complete loyalty.

4. The prohibition of making a graven image cannot mean only if it is worshipped, since the worship of idols is covered by the previous verses. It must mean that the very fashioning of the image is forbidden.

5. Sforno grapples here with the problem of the justice of God punishing children for the sins of their parents. Following the Rabbis, he says that it only applies if the children are themselves wicked and add to the evil of their ancestors. After many generations evil becomes so deeply rooted in a family that there is no hope that they will ever change. Sforno's illustrations are from the dynasties of the wicked kings of the Northern Kingdom.

6. Although God does not punish children because of the sins of their parents, he does exempt children from the punishment they deserve because of the virtue of their parents.

7. The word in "vain" means falsely. But it can also be taken literally to mean "pointlessly." Hence Sforno's comment. It is not right to take even a true oath if such a thing is not absolutely essential; how much more then, is it wrong to swear falsely.

8. See the comment of Rashbam to this verse (in the section in this book on Rashbam). Rashbam is bothered by the meaning of "Remember" here. Since the sabbath comes round once a week, how could we forget it? Rashbam replies that the "sabbath" referred to is the first sabbath of creation. But Sforno has a different solution. The meaning is that we should always have the sabbath in mind. Even on the weekdays one should remember that the sabbath will come at the end of the week. One should order one's days so well that all business concerns, for example, will have been attended to during the week and there will then be complete rest from anxiety on the sabbath.

9. The word for "shalt thou labour" is taavod and has the same root as the word eved, "slave." For Sforno, a basic sabbath idea is that the day frees man from bondage to worldly things and anxieties.

10. For Sforno, the sabbath is to be a day devoted entirely to spiritual things. But is it not a religious duty to eat and drink on the sabbath? Yes, replies Sforno, but this should be done as an aid to the spiritual. He quotes a Rabbinic saying to show that physical delights can assist a man in his intellectual endeavors by stimulating and broadening his mind. In his comment about children, Sforno means that the verse cannot refer to grown-up children, for grown-ups are embraced by the term "thou" in the verse.

11. The Rabbis speak of the "extra soul" with which a man is endowed on the sabbath. Sforno understands this to mean that on the sabbath the atmosphere is especially conducive to the worship of God.

12. Sforno understands the promise of long life as referring not alone to the fifth commandment but to all the previous four as well. Since these all have to do with honoring God, eternal life is promised as a reward for their observance. The next five commandments do not require this reward (though Sforno does not say that it is not given) since they are obviously essential if human society is to be established. The Rabbis observe that it is hardly true that everyone who honors his parents lives long, so that they suggest that the reference is not to length of days in this world but in the Hereafter where "there is only length of days." The Rabbis probably mean by this that in the Hereafter life is unending, but note the neat twist Sforno gives to the saying. In the Hereafter there is only "length" of days not "breadth", i.e., it is a purely spiritual state and is not spatial ("breadth" = "space"). But he seems to contradict himself when he goes on to speak of "on the land." Probably he means that two kinds of reward are promised.

13. Sforno extends the meaning of these three commandments. His reference to kidnapping and its context is to the Rabbinic observation that "Thou shalt not steal" means here "Thou shalt not steal a man" since it follows the command against murder and murder is a capital offence.

14. How can a man help coveting that which is not his? Sforno says that he can do this by reflecting that it is a sheer impossibility for a man ever to acquire that which God has destined for his neighbor. Here Sforno follows Ibn Ezra (see the section on Ibn Ezra in this book).

Alshech

How did· David fight Goliath?

Rabbi Moses Alshech (=Al-Sheik, "The Sheik") was a famous Talmu-
dist and preacher in sixteenth century Safed. His Commentaries
to the Bible were based on the sermons he delivered regularly in
Safed, so that there is a distinct homiletical flavor about them.
Typical of his method is to raise a number of difficulties presented
by the text and then to remove them all by a fresh interpretation of
the text. Alshech called his Commentary to the Pentateuch Torat
Moshe, "The Torah of Moses" (after his own name), but it is said
that his readers considered this to be too presumptuous, so this and
his other works are always referred to as "The Alshech."

Considerations of space prevent us from giving more than one
example of Alshech's prolix method. We give a typical example of
his work at length. This is his comment on the story of David and
Goliath, especially on the verse: "And he took his staff in his hand,
and he chose five smooth stones out of the brook, and put them in
the shepherd's bag which he had, even in his pouch; and his sling
was in his hand; and he drew near to the Philistine" (I Samuel 17:
40).

A. HOW DID DAVID FIGHT GOLIATH?

One should consider the following questions. David did not do anything with his staff. Why, then, did he take it in his hand? A second difficulty is presented by the words: "and he chose five smooth stones out of the brook." It should have said: "and he took five smooth stones." For even if he did choose these stones from among the others that were in the brook, why do we have to be told that he chose good or smooth stones out of the others that were there? Furthermore, why do we have to be told that he took the shepherd's bag and held the sling in his hand? Would we have thought that he hurled the stones if the sling was not in his hand? Again, why do we have to be told that the man who bore the shield went before Goliath (verse 41) and that Goliath disdained David: "for he was but a youth, and ruddy, and withal of a fair countenance" (verse 42)? The fact that David was ruddy and of a fair countenance was no reason to disdain him. And why did Goliath say (verse 44): "Go" (lechah) instead of "Come" (bo)? And why did he say (verse 44); "and to the beasts (behemat) of the field" instead of "and the wild beasts (ḥayat) of the field"? Furthermore, why does it repeat (verses 46 and 47): "that all this assembly may know"? Is it not simply a repetition of the same idea in different words? And if there is a reason for the repetition, why does it have to be in different words? Furthermore, it says: "for the battle is the Lord's" (verse 47). Why was it necessary to state this, since it is implied in the previous statement (verse 46): "This day the Lord will deliver thee into my hand"? The words: "And he will give you into our hand" (verse 47) are also superfluous since this, too, is implied in the previous statement. Similarly, why does it repeat (verse 50) "So David prevailed over the Philistine with a sling and with a stone" since this has already been stated? The same applies to the words "and smote the Philistine" (verse 50). The same applies to: "but there was no sword in the hand of David" (verse 50). This has been stated previously.

Alshech subjects the text to a close scrutiny. Many of his objections are more than a little artificial, but he wishes to call attention to these points in order to build up his novel interpretation of the narrative. It is as if he is saying: There are some curious expressions here and I shall demonstrate to you that they point to a meaning of the whole narrative that is not evident on the surface.

However, the matter is as follows. David said to himself, there will be no possibility of slaying Goliath with a sword or a spear since every part of his body is covered by brass (verses 5-6). The only possibility is to thrust the edge of the sword into the tiny portion of his forehead that was left bare, but if anyone tried to come near enough to do this the Philistine, whose hands were not bound, would smite him with fifty blows. That is why Abner (the captain of the Israelite army) for all his courage, did not dare to fight him. Consequently, the only way it could be done was to hurl a stone at him from a sling at a distance. It was essential to hurl the stone skillfully or with trust in God's providence so that it would not fail to hit him straight between the eyes, namely, on the tiny part of his forehead that was left bare. Now if the Philistine had the slightest suspicion that David had a sling in his hand, he would have covered up that part as well, until David would be too close for the sling to have any effect. A sling can only be operated successfully at a distance from its target. Therefore, David cunningly concealed the sling and the stone and he took his staff in his hand so that the Philistine would imagine that he intended to fight him with the staff. That is why the Philistine said: "Am I a dog, that thou comest to me with staves?" (verse 43). He did not realise that David only took the staff to fool him and that David really intended to fight with the sling he had concealed. And that is why it says that he chose five stones. This means that he chose to fight with stones rather than with a sword or a spear. David did not carry these stones in his hand. Before the encounter he had placed them in the shepherd's bag he had with him, the container for his food and drink. He placed this bag in the larger pouch he also had with him. This latter resembled a leather bottle as used by shepherds. He did all this so that Goliath would have no suspicion that the bag contained stones. It was unusual to place in that kind of bag anything but food and drink, so that those who saw the bag in the pouch would imagine that it contained only food and drink. The reason he placed the stones in the bag rather than in the larger pouch was to enable him to take the stones from there easily when they were needed. The bag, shaped rather like a wooden bowl, was an open receptacle so that whatever was in it could easily be taken out without delay, whereas the pouch was more like a bottle with its sides close together. Effort would have been required to draw a stone from the pouch and there would have been delay when delay was fatal. Consequently, David placed the stones in the open receptacle and he then placed this in the pouch in such a way as to prevent the sides of the pouch coming close together. It was thus an easy matter to extract the stones from the receptacle. That is why it says (verse 49): "And David put his hand in his bag, and took thence a stone, and slung it." Since the stones were in the bag, he was able to take the stone as soon as he put his hand there. After he had hidden the stones in the bag, he made the sling ready. Therefore it says (verse 40): "and his sling was in his hand." This means that he held the sling in the hand which held the staff, but concealed in such a way that those who observed David were unaware that he held a sling.

Alshech understands our verse to mean that David had two receptacles, a smaller but open bag and a larger pouch, as he explains. He has now answered some of his original questions. Why does Scripture tell us that David chose the stones? The answer is that the verse does not mean to inform us that he chose these stones rather than any others—this we would know without being told—but that he chose to fight with stones rather than with a sword or a spear which, he realised, would be totally ineffective. Why does Scripture say that he held the sling in his hand? The answer is that Scripture means to tell us that he cunningly concealed the sling in the hand which held the staff. Note, too, how skillfully Alshech describes Goliath's taunt about fighting dogs with staves. David had successfully tricked Goliath into overlooking entirely where the real danger to him lay, in the concealed sling and the stones. Alshech's interpretation no doubt makes the whole episode less heroic and "sportsmanlike," but Alshech would probably say that David was not playing games. He was fighting against a ruthless foe who had all the advantages on his side.

The reason why David took five stones is explained as follows by our Rabbis of blessed memory. One was for God, as if to declare that in spite of that wicked one, God would help David to defend

His honor which had been desecrated. The second was in the merit of Aaron who was Goliath's adversary because Goliath had slain Hophni and Phinehas, the priests of the Lord at Shiloh (I Samuel 1:3; 4:11). The other three stones corresponded to the three patriarchs whose descendants Goliath had taunted. Following this line of thought, it is possible that when it says that David took the stones from the brook it hints at the Jacob narrative, in which it is said: "and sent them over the brook . . . and there wrestled a man with him" (Genesis 32:24,25), the man being the guardian angel of Esau. David's prayer was that just as God had helped Jacob to wrestle with the angel at the brook, so should He help him in his struggle with Goliath. David drew near to the Philistine. "And the Philistine came near and nearer unto David" but he did not see him because "and the man that bore the shield went before him" (verse 41). But when they came closer to one another, then: "And when the Philistine looked about, and saw David, he disdained him" (verse 42). Goliath said: It cannot be that this one's power lies in his knowledge of battles since he is a "youth" untrained in warfare. Nor can it be that he comes to fight equipped with great heroism. His enthusiasm for the fight and his daring is because he is "ruddy". But he must surely be lacking in true heroism since he is "withal of a fair countenance" and handsome men are not by nature great heroes, so his keenness and his self-confidence will be of no avail. If he means to frighten me into flight by his boldness, then I say: "Am I a dog" (verse 43) to be driven away by sticks? No sticks will cause me to flee in terror. Goliath then proceeded to curse David by his own gods and he said to David "Go" (verse 44) away from me and all will be well. But if you dare to come near me "I will give thy flesh to the fowl of the heaven . ." without even having to fight, for you will die there and then in front of me by my gods' curse. That is why it says: "Go" and not "Come". The reason why he said "and to the beasts of the field" was dealt with by the Rabbis who ask: "Does a beast eat a beast?" The Rabbis were moved to say this because the verse does not say "the wild beasts of the field." The Rabbis observe, in fact, that David saw from this that Goliath's mind had begun to be confused, for he had fallen from grace and his fortunes had turned for the worse. Consequently, "And David said . . . This day the Lord will deliver thee into my hand" (verses 45-46). But according to the plain meaning, it is

**possible that Goliath said: "Since you are a youth and of good
appearance your flesh is so tender that even the beasts can eat
you."**

*Alshech first quotes a Midrash on why David took five stones. The
second stone was for Aaron, the priest, the ancestor of Hophni and
Phinehas, who, say the Rabbis, were slain by none other than
Goliath. Alshech adds a little Midrash of his own, on the reason
why David took the stones from a brook. The Rabbis say that the
angel who wrestled with Jacob was Esau's guardian angel. Alshech
then proceeds to give further answers to some of his original
questions. Why the reference to the man carrying the shield? The
answer is because this explains why it took some time before
Goliath saw David because the shield acted as a screen. Why the
reference to "young" and "ruddy" and "a fair countenance"? The
answer is that these belong to Goliath's taunts. David surely did not
come equipped with skill in battle since he was too young to have
gained any experience. David's evident self-confidence was due to
his sanguinity; he was simply impetuous as ruddy people are.
(Compare the folk-belief nowadays that red-haired people are
impulsive and quick-tempered). It was really, Goliath believed, a
bad case of over-confidence. He could not believe that David was
really a hero since a great warrior ought to look fierce and even
ugly, not to have a handsome appearance. Why "Go" in the verse
rather than "Come"? The answer is that Goliath said to David:
"If you have any sense, you had better go from here as soon as you
can. If you do decide to come nearer, the curse of my gods will
strike you dead." Why the beasts of the field and not the wild
beasts of the field? Now here the Rabbis give the interesting
answer that this does not, in fact, make sense and hence David
concluded that Goliath's mind was beginning to crack because God
had pronounced his doom. Alshech gives another reason. Goliath
said that even the beasts (=the cattle) will be able to eat David's
tender flesh.*

**David replied: You imagine that I will die in your presence, but
this will not be. Your trust in your gods by whom you have cursed
me is nonsense. And as for your trust in your sword and spear,
none of which I have, you should know that: "I come to thee in
the name of the Lord of hosts, the God of the armies of Israel,
whom thou hast taunted" (verse 45). For in reality your quarrel is**

not with me at all but with God whom you have taunted. I have no need, therefore, for any weapons for "the Lord will deliver thee into my hand" (verse 46). This means, I will slay you by my hand and not with a sword. Though it would have been God's doing even if I were to slay you with a sword, but God wishes to sanctify His name both among the heathen and among Israel. He will sanctify His name among the heathen because by the mere fact that I will slay you the heathen will know that Israel has a God, otherwise how would I be able to overcome you? That is why it says: "that all the earth may know that there is a God in Israel" (verse 46). This would be known even if I were to slay you with a sword or spear. But God wishes His name also to be sanctified among Israel, who know already that there is a God in Israel. That is why it says (verse 47): "And that all this assembly may know that the Lord saveth not with sword and spear." For nothing can prevent God from saving even without weapons, as He will do for me this day. You might ask, how can I be so confident that I will achieve this, that "I will smite thee, and take thy head from off thee" (verse 46)? Perhaps, even though it is true that the Lord is God, I may not be worthy that all this should be achieved by me. My answer is: "for the battle is the Lord's." The battle is on His behalf and to defend His honor and not to defend ours. Therefore we know that: "He will give you into our hand" (verse 47). For this is His way, that who- ever does anything for the sake of His honor, He does it for that one's sake. This follows the idea of the Rabbis that whoever needs something for himself and yet prays for that very thing on some- one else's behalf, he will be answered first.

Some further answers to some of the original questions. Why the repetitions to which Alshech called attention at the beginning? For the reasons he mentions here. Each verse has its own part to play in the dialogue as a whole. The final remarks of Alshech here mean that when a man needs something for himself, good health, for example, and yet is unselfish enough to pray on behalf of another sick person, forgetting his own needs, he will be answered first with God's healing.

Then "when the Philistine arose, and came and drew nigh" (verse 48) then, with a sense of victory, "David hastened, and ran toward the army to meet the Philistine." "And David put his hand in his bag, and took thence a stone, and slung it, and smote the Philistine in his forehead" (verse 49). This means that all David did was to make some contribution of his own. The stone would by nature have fallen to the ground, but it was from the Lord that "the stone sank into his forehead" of its own accord. This is especially so, since the Rabbis say of the five stones that one was for God, the second was for Aaron, and the other three for the patriarchs. I assume that the first stone, which did all this, was the one assigned to God. That is why David said: "But I come to thee in the name of the Lord of hosts" (verse 45). For right from the beginning he came in the name of the Lord, that is with the first stone, as we have said, and it was capable of doing all this.

The point about the stone finding its own way into Goliath's forehead is this. The word for "it sank" is va-titba. *Alshech puns on this word which resembles the word* teva, *"nature." (Actually, this is anachronistic since the word* teva *for "nature" is not Biblical but medieval). The nature of the stone was to fall to the ground under the force of gravity, but God made its "nature" such that it made its own way into Goliath's forehead. All that David had to do was to make the very minor contribution of slinging the stone which then wended into own way to its destination.*

The narrative continues: "So David prevailed over the Philistine with a sling and with a stone, and smote the Philistine and slew him; but there was no sword in the hand of David" (verse 50). This verse discloses all that we have written previously. David concealed the sling and the stones from Goliath, allowing him to see only the staff in his hand. This was to prevent Goliath covering his forehead until David would be so near to him as to render the sling in- effective. Goliath knew nothing of the sling until suddenly the stone became embedded in his forehead. Hence it says: "So David pre- vailed over the Philistine with a sling and with a stone." This means: Know that the reason why David prevailed over the Philistine was because of the sling and the stone which Goliath did not see and so could not protect himself against them. All he saw, as we have noted, was the staff in David's hand. Therefore he "smote the Philistine" since he did not cover his forehead to render the sling harmless. Now David had said: "and I will smite thee, and take thy head from thee" (verse 46). Therefore it now says "and smote the Philistine" in order that David might be true to his word. He also wishes to be true to his further word that he would take Goliath's head from him "but there was no sword in the hand of David." Therefore: "And David ran, and stood over the Philistine, and took his sword . . . cut off his head therewith" (verse 51). "And he brought it to Jerusalem" (verse 54) to give thanks to God "but he put his armour in his tent" with the exception of the sword. Possibly, he brought the sword to the king and then sent it to Nob (I Samuel 21:1-10) where the Lord's sanctuary was situated. It belonged to the Lord, for it came about through a miracle.

Whether Alshech's interpretation is the correct one is another matter, but we cannot help admiring the skillful manner in which he interprets the narrative so that it contains nothing superfluous and nothing out of place. Alshech's rich vocabulary and style should also be noted. Of all the traditional Biblical commentators, Alshech is the greatest Hebrew stylist.

Ephraim Lunshitz

How is injustice to be avoided?
Why is there no reference in the Bible to the immortality of the soul?

Ephraim Solomon ben Aaron Lunshitz (died Prague 1619) was a famous Polish teacher and preacher. His Commentary to the Pentateuch entitled Keli Yakar (Precious Vessel) was first published in Lublin in 1602 and since then its popularity ensured that it was frequently printed in editions of the Pentateuch.

A. HOW IS INJUSTICE TO BE AVOIDED?

Comment on: "Ye shall do no unrighteousness in judgment; thou shalt not respect the person of the poor, nor favour the person of the mighty, but in righteousness shalt thou judge thy neighbour" (Leviticus 19:15). Keli Yakar's main point is that the verse means that judgment (i.e., the court of law and so forth) must be entirely free of the slightest taint of injustice because even acts not themselves unjust might be held unjust if perpetrated under the guise of the law.

"Ye shall do no unrighteousness in judgment." The same expression occurs at the end of this portion: "Ye shall do no unrighteousness in judgment, in meteyard, in weight, or in measure" (Leviticus 19: 35). It seems to me that both verses have to be understood in the

same way. This is that a man should not carry out an unrighteous act that is true and just. By this I mean an act can be just and right in itself, and yet it may involve unrighteousness. How can this be? The verse goes on to explain: "Thou shalt not respect the person of the poor." Rashi explains this as follows. "You should not say: 'He is a poor man and the rich man with whom he contends in the court of law is obliged to support him. Very well, then, I shall decide in his favor, even if he is wrong, and thus cause him to be supported in a dignified way.'" Now, in itself, this is quite right and proper since it is true that the rich man is obliged to support his poor brother and can even be compelled to do so, but it is nonetheless an unrighteous act if it is done "in judgment." These words are intended to exclude any other place that is not a place of judgment. That is to say, in any other place or circumstance it would be no act of unrighteousness. For there is no doubt that the rich man is obliged to support the poor and he can even be compelled to do so, but it is nonetheless an unrighteous act if it is done in the place of judgment. This is no reason for departing from the clear demands of justice. Rather justice should be allowed to pursue its course and on another occasion let the rich man be compelled to support the poor. Similarly, in the case of weights and measures. It is possible for a man to act justly and yet unrighteousness can be involved in what he does. How can this be? Supposing a shopkeeper cheats by underweighing, but sells at a cheaper price than other shopkeepers. He does this so that people should patronize his shop thinking that his prices are lower, but do not realize that, in fact, he is selling them short weight. Now, in reality, he acts justly since his customers do get value for their money. Yet what he does is unrighteous because he cheats and causes unfair competition to the other shopkeepers. Every other example where there is justice from one point of view but unrighteousness from another is included in this prohibition.

A fine comment on this verse. Even an act just in itself may be the occasion for a perversion of justice as in the examples Keli Yakar quotes. He now proceeds to interpret the verse in another way. The verse refers to a judge who "does unrighteousness." But how can one do unrighteousness? Unrighteousness is a negative thing in that one does not do justice. Keli Yakar's interpretation is that the judge should not himself be guilty of acting lawlessly. It is as if the verse says: "You, who are called upon to administer justice, do not do any act that results in unrighteousness, in the sense that it brings the law into disrepute."

Since the verse says: "Ye shall do no unrighteousness," it seems to me that it does not speak of a perversion of justice, for that is not to do something but to fail to do something. The verse is rather an admonition to the judge not to allow himself to do that which, in his capacity as judge, he declares to be forbidden to others. The Rabbis say that any judge against whom another has a successful case in a court of law is no judge. This does not mean where, for example, he sets afire another's haystack but there is a hint here, too, that the judge should first clear himself of the slightest suspicion of sharp practice and then and only then will he be fit to judge others. The Rabbis tell us of a judge who was called upon to issue a court order that all trees causing a nuisance by overhanging the public domain should be cut down. He cut down his own overhanging tree on the night before he gave the ruling. Therefore the verse says to the judges, do not do yourselves that which you decide in court to be unrighteous. It may be that Rashi refers to this when he comments that a judge who destroys the law is called unjust, hated and detested. Now since Rashi uses a word like "destroy" he cannot be referring to a failure to render a just decision, but to a positive act which destroys confidence in the law. If the judge himself does not obey the law he lays down for others, he destroys all respect for the law. The public then complains of the law and refuses to comply with it, relying on the unlawful way in which the judge himself behaves. That is why Rashi quotes in support the verse: "For all that do such things, even all that do unrighteously, are an abomination to the Lord thy God" (Deuteronomy 25:16), a reference in the context to false weights and measures. In that section it is said: "Thou shalt not have in thy bag diverse weights, a great and a small" (verse 13). This refers to the man who uses small weights when weighing out to sell to others but large weights when buying for himself. This is precisely the same offence of which the judge is guilty when he allows himself to do that which he declares forbidden to others. Rashi then quotes the verse: "And thou shalt not bring an abomination into thy house" (Deuteronomy 7:26). For the judge who places himself in the position of having a case against him decided in favor of the other party because he has been unjust, thereby brings an abomination into his own house. When he renders decisions he does so with an abomination in his house. This is a clear and correct hint and contains a very fine idea.

It is extremely unlikely that Rashi really hints at the idea mentioned by Keli Yakar, but that does not affect the value of the idea itself.

B. WHY IS THERE NO REFERENCE IN THE BIBLE TO THE IMMORTALITY OF THE SOUL?

Comment on: "And I will walk among you" (Leviticus 26:12). We know from a number of sources that in the Middle Ages some Christian scholars declared that the Christian religion was more spiritual than the Jewish because the Torah only refers to material rewards, as in this section of Leviticus, and contains no reference to spiritual bliss in the Hereafter. Keli Yakar follows Don Isaac Abravanel in his Commentary to this verse in stating a number of reasons for the apparent silence of the Torah on the whole question of spiritual bliss in Heaven.

"And I will walk among you." Rashi comments: "I will walk among you in the Garden of Eden." Rashi's intention is to remove from our holy Torah every complaint and objection. For such objectors say that since the Torah does not mention the main reward, which is that given to the soul, it follows that the laws of the Torah do not have the power of endowing those who keep them with spiritual bliss in the world to come, and the purpose for which these rules are to be obeyed is solely for the attainment of reward in this miserable world. Many worthy scholars have addressed themselves to this question. There are seven different opinions as to how the problem can be resolved. Rabbi Isaac Abravanel records these and explains them in detail. I shall state them as briefly as possible and set them out here in order to close the mouths of those who speak arrogantly of our holy Torah. The first opinion is that of Maimonides, that all these promises are not in the nature of reward for keeping the laws. All the evil and good things mentioned in this portion of Leviticus refer only to the removal of hindrances to the pursuit of perfection. Their meaning is: "If you will keep My laws, I will re-

move from you anything that hinders the pursuit of perfection such as wars, sickness, hunger and sorrow, so that you will be able to serve the Lord without hindrance." The main reward of the world to come is not mentioned here so that a man should serve his Maker because it is right to do so, not in order to receive a reward or because of the threat of punishment. Consult Maimonides' *Book of Knowledge.*

According to Maimonides, no reward at all is mentioned in the Torah because the good man ought to serve God in love, without thought of reward (though there is, in fact, great reward in the Hereafter). The promise of material benefits is not as a reward but as a means to an end. No reward is promised, but it is simply stated that if a man desires sincerely to serve God, then God will help him by removing such hindrances as sickness and sorrow. This is a very lofty idea. A man should not even think of reward in Heaven when he does good and should do it solely because it is right and out of love of God. Book of Knowledge is the first of the fourteen books into which Maimonides' great Code of Law is divided. (See the section on Maimonides in the first volume of this series). Later on Keli Yakar quotes Maimonides' Guide for the Perplexed as expressing a different opinion, but it is well-known that Maimonides' approach in his Code is different in many respects from that which he adopts in his Guide.

The second opinion is that of Abraham ibn Ezra in his Commentary at the end of Deuteronomy. There he observes: "In my opinion, it is because the Torah was given to all, not to one individual. Only one in a thousand can grasp the idea of the world to come because it is so deep." He means that it is extremely difficult to grasp the nature of that kind of reward since that which is material cannot comprehend that which is purely spiritual. Therefore, the Torah conceals this very profound matter from the masses, who, in the weakness of their minds, could not possibly understand it.

Purely spiritual bliss is such a profound idea that it cannot be mentioned even in the Torah. The Torah is a work for the guidance of all men, not only for the spiritually elite.

The third opinion is that of Rabbi Bahya the elder. Ibn Ezra refers to it in his above-mentioned Commentary and leans towards it, as does Nahmanides. In this view all the promises given in the Torah are supernatural. It is not a natural thing that when people obey God's laws, this should cause rain to fall or that when they disobey, this should cause rain to be withheld. That the soul should return to her Source, on the other hand, is natural and there is nothing miraculous about it. Since we find in the Torah the punishment of *karet* ("cutting off") for the soul of the sinner, which is cut off from her Source, it follows that if a man is not a sinner, his soul returns to her Lodging, to her place of residence as before. It seems to me that this is the meaning of the verse: "Wait for the Lord, and keep His way, and He will exalt thee to inherit the land; when the wicked are cut off, thou shalt see it" (Psalms 37:34). This means: From the fact that to be cut off is, according to the Torah, the fate of the wicked, you can see that there is a spiritual reward, that God will exalt you to inherit the land of the living, for the soul will ascend to the place whence she had been hewn. This you can see from the fact that the wicked have to be excluded explicitly from entering there.

Bahya the elder is Bahya ibn Pakudah, author of Duties of the Heart (a selection from which is given in the second volume of this series). The term "the elder" is used to distinguish him from the other and later Bahya (Ibn Asher), from whose work there are selections in this volume. Only supernatural rewards require to be recorded in the Torah, not purely natural ones. The Torah has no need to mention spiritual reward specifically, since it is altogether natural for the soul to return to her Source. Indeed, a special statement is required to record that some persons, the wicked, do not merit this natural fate of the soul and their souls are "cut off." Karet is mentioned as a punishment in a number of places and there is considerable debate as to its meaning. Here it is taken to mean the "cutting off" of the soul from heavenly bliss. Keli Yakar adds a homiletical interpretation of the verse in Psalms so that it yields his idea here.

The fourth opinion is that in those days all the world's inhabitants denied God's providence. They argued that everything that happens in the world is fated so to happen and is not determined by the will of the Holy One, blessed be He. Therefore it was necessary to strengthen belief in providence by means of these promises, by pointing out that anyone can see how beneficial providence extends over all who do His will. But if He had promised them spiritual reward, they would still have remained unbelievers so far as providence is concerned since it is a well-known principle, they would have argued, that whoever wishes to testify falsely has only to testify to something that is hard to verify. This is the opinion of Rabbi Nisim in his Commentary to Genesis. It is based on the argument in the book *Kuzari*. When the King of the Khazars puts the objection to the Rabbi that the promises of other religions are richer than those which Judaism offers, the Rabbi replies: "But all the promises of the other religions are in connection with life after death and nothing is promised for life here on earth. They promise nothing, in other words, that can be verified by experience. What is more, no believer in these promises is anxious to attain them as soon as he can. On the contrary, if he could postpone them for a thousand years, he would freely choose so to do in order to stay longer in this world with all its burdens and sorrows." This is truly an irrefutable argument, that the Torah promises that for which man has a strong desire.

A very frank reply. For all our belief in spiritual bliss in the Hereafter, Judaism wishes to stress that God is concerned with what we do with our lives in the here and now. What was needed at the time when the Torah was given was not a promise of spiritual bliss in Heaven, which, after all, is remote from all man's experience, but the promise of happiness on earth, which, so the Torah teaches, stems from obedience to God's will. For Rabbi Nisim Gerondi, see the note to the section on Abravanel in this book. The Kuzari is the famous book by Judah Ha-Levi in the form of a dialogue between a Rabbi and the King of Khazars who eventually was converted to Judaism. (For a selection from the Kuzari, see the second volume in this series.)

The fifth opinion is that before the Torah was given, the people worshipped the heavenly bodies. They used to perform certain rites in order to bring down blessings from the heavenly bodies, in order for the rain to fall in its season and in order to obtain other material goods. When the Holy One, blessed be He, gave them the Torah and forbade them to practice these idolatrous rites, He had to promise them that they would still have these material benefits even if they kept the Torah and that, on the contrary, they would not have them if they continued to worship the heavenly bodies. But He had no need to promise them spiritual bliss, since this was not promoted by the idolatrous rites which they had previously carried out. **This is the view of Rabbi Saadia in his book** Beliefs and Opinions **and it is also the view of the** Guide for the Perplexed **Part III.**

For Saadia and Maimonides' Guide for the Perplexed, see the selections and notes in the second volume of this series. In this view, the Torah has to be seen against its background. The aim of religion at that time was certainly not in order to attain to spiritual bliss in the Hereafter. It was very much a worldly affair. Certain magical rites, the idolators believed, brought beneficial material consequences. The Torah says, as it were, that these consequences can result from the service of the true God, and, indeed, only from this service. The aim of the Torah was to wean an idolatrous people away from idolatry, and the most effective weapon in the struggle was the promise of the kind of reward the people really desired and which was at the heart of the popular religion.

The sixth opinion is that since Scripture says: "And I will walk among you" (Leviticus 26:12) and "I will set My dwelling-place among you" (Leviticus 26:11), that the Shechinah (the Divine Presence) will be attached to Israel even in this world where the soul is involved with matter. How much more then will the Shechinah be with them after the soul has parted with matter. So you see that all those spiritual promises which are held out by the false religions for men after death are promised to us by the Torah even in the life of this world. The fact that we have produced prophets demonstrates that this is so. This opinion, too, you will find in the reply of the Rabbi to the King of the Khazars at the end of the first part of the Kuzari. **Rabbi Nisim in a sermon also accepts this idea.**

The Torah does in fact speak of elevated spiritual bliss, but not as reserved solely for the Hereafter. Holy men like the prophets can "walk with God" even in this life.

The seventh opinion is that all the promises mentioned in the Torah are to the nation as a whole, since the world is judged according to the deeds of the majority. The promise of material rewards, good

crops, peace and so forth, are for the people of Israel as a body. But the spiritual reward of the world to come is not for the nation as a body, but each individual is judged there according to his own deeds. This is hinted at in the command to honor parents (Exodus 20:12) and to send away the mother bird (Deuteronomy 22:6,7). This is the opinion of the book *Ikkarim* and of Naḥmanides in his comment to the verse: "with all your heart" (Deuteronomy 11:13).

The material rewards are those of national well-being and prosperity. But the reward of the soul in the Hereafter is for each individual. The Torah wishes to promote the idea of a holy nation, hence its appeal to national prosperity. The fate of the individual soul is naturally also the concern of the Torah but this is axiomatic. The book Ikkarim is by Joseph Albo. A selection from it is given in the second volume of this series. In the commands to honor parents and to send away the mother bird, the promise of long life is given. The Rabbis understood this to mean long life in the Hereafter (see the section on Sforno in this volume). Since these two commands are not addressed to the nation as a whole but to the individual, the promise of spiritual, not material, bliss is recorded.

Let all those who speak arrogantly against our holy Torah flee in these seven ways. All this is quite apart from the fact that we can see with our own eyes how much God loved the patriarchs, Abraham, Isaac and Jacob. But if their happiness were to be measured solely in worldly terms, in what way was Abraham more successful than Nimrod? Nimrod was a world ruler, but Abraham was a wanderer all his days, going from one tent to another and from one nation to another. And so it was with Isaac and with Jacob. We do not know what reward they had. For if the sum total of their reward was that promised to their seed, what advantage was it for them that after their death their seed would inherit the land while they themselves departed this world without any advantage from all their toil? And even the people of Israel who did inherit the land, what was their advantage even in times of peace, over all the kingdoms of the world that reigned as successfully as they did and some of them even more successfully? It can only be that the great goodness stored up for the righteous in the Hereafter is the portion reserved for the patriarchs and for all their offspring, for the same law is for all.

Keli Yakar now adds a further idea of his own. If reward in this life is all there is, where is God's justice since good men like the patriarchs did not have much success in this world?

Ḥayim ibn Attar

Why should one help the poor?
What is the significance of the command against idolatry?
How should a good man help sinners?

Ḥayim ben Moses ibn Attar (born Morocco 1696; died Jerusalem, 1743) wrote a Commentary to the Pentateuch entitled Or Ha-Ḥayim, The Light of Life (a play on his name). The Or Ha-Ḥayim, as can be seen from the examples given here, is written in a mystical vein. It was first printed in Venice in 1742. Since then it has been printed together with the text in many editions of the Pentateuch. The Or Ha-Ḥayim is especially popular among the Ḥasidim, partly because it is reported that the Baal Shem Tov, the founder of the Ḥasidic movement, thought very highly of its author. The Ḥasidim call the book and its author "The Holy Or Ha-Ḥayim."

A. WHY SHOULD ONE HELP THE POOR?

Comment on: "neither shalt thou favor a poor man in his quarrel" (Exodus 23:3). The plain meaning of the verse, as Or Ha-Ḥayim knows full well, is that the judge should not show favor to a poor man in his lawsuit with a rich man if the poor man is in the wrong (see the comment of Ephraim Lunshitz in this volume). But our author interprets the verse allegorically.

"Neither shalt thou favor a poor man in his quarrel." In the words "in his quarrel" there is a hint to the saying of our Rabbis, of blessed memory, that the poor man has a quarrel with his Maker. Why does He feed everyone and yet leaves me hungry and without clothes? Whoever gives alms to the poor man and supports him, thereby causes that poor man's quarrel with Heaven to cease. But when a man refuses to help the poor, then the complaint of the poor man against God is rendered favorable and plausible. Therefore our verse commands us not to encourage the poor man in his quarrel with his Maker, but to help him as befits those who obey the laws concerning charity.

A fine comment. The implication is that the poor man cannot be blamed if in his distress he quarrels with God. The blame is at the door of those who can help the poor but refuse to do so. They "favor" the poor man in his quarrel with his Maker. It is sometimes claimed that religion, by turning men's minds away from the sufferings of this world, fails to encourage men to alleviate that suffering. The Or Ha-Hayim's note is to the exact opposite effect. The truly religious man will acknowledge the justice of the poor man's quarrel and will fight for his Maker by removing the poor man's cause for complaint.

B. WHAT IS THE SIGNIFICANCE OF THE COMMAND AGAINST IDOLATRY?

Comment on: "Turn ye not unto the idols, nor make to yourselves molten gods: I am the Lord your God" (Leviticus 19:4).

The reason this verse uses the expression "turning" is in order to prohibit even idolatrous thoughts. The meaning of the verse is that man should not allow his mind to turn towards idols, to think of them. To enable you to understand this in accordance with the way of truth, you must know that "other gods" belong in the category of the hindparts. When a man thinks on them he causes them to turn to face inwards. He who is wise will understand.

Or Ha-Hayim understands "Turn ye not unto the idols" to mean that even a turning in thought is strictly forbidden. As a general principle, the Rabbis remark that an intention to sin is not counted as a sin. If, for example, a man intended to steal but did not actually steal, God does not hold him guilty for the intention or thought alone, only if he actually did the forbidden act. Idolatry is, however, an exception. Even the intention to worship idols is a grievous sin. Or Ha-Hayim then adds a further elaboration in the spirit of the Kabbalah ("the way of truth"). Since he held that Kabbalistic mysteries should only be conveyed to the wise, the initiates, he is very circumspect and wraps around his comment with secrecy. It is consequently more than a little difficult to know what he is trying to say. His meaning appears to be something like this. According to the Kabbalah, even evil is nourished by the good because even evil, to exist at all, must be kept in being by God's power which sustains all things. God allows people to worship idols if they so desire or, rather, He does not destroy idols, so that sinful folk are free to worship them, although God strictly forbids this and other evils. Figuratively speaking, it can be said that the realm of the holy represents the "face." It has nothing to hide, it is good in itself, it is open and smiling, as it were. The unholy, on the other hand, is represented by the hindquarters (which are shameful and need to be concealed). Now, according to the Kabbalah, man's thoughts mirror God's thoughts and they have an effect on God's control of the universe. Consequently, by using his mind, the part of him that is closest to the divine, to dwell on idolatrous thoughts, he causes extra power to be added to the forces of evil. He makes the "posterior gods" turn around. They are no longer ashamed and confused. Or Ha-Hayim interprets the verse mythologically to mean: "Do not cause the idols to turn inwards." There is a pun here, too, since the Hebrew for "other gods" is elohim aherim which he reads as elohim ahoraim, "posterior gods."

"The idols." The plural form is used because the category of evil is the category of separation and has no unifying principle. That is why whenever the Torah refers to idols it uses the plural form.

An interesting idea. God's unity is the exact opposite of evil. Evil only exists in opposition to God's unity. Consequently, it is typical of evil to pursue division and separateness. A simple illustration is that of good men submerging their differences and selfish interests for the sake of the common good, whereas even when evil men do work together, each is in fact thinking only of what he can get out of it and he would willingly betray the others if his interests demand it. Each idol, each strange god, pulls its worshipers in a different direction. Hence the Torah always uses the plural form when speaking of idols.

"Nor make to yourselves molten gods." There is a difficulty here. The verse has already forbidden man to turn to any idols. What need was there for it to repeat this? Furthermore, why does it say "to yourselves"? It is possible that the reference is to the idea found in the Rabbinic literature that whenever a man performs a good deed the Divine Presence rests upon him, but whenever he disobeys God's laws, a spirit of impurity rests on the organ with which he sins. This forms a screen to separate man from his God, as it is said: "Your iniquities have separated between you and your God" (Isaiah 59:2). This is the meaning of our verse: "Nor make to yourselves gods which form a screen between you and the Source of life." This teaches you that whoever turns his mind to idolatrous thoughts causes a screen to be erected between him and his Maker. Therefore the verse concludes: "I am the Lord your God" to inform us that it is from his God that a man becomes separated when he erects that screen.

A mystical idea that the pursuit of goodness and holiness brings a man nearer to God, whereas disobedience of God's laws separates man from God, since evil and God's holiness are incompatible. There is no greater impurity than idolatry. So the verse means: "Turn not unto the idols, for if you do you will make gods which form a screen between God and yourselves." The pun here is on the word for "molten", massechah, connecting it with the word masach, "a screen."

The verse also means when it says "I am the Lord thy God," that by keeping himself apart from idolatry, a man makes the Lord his God. As the Rabbis say: Whoever denies idolatry, it is as if he had acknowledged the whole of the Torah. Interpreting the verse allegorically, one can say that it refers to the idea mentioned by the Rabbis in their comment on the verse: "Were it not that I regard the presence of Jehoshaphat the king of Judah, I would not look toward thee nor see thee" (II Kings 3:14). The Rabbis comment that we learn from this verse that it is forbidden to gaze at the face of a wicked man. Therefore it says here: "nor make yourselves molten gods," namely, do not be wicked and thus turn yourselves into molten gods at whose faces it is forbidden to gaze.

First Or Ha-Ḥayim reads into our verse the Rabbinic idea that since Judaism is to combat idolatry, therefore anyone who rejects idolatry is treated as if he had kept the whole of the Torah. His second comment is allegorical. In the verse from II Kings, the prophet Elisha says to the wicked king Jehoram that were it not for Jehoshaphat, he would not look at Jehoram. The Rabbis take "looking" in this verse literally, and observe that one must not gaze at the face of a wicked man. Now it is also forbidden to gaze at idols. The verse is then interpreted to mean: "Do not make yourselves into molten gods," i.e., do not pursue wickedness, for if you do, you become as the molten gods at whom it is forbidden to gaze.

C. HOW SHOULD A GOOD MAN HELP SINNERS?

Allegorical comment on Deuteronomy 22:1-3: "Thou shalt not see thy brother's ox or his sheep driven away, and hide thyself from them; thou shalt surely bring them back unto thy brother. And if thy brother be not nigh unto thee, and thou know him not, then thou shalt bring it home to thy house, and it shall be with thee until thy brother require it, and thou shalt restore it to him. And so shalt thou do with his ass; and so shalt thou do with his garment; and so shalt thou do with every lost thing of thy brother's, which he hath lost, and thou hast found; thou mayest not hide thyself."

This portion refers in detail to the obligations in the matter of re-uke which the sons of the living God, the righteous of the world, have towards the rest of God's people. As I have stated elsewhere, the title "brother," the highest of all titles, is given to these right-eous men. They are here commanded not to hide themselves from the ox and sheep of their Brother, God. The name Brother was given Him to denote to which of His holy ones the command is di-rected, namely, as we have said, to the righteous. The "ox and sheep" are those men who behave as beasts, but who are for all that the holy flock of God. "Drive away" refers to the verse: "thou be driven away and worship them" (Deuteronomy 4:19). Whoever disobeys God's laws is called one who is driven away. The verse commands the righteous not to hide themselves from these sinners, but to restore them to their Brother, the Eternal. The reason the verse uses the emphatic form "thou shalt surely bring them back" is to command the righteous first to restore the sinners to the right path, and then they will be brought back to God. "And if thy brother be not nigh unto thee." By stating this, the verse speaks of the pe-

riod of this last exile, as it says: "I behold him, but not nigh" (Numbers 24:17), so that God is not nigh, "and thou knowest it not," for when the end will be is hidden and no one knows when it will be. As a result the heart loses faith and the feet totter, as we see with our own eyes in this generation. For all that, the Lord commands: "thou shalt bring him unto thy house", referring to the house of learning. There you must teach him the paths of life, the way upon which the light shines, so that he no longer turns aside from the way and his enemy does not find him by means of false thoughts and opinions, for the light of the Torah will save him from these. This should continue until God will find him acceptable and seek him. Therefore it says: "until thy Brother seeks him and thou shalt restore him to Him." This means that Scripture treats the righteous man who does this as if he had restored him and saved him from destruction.

There is no neuter gender in Hebrew, so that the pronouns referring to the ox or the sheep can be translated "him" and made to refer to the "lost sheep," those who are "driven away," the "wanderers." The righteous men, to whom God is a Brother, are called upon to lead these wandering sheep back to God, to their Brother who has lost His sheep. These folk who stray are called "oxen" and "sheep" because they behave in a brutish way, and yet are still God's sheep about whom He cares. The point about the emphatic form is that in the Hebrew this reads as hashev teshivem, "restore, restore them," which is taken to mean, first restore them to the good life and then automatically God will find them again. "And thou know him not" can be read as "and thou know it not." Hence Or Ha-Ḥayim translates: "If your Brother is not near," to mean "because you are in exile and the end (the Messianic age) is not nigh and you do not know when it will be and so people lose their hope and faith." In the time of exile men are prone to sin and lose their faith. The righteous cannot in such a time succeed directly in restoring those who have strayed. What they can do is to take them into the house of learning and teach them the Torah. This will help them resist the blandishments of the enemy (= the evil in man) and as a result they will become worthy of God seeking them out ("to require" and "to seek out" are the same in Hebrew). Or Ha-Ḥayim then gives a second interpretation of God "seeking out." This means at the time when God will require the soul, i.e., at the time of death.

Or the verse may mean that the wise man must continue his endeavors to teach the children of Israel the Torah and reprove them until the day of visitation, when God will require the soul and the spirit will return to God. The verse stresses "and thou shalt restore it to *Him*" because if the sinner's feet slip, his soul will not return to God but will be banished in shame. The next verse states: "And so shalt thou do. . . ." There are three parts of man. The first is his body. The second is the spiritual part. The third is the part of the Torah, the betrothed bride of every man of Israel. Corresponding to the bodily part, the verse says: "And so shalt thou do with his ass." Corresponding to the spiritual part, the verse says: "and so shalt thou do with his garment," for this part of man is called a "garment," as, in the Rabbinic parable in tractate Sabbath, the soul is compared to a royal garment distributed by a king. Corresponding to the Torah part, the verse says: "and so shalt thou do with every lost thing of thy brother's." This part is called a "lost thing" on the analogy of Rabbi Simeon ben Yohai's parable of the man who loses something and is always looking for it. For the portion of the Torah allotted to this person would be lost entirely, since no one else can ever attain it, as the Kabbalists say. And by causing that man to repent, the righteous man allows him to find that portion once again.

The physical side of man has to be restored to God, i.e., he must no longer sin with his body. There is a pun here (Or Ha-Ḥayim appears to be very fond of these). The Hebrew word for "ass" is ḥamor, and Or Ha-Hayim connects it with ḥomer, "matter." Man's soul must also be restored to God. This is his royal garment given to him by God and is therefore referred to as "his garment." But each Jew has his own portion in the Torah. Now the Torah is compared by the Rabbis to Israel's bride. Rabbi Simeon ben Yohai (Second Century) in the Talmud says that the reason that a man goes out to look for a wife, rather than the other way round, is because he has lost her (a reference to the story of Eve being created out of Adam's rib) and he looks for that which he has lost. Or Ha-Ḥayim applies this to the Torah, Israel's bride. Each Jew should be busy looking for the part of the Torah that is his, i.e., each Jew has his own special insights into the Torah and if he does not reveal them, no one else can possibly do so and they will be lost. By restoring the sinner to the way of the Torah, the righteous man helps him to find that for which he has been looking and which is also lost from God until he finds it again.

The next verse (verse 4) stated: "Thou shalt not see thy brother's ass or his ox fallen by the way, and hide thyself from them; thou shalt surely help him to lift them up again." This means, the righteous man must not imagine that he has only been commanded to assist a sinner who has strayed from the path but for whom there is still hope that he will repent. One who has fallen, however, and become exceedingly wicked, can he ever be raised up again? There is no hope for such as he. The verse states that such an attitude is wrong. You must not see him fallen and hide yourself from him, but you must help him to lift himself up again. The verse states: "shall help him," as if to say, it only applies if he assists you and wishes to repent. But if he has fallen and has no wish for you to raise him up again, then you have no obligation. Such a person can be considered to be a scorner and Scripture says: "Reprove not a scorner, lest he hate thee" (Proverbs 9:8).

In his last comment, Or Ha-Ḥayim understands "him" not as referring to God, as in the previous comment, but to the sinner. He evidently takes this verse to mean: If you see your brother behaving like a beast and fallen by the way, do not say that he is too far gone for me to help him. You must still help him because there is still hope. If, however, he refuses to have anything to do with you and is perfectly happy as he is, then he should be left alone. There is no point in rebuking a scorner because it will all be of no avail.

Kalonymus Kalman Epstein

Which is higher, prayer or Torah study?
How can a man be a hermit and yet be social?
How can a man be pure?

Once the Ḥasidic movement had established itself at the end of the Eighteenth Century, a number of Commentaries to the Pentateuch in the spirit of Ḥasidism began to be published. One of these became so popular that it has been printed in editions of the Pentateuch together with the text. This is the work Maor Va-Shemesh, Light and Sun, by Rabbi Kalonymus Kalman Epstein of Cracow (died 1827). The work is naturally written from the Ḥasidic point of view, the author's chief aim being the inculcation of Ḥasidic ideas as derived, he believed, from the Torah.

A. WHICH IS HIGHER, PRAYER OR TORAH STUDY?

Comment on the verses describing how Jacob awoke from his dream of the ladder reaching to heaven, Genesis 28:10-22, especially verses 16-17: "And Jacob awoke from his sleep, and he said: 'Surely the Lord is in this place; and I knew it not.' And he was afraid, and said: 'How full of awe is this place! this is none other than the house of God, and this is the gate of heaven.'"

The Midrash comments on the verse: "And Jacob awoke from his sleep" (mi-shenato) **and reads it as: "And Jacob awoke from his**

learning" (mi-mishnato), a very strange comment. It appears to me that the following interpretation is the correct one. It is well-known that man's chief mode of worship, by means of which he can attain to complete perfection in God's service and to the comprehension of His divinity, is through the study of the Torah and through prayer. One without the other is inadequate. The Rabbis say that a man ignorant of the Torah cannot be a saint. But, on the other hand, a man cannot perfect his soul by the study of the Torah alone. As the Rabbis declare: Whoever says that he will have only the Torah, does not even have the Torah. There is no doubt that a man who studies the Torah for its own sake can attain to great sanctity, provided always that he studies for its own sake and attaches all his vitality, spirit and soul to the letters of the Torah. For all that, the only way he can attain to real fear and love of God, to the longing for God's service, and to the comprehension of His divinity, is through prayer, offered with self-sacrifice and with burning enthusiasm. All this is well-known and is stated in all the holy books. Now the saying of the Rabbis on the verse: "And he lighted upon the place" (verse 11) is well-known. They remark that Jacob prayed there and was the first to introduce the evening prayer. From this it follows that until then Jacob did not know the secret of prayer and in what its greatness consisted. We find that Jacob secluded himself in the house of learning founded by Shem and Eber where he studied the Torah. It follows that Jacob knew the secret of the Torah, yet the revelation of God's divinity did not come to him until now, appearing to him only when he had grasped the secret of prayer. This is what the Midrash means when it says that Jacob awoke from his learning, that is to say, from his study of the Torah. Through the prayer he had uttered he awoke to the realization that he had not hitherto attained to the full extent of comprehension of God because he had tried to achieve it by the study of the Torah alone. Therefore he said: "Surely the Lord is in this place," as if to say, through prayer one can grasp more of God's revelation, more than Jacob had grasped beforehand when he had only studied the Torah; "and I knew it not," I did not appreciate this secret. "This is none other than the house of God." This means that through prayer, in which man bestirs himself in a spirit of burning enthusiasm, he can attain to dread in the presence of God's elevated majesty. This dread is called by the Rabbis a "house", as in the Rabbinic saying: "Woe to the man who has no house, only a door to the house." "And this is the gate of heaven." For prayer is the main gateway to heaven; the way in which a man can attain to the comprehension of divinity and the fear of heaven; the good treasure house that is heaven, for the fear of the Lord is his treasure. Take note of this for it is an excellent observation.

It need hardly be said that Maor Va-Shemesh's interpretation is the intention neither of the text nor of the Midrash. We have here, in fact, an attempt at reading Ḥasidic ideas into the sources. In the traditional Rabbinic scheme, there is no higher religious duty than the study of the Torah. This takes precedence over prayer. We find, indeed, that some Rabbis in Talmudic times only prayed occasionally because all their time and energy were devoted to the study of the Torah. But the Ḥasidim believed that the highest degree of religious experience was only possible through prayer. Note that Maor Va-Shemesh does not decry the immense value of Torah study, but he argues that man must pray if he is to reach a more complete apprehension of the divine. It should also be noted that he speaks of Torah study for its own sake. This means without any ulterior motive, to acquire fame or wealth and the like. The opponents of Ḥasidim believed that Torah study was so important that even such ulterior motives could be excused, but Ḥasidism would have none of this. The reference to the "letters of the Torah" is also a typical Ḥasidic idea. The letters of the Torah are sacred. They represent spiritual forces on high. Therefore when a man has his mind on these, his thoughts are "attached" to the divine in a very special way. Maor Va-Shemesh speaks, too, of burning enthusiasm (hitlahavut). The Ḥasidim believed that a mere mouthing of the words of the prayers is as nothing. The worshipper in his prayer must burn in his enthusiasm for the divine. He must forget all about his ego and his selfish needs and lose himself, as it were, in the divine, hence the reference to "self-sacrifice." The Rabbinic reference to the "house" is that if a man has studied the Torah but has no fear of God, it is as if he had made a door for his house without having any house where to put the door. The Rabbis further say that Jacob spent ten years studying the Torah at the house of learning founded by Shem, son of Noah, and his grandson Eber. This is, of course anachronistic. There were no "houses of learning" in the Rabbinic sense in the days of Shem and Eber, but is a typical Rabbinic idea that the great institutions of Rabbinic times had their

*origin in much earlier times, so that the Biblical heroes are
described as Rabbinic scholars. The rest of the comment is self-
explanatory.*

B. HOW CAN A MAN BE A HERMIT AND YET BE SOCIAL?

*Comment on: "And the Lord spoke unto Moses, saying: Speak unto
all the congregation of the children of Israel, and say unto them: Ye
shall be holy; for I the Lord your God am holy" (Leviticus 19:1,2).*

The Midrash comments as follows on our text: The Holy One, blessed
be He, said to Moses: Go, say to Israel, My sons! Just as I am separate
from the world, so you should be separate from the world. Just as I
am holy, so you should be holy. Therefore it says: "Ye shall be holy."
This Midrash is very strange. For one thing, God does not make excessive demands on His creatures, God forbid. It is surely quite impossible for all the congregation of the children of Israel to be separate from the world, and, especially to be as separate as God is
separate, as it were? It seems to me that this can be explained
quite simply. The ways of God, in which man must walk in order to
serve God, are many. But the main way of serving God is for man to
love God and so attach himself to God. Now some people imagine
that the only way in which a man can serve God by becoming attached to Him is through solitude. They imagine that the way in
which a man can attain to attachment to God is for him to seclude
himself in a lonely room to study there, conversing with no one at
all and showing himself to no one at all. But this is not entirely true.
A man can live for many years in solitude, speaking to no other human being at all, and yet never arrive at the truth. I once heard a
comment on the verse: "If a man hide himself in secret places and I
shall not see him, saith the Lord" (Jeremiah 23:24) from our master
and teacher, the famous Rabbi, our master Rabbi Elimelech of Li-
zensk, may the memory of the righteous and holy be for a blessing.
He explained the verse to mean that if a man secludes himself in a
secret room and imagines that this is the main way to serve God,
God says: "And I shall not see him," as if to say, I, too, as it were,
shall not see him there. On the contrary, the main way for a man
to serve God is to associate with the children of Israel, with the
righteous and worthy among them, and as a result man can reach
the true service of God by learning good conduct from these right-

eous men. The main idea of solitude is in the mind, that is, to think of the majesty of God at all times. Even when a man is part of a huge assembly, his thoughts should be attached to the Creator, blessed be He. As the author of *The Duties of the Heart* writes in *The Gate of Separation from the World*, separation chiefly requires that even when a man is in a room full of people, he should imagine that it is empty. He means by this that a man's thoughts should be so attached to God that he is hardly aware that other people are present. Especially when he prays, a man should attain to such attachment to God that he is no longer aware that any other creature is present, and he should be alone with his Creator, blessed be He. This is chiefly what the ideal of solitude means. When a man converses, too, with inferior folk he should not allow his soul to become completely associated with them. His thoughts should be detached, dwelling on the exalted majesty of God. This is the meaning of our text which speaks to the whole assembly of the congregation of Israel. "Ye shall be holy," namely, you shall be separate from the world. That is to say, even in a huge assembly of the holy congregation, when all are together, each one should yet be on his own, attaching and binding his thoughts to God, so that it will be as if each were entirely alone, without any other human being present there, as the afore-mentioned sage remarks that in a room full of people, it should be as if the room were empty. This is the meaning of the Midrash we have quoted: "Just as I am separate from the world." Even though He fills all worlds and encompasses all worlds and no place is void of Him, yet He is separate from anything material. So it should be with you. Even when you are in a huge crowd of people, you should be separate from them. Your thoughts should be attached only to God and you should have no association with the material aspect of the crowd, and you will then be holy.

First, it should be noted that the saying of the famous Ḥasidic Rabbi Elimelech, the teacher of Maor Va-Shemesh, can be read into the Hebrew of the verse in Jeremiah, but it is not, of course, the plain meaning of the verse. Rabbi Elimelech takes the verse to mean that if a man imagines that he can find God by hiding himself, by living as a hermit, so that others cannot see him, he is bound to fail. God, too, as it were, will not see him. We have in this passage a typical statement of the Ḥasidic ideal of "attachment" (devekut) to God. This *means that God should always be in men's thoughts. The Rabbis who opposed the Ḥasidim, and they were many, believed that even if it is possible for man always to have his thoughts on God, it is not desirable, because this would affect his complete concentration on the things God would have him do, his obligations to his fellows and the study of the Torah, for example. Now the Ḥasidim, as good Jews, could not deny that a man has very strong social obligations. Indeed, Ḥasidism encouraged special life. The dilemma is solved by Hasidic thinkers like Maor Va-Shemesh by drawing on the idea that a man can and should be a good "mixer," friendly and helpful and taking his full part in the social life of his community, but, at the same time, having his mind on God. Solitude is a great ideal, but only solitude in thought. This is the reasoning behind this comment of the Maor Va-Shemesh. (For The Duties of the Heart by Baḥya ibn Pakuda, see the section of the work quoted at the beginning of the second volume in this series. The Gate of Separation is a chapter in Baḥya's work.) Note Maor Va-Shemesh's novel interpretation of the Midrash. God is immanent in the world and yet He is also transcendent. Hence the Midrash understands God as demanding that man should be like Him in this respect; he should be in the world but not of it.*

C. HOW CAN A MAN BE PURE?

Allegorical interpretation of: "Thou shalt not plow with an ox and an ass together" (Deuteronomy 22:10). Maor Va-Shemesh puns on the word ḥamor, "ass," and connects it with ḥomer, "matter" (as does Ḥayim ibn Attar in this volume). He also puns on the word shor, "ox," and connects it with shur, "to gaze," i.e., to gaze in mystical reflection on the mysteries of the upper worlds, the heavens and their spiritual illuminations.

The following is the allegorical interpretation of this verse. Some men serve God by studying the Torah and praying, but have no desire to worship God by breaking their bodily appetites. This is not the good way. A man should worship God by breaking his bodily and material appetites. Now it is well-known that the "ox" represents allegorically a high stage of divine worship. The word *shur* **means to gaze on the upper worlds and the illuminations on high. The righteous are called "oxen" for this reason, as we find that the righteous Joseph is called an "ox" (Deuteronomy 33:17 and, accord-**

ing to the Rabbinic interpretation, Genesis 49:26). The ass, on the other hand, represents materialism, hinting at the body and its appetites. This, then, is the meaning of: "Thou shalt not plow with an ox and an ass together." This means: You must not serve God with the soul and the material side together; namely, a man should not serve God without first breaking the coarseness of his material nature. Such worship is of no value, but a man must first break all his material longings.

"Breaking" one's material nature means denying oneself, leading an ascetic life, rejecting undue coarseness and materialism, refining one's physical appetites. It is sometimes assumed that Hasidism is non-ascetic but there are also ascetic Hasidic trends, represented particularly by Maor Va-Shemesh's teacher, Rabbi Elimelech.

Malbim

Can a man love his neighbor as himself?
What is the secret of happiness?

Rabbi Meir Laib ben Yeḥiel Michael formed his family name from the initial letters of his name, so he is known as Malbim. This famous Russian Rabbi was born in 1809 and he died in 1879. He wrote a Commentary to the whole of the Bible which is nowadays known as the Malbim Commentary. It has been published in twelve volumes, six on the Pentateuch and six on the other books of the Bible. Malbim is completely and uncompromisingly traditional in his view but, as can be seen from the extracts given here, is thoroughly conversant with modern thought.

A. CAN A MAN LOVE HIS NEIGHBOR AS HIMSELF?

Comment on: "Thou shalt love thy neighbor as thyself" (Leviticus 19:18).

"Thou shalt love thy neighbor as thyself." The commentators have observed that the verse cannot possibly mean that a man should love his neighbor as much as he loves himself, for such a thing is contrary to human psychology. Furthermore, since neither love nor hate are in man's control, he cannot be commanded to feel one or the other. The truth is that when Scripture does refer to love in the

conventional sense, it always uses the word *nafsho* ("his soul"), as when it says: "And Jonathan loved him as his own soul" (I Samuel 18:1), and "for he loved him as he loved his own soul" (I Samuel 20:17), and it does not use the expression: "as thyself." The root *ahav* ("to love") is usually attached to the word *et* (the sign of the accusative), yet here it is attached to the letter *lamed* ("to"), and so, also, later on: "and thou shalt love him *(lo)* as thyself" (Leviticus 19:34). There is a clear distinction between the word *et*, which is the sign of the accusative, and the use of the *lamed*, which denotes a reaching out towards something. For instance, when the verse says: "And He shall deliver *et* their kings into thy hands" (Deuteronomy 7:24), the *et* denotes the accusative. But to say: "And he shall deliver to him" *(lo)* would denote something to be attained. And so it is always.

Malbim repeats an obvious question raised by the earlier commentators. How can love be commanded at all, and, even if it could, is it psychologically possible to love another as oneself? Malbim's reply is, as he says later on, that the command is for a man to behave in a loving way to his neighbor. It is not directed to the emotions, but to man's conduct. He should do good to his neighbor and refrain from harming him, just as he wishes his neighbor to behave towards him in this way. The meaning of the verse according to Malbim is: "Do loving acts to your neighbor just as you do loving acts to yourself, and refrain from harming him just as you refrain from harming yourself." Malbim tries to prove that this must be the meaning of the verse. As a grammarian he notes the unusual form of this verse. If it were really intended as an appeal to the emotions, it would have said: "Thou shalt love thy neighbor as thine own soul." Moreover, the little word et represents in Hebrew the sign of the accusative. Here, however, the verse does not say: Ve-ahavta et reacha but Ve-ahavta le-reacha, hence the meaning is: "love towards thy neighbor," i.e., loving deeds expressed to him or on his behalf.

Indeed Hillel the elder defined it (in tractate Sabbath when he taught the convert the whole Torah while the latter stood on one leg) when he said: "That which is hateful unto thee do not do unto thy neighbor." This means that a man should wish his neighbor to have that which he wants for himself, namely, advantage and protection from harm. He should endeavor to do everything that is to the advantage of his neighbor, whether in terms of bodily health or success in business, just as he makes such endeavors on his own behalf. And it goes without saying that he should not be responsible for doing anything to his neighbor that he would not wish to be done to him. Our verse states this by using the *lamed*, indicating that which is *for* his neighbor. He should desire *for* his neighbor that which he desires for himself.

The story of Hillel and the prospective convert to Judaism is well-known. This man said that he wanted to become a Jew, but only if Hillel would teach him the whole Torah in the short space of time that he stood on one leg. Hillel replied: "That which is hateful unto thee do not do unto thy neighbor. This is the whole of the Torah. The rest is commentary. Go and learn!" Malbim points to the fact that Hillel speaks of not "doing" to the neighbor that which is hateful to the man himself. Hence he finds in Hillel his idea of the use of the lamed *as stated previously. It might be mentioned that many modern Biblical scholars make a distinction similar to that of Malbim and understand the verse in more or less the same way, except that many of them argue that the expression "as thyself" does not refer to "thou shalt love" but to "thy neighbor," i.e., "thy neighbor (who is) as thyself."*

Now the philosophers have laid it down as the first principle in ethics that a man should only do that which he would wish to be a universal rule. For instance, if a man is prepared to harm his neighbor for the sake of his own advantage, he should ask himself whether he would wish this kind of conduct to become a universal rule. If it did, then the rule would apply to all, that for personal gain one could harm another. But no one really wishes to be harmed by another for the sake of the other's gain. Therefore he will not behave in this way himself. Similarly, if a man is ready to refrain from helping his neighbor when he has the opportunity of so doing, he should ask himself whether he wishes this to be a universal rule. If it were, then no one would ever help him. That is why Rabbi Akiba said that our verse is the great rule of the Torah. However, the speculative philosophers have objected that this rule is not sufficiently inclusive. For in obedience to this rule everything a man does is measured in terms of self-interest, whereas the ideal is for man to behave in accordance with the higher reason, without any taint of self-interest. That is why Ben Azzai applies the rule on a much more elevated plane, relying on the verse: "This is the book of the generation of Adam" (Genesis 5:1). Ben Azzai means that all human beings are bound to one another as if they were, in reality, a single person. They have all been created in God's image, and it is their duty to perfect the image and to resemble the image on high which embraces the souls of all men. All men are like a single body composed of various organs, in which the head loves the hand as itself. As Ben Azzai says in *Ethics of the Fathers:* "Despise no man." And he says further in the Talmud: "The whole world was only created for the sake of providing the righteous man with company." For since all human beings are like one single person, then although the perfect man is the heart and the special treasure, yet the masses are like the flesh, sinews, bones, skin and muscles of the body which surround the heart and protect it. The heart feels it when any organ of the body is lacking or when any organ is sick or functions inadequately, even when there is pain in the skin or in the lobe of the ear. That is why a man should want for another that which he wants for himself, for others are flesh of his flesh and bone of his bone.

Malbim discusses here the views of Kant, with whom he was evidently familiar, and other modern ethical theorists. The universal rule Malbim speaks of is Kant's "categorical imperative." In the Midrash known as Siphra and in other Rabbinic passages quoted by Malbim later on, the two second century teachers Rabbi Akiba and Ben Azzai debate which Biblical verse contains "the great rule of the Torah," i.e., which verse contains the best summary of what Judaism is all about. Rabbi Akiba states that it is our verse, but Ben Azzai states it is the verse: "This is the book of the generations of Adam," in which it is implied that all men are brothers. Malbim has his own understanding of the debate. Rabbi Akiba takes our verse as the golden rule. A man should do good to others just as he wishes others to do good to him. But Ben Azzai has the mystical view that, in reality, there is not self and others as distinct entities since all men are one. To love one's neighbor is to love oneself. This should be compared to John Donne's famous: "No man is an island."

This idea is stated in the Jerusalem Talmud, tractate Nedarim. Rabbi Meir rules in the Mishnah that if a man vows that his goods are forbidden to another, the vow can be anulled if he expresses remorse at having made it. The suggestion should be made to him, says Rabbi Meir, that he ought to feel remorse since the Torah states that a man should not take revenge and that he should love his neighbor. On this the Jerusalem Talmud comments: "Because a man has cut off one of his hands should he then cut off the other?" The meaning is that since all men are as one single person, it is only right that a man should love his neighbor as himself. The Jerusalem Talmud after having made this observation quotes the debate between Rabbi Akiba and Ben Azzai. In the light of our interpretation, all is clear. The debate is also quoted in the Midrash, Genesis Rabbah. It may be conjectured that Rabbi Akiba follows his own argument (in the *Siphra* near the end of Leviticus) that the saving of a man's own life takes precedence over that of his neighbor, while Ben Azzai would follow the view of Ben Petura recorded there. Here is not the place to go into this matter at greater length.

For the Jerusalem Talmud, see the first volume in this series. The Jerusalem Talmud states that a man ought to feel remorse at having placed a ban on his goods so that another should not be able to enjoy them, even if the other has harmed him. The illustration given by the Jerusalem Talmud reminds us of our saying about cutting off the nose to spite the face. Malbim's final quote means this. There is a debate between Rabbi Akiba and Ben Petura on the case (see the first volume in this series where the case is discussed in detail) of two men travelling through the desert and one of them has no water while the other only has enough water to keep himself alive. Is he obliged to share the water with his friend? Rabbi Akiba rules that his own life comes first, but Ben Petura rules that he must share the water even though, as a result, they will both die. Malbim suggests that Rabbi Akiba in both our instances follows the same principle, of enlightened self-interest. But Ben Azzai has a different view and presumably he would agree with Ben Petura.

B. WHAT IS THE SECRET OF HAPPINESS?

Comment on the first Psalm. The numbers are those of the verses on which Malbim comments.

[1] "Happy is the man that hath not walked in the counsel of the wicked, nor stood in the way of sinners, nor sat in the seat of the

scornful." The Psalmist intends to expound the conditions necessary for a man to be happy. There is a difference between the term *meushar* ("happy") and *matzliaḥ* "prosperous"). Prosperity generally refers to this worldly things, while happiness refers to other-worldly, spiritual things. Now perfection can be attained with regard to three things: possessions, bodily health and the human spirit. Hence the Psalmist declares at the outset that he speaks of "happy is the *man*." He refers to that happiness which is peculiar to man, to the human being by virtue of his human nature, not of the kind of happiness man shares, in the animal part of his nature, with the whole genus of animals. That is to say, perfection in possessions and perfection of body are to be found among the animals as well. For we find that many animals procure their food and sustenance more easily and more effectively than man and none is richer than the pig. And they have more bodily vigor than man, the elephant and the lion, for instance. And their senses are more acute than those of man, the vision of the eagle and the vulture, for instance. So that the only type of happiness peculiar to man is that which stems from improvement of the character and ethical traits. This is typical of man alone. The Psalmist declares that in the first instance man's happiness depends on his avoiding sin. "That hath not walked in the counsel of the wicked." The difference between "the wicked" and "sinners" is that the term "the wicked" refers to those who sin intentionally and presumptuously, whether against God or against their fellows. The Psalmist, consequently, speaks of "the counsel of the wicked," for these sin by taking counsel and by using their mind. But when speaking of "sinners," the Psalmist cannot use the word "counsel" for they do not sin by taking counsel. He adds, therefore, "nor stood in the way of sinners," as if to say, not even this. For the "sinners" only commit their sins out of lust and he means to say that the good man does not even commit this type of sin. He states further that not only does such a man not "walk" in the way of sinners (i.e., does not sin constantly), but that he does not even "stand" in their way, that is to say, not even occasionally. "Nor sat in the seat of the scornful." The "scornful" are those who sit around doing nothing. They commit no evil deed but neither do they do good. All they do is pursue the wind and vanity and frivolity and they do not study the Torah.

Malbim's method, which he sometimes pursues to inordinate lengths, is to find a meaning for every single nuance of the text. Thus here he tries to account for the use by the Psalmist of a number of different nouns and verbs. One reply would be that the Psalmist simply rings the changes for the sake of dramatic effect. But Malbim wishes to find something more than this in the text. The Psalmist, he says, speaks of the "counsel" of the "wicked" because he is thinking of those who have a philosophy of evil, backing up their evil deeds by a supposed rationale. The "sinners," on the other hand, are those who sin out of personal greed, lust or gain but do not seek to defend their deeds by pseudo-sophisticated arguments. They have a "way" but not a "counsel." The good man does not even "stand" for a while in this way, let alone walk in it. The "scornful" have neither evil "way" nor "counsel." They do not do anything. They only "sit" and the good man refuses to sit with them in idleness.

[2] **"But his delight is in the law of the Lord; and in His law doth he meditate day and night." However, it is not enough just to refrain from doing evil. It belongs among the conditions for attaining happiness that man should do good positively. This does not mean doing good in the conventional sense like the philosophers who invent purely human ethical systems, but that man should keep God's law and His precepts. The Psalmist explains, too, that it belongs to the ideal of doing good that man should only do it because it is good and in order to carry out God's command. He should not have ulterior motives for doing good, in anticipation of some personal advantage or reward for serving God. For then he would not be delighting in the law of the Lord, but rather in the pleasure and personal advantage he hopes for. Consequently, the Psalmist makes it conditional: "But his delight is in the law of the Lord." Now this type of perfection consists of two things, perfection of thought and perfection in the deed. Perfection of thought is called the law of the Lord, which teaches man the knowledge of the Lord, His ways and His truth. But this aspect can never be completely attained by man. It is sufficient if man's delight and his desire is in the law of the Lord so that he tries hard to comprehend it and he searches for it, even though he can never really comprehend God and can never see His face. But as for perfection in deed, this is the law of man, teaching him what he must do and what he must not do. This is**

called "his law." In this man must "meditate day and night," study-ing in order to practice.

Malbim says that in the second verse the Psalmist turns to the positive good man must do in order to be "happy." It is not conventional or merely human goodness, but the pursuit of God's laws. Man's "delight" moreover should be in doing God's will, not for the fame, honor and wealth and so forth he hopes to attain from doing good. Malbim takes the pronoun in "his law" in the second part of the verse as referring to man (so that, unlike in the current English translations, it should be written with a small "h"). Thus there are, as it were, two "laws." The first is the law of God, i.e., of knowing God. The second is man's law, i.e., the way in which man must conduct himself. Of the first the Psalmist states that man can never fully attain it, but he can and should have "delight" in it. How can finite man ever hope to comprehend the Infinite? The second, dealing as it does with man's duties, can be fully grasped by man. Therefore, the Psalmist says of "his" law that the good man meditates therein day and night.

[3] "And he shall be like a tree planted by streams of water, that bringeth forth its fruit in its season, and whose leaf doth not wither; and in whatsoever he doeth he shall prosper." If we think of man in terms of his capacity for growth, by virtue of which he belongs in the same genus as plants and trees, then we can understand him in terms of a tree with its roots reaching upwards and its trunk downwards. For man's brain corresponds to the roots of the tree. All sensations proceed from the roots to the branches, that is, to the bodily organs, and to the brain they return, just as the tree sends moisture and nourishment from the roots to the branches. Man should therefore realise that he is not really like a tree, the vitality of which stems from the soil, for man's roots and stock are planted in the higher worlds. It is from there that man receives his flow of the life-force; it is by the mouth of the Lord that man lives. Conse-quently, if man lives by bread alone and turns only earthwards, it is as if he walked upside down with his head downwards and his legs in the air. The Rabbis say that the righteous are like a tree whose roots extend to a place of purity but whose branches extend to a place of impurity. The opposite is true of the wicked. There is a clear distinction between a tree and grass. Grass sprouts in the

spring, producing seed after its kind. But then it withers and vanishes so that it seems as if its whole purpose is realised in the species as a whole, not in the individuals of the species. It is otherwise with the tree which endures for many a year, producing blossoms, flowers and fruit, with its seed perpetuated year by year. It is as if, in addition to the preservation of the species, the individual tree is preserved for many days, with its fruit for food and its leaves for refreshment. On this analogy the Psalmist speaks of the happiness of the perfect man and his excellence.

a). He is like a tree. This means that he is not like grass of which the species alone is the ultimate purpose. The masses behave, indeed, as if this were true of them. They do nothing to make sure that they will survive as individuals but only to make sure of the survival of the human species, and to leave to their offspring whatever advantages they have attained, as if they had no other purpose in life than the survival of the species. But the good man is like the tree. Apart from the survival of the human species as a whole he survives as an individual, producing the fruit of Torah and good deeds in praise of God, so that his soul is immortal.

b). "He shall be like a tree replanted" (shatul). There is a clear distinction between that which is planted and that which is replanted. That which is planted remains in the same place, but that which is replanted has grown elsewhere but is replanted in order to improve it and enable it to reach a higher stage of perfection. Now there are plants, fresh and green, which, because they are so moist, cannot be replanted. Such plants can never be improved and they cannot last very long. But a tree, precisely because it is green in the sun, is improved and lasts longer when it is uprooted from one place and replanted in another. As I have expounded the verse: "Can the rush shoot up without mire . . . He is green before the sun" (Job 8:11-16), consult my commentary to Job. There the wicked is compared to grass planted in one place which cannot be moved from place to place because of its excessive moisture and which, therefore, eventually withers. But the righteous is compared to a plant that is not so moist. He is made to wander from place to place, but this is his joyous way and he can take root in a different soil to sprout afresh. The wicked has the world as his home. Here alone is he planted. But the righteous is removed from this world and its desires, to be replanted by the streams of water on high, as it is said: "Planted in the house of the Lord" (Psalms 92:14).

c). "By streams of water." For the tree planted in a dry place is anxious in the year of drought and either ceases from yielding fruit or does not yield fruit in the right season (as it is said in Jeremiah, Chapter 17). It is otherwise with a tree planted by streams of water which can find its nourishment and moisture ready to hand. The upright men among the philosophers, who lead righteous and benevolent lives in obedience to the ethical rules they have worked out for themselves, cannot always find enough to sustain them since the human mind becomes tired of reaching out for the goal all the time and it falls into error in many of its judgments. It is otherwise with regard to one planted near the law of the Lord and His commandments. Such a person will find his way unerringly.

d). "That bringeth forth its fruit." This tree will produce *its* fruit, that is to say, unlike grass and herbs which only produce seed and do not survive as individuals, only as a species, and unlike a tree planted in the desert, which loses his character and fails to produce the fruit it is capable of producing, only producing rotten and inferior fruit. This tree will produce the fruit it is capable of producing. So it is with regard to the righteous. He is not like the intellectuals among the heathens who produce fruit as a result of speculative and deductive reasoning. These are not really the special fruits of the soul. Since the soul is divine, her fruit is holy and can only be actualised by means of the divine Torah and its precepts.

e). "In its season." This tree will produce its fruit in *its* season. And so, too, the bliss of soul and the happiness of the righteous will be in the right time, the time when the soul returns to reap her harvest in the place whence she came.

f). Also "whose leaf doth not wither." For the leaves protect the fruit and shield it from harm. So, too, even the temporal prosperity of the righteous will be preserved, his wealth, property and health, and they will not wither so that they can assist him to attain his ultimate bliss, which is the fruit. The fruit of the righteous, the Torah he studies and the precepts he carries out, are easily protected by the leaves of possessions and health and if these were to wither, his poverty or ill health would prevent him from serving God.

g). "And in whatsoever he doeth he shall prosper." The tree shall make its seed prosperous, too, so that whatever is sown or planted from it will be as the tree itself. So it is with regard to the righteous. His children, too, will prosper in his merit. His seed will be mighty in the land and will be a generation that is blessed.

*Note how, in this lengthy comment, Malbim treats every word of
the verse as if to make it yield the thought that the righteous
enjoys, in the analogy of the tree, seven advantages. These are:
1) individuality; 2) greater perfection; 3) divine guidance;
4) spiritual fulfilment; 5) spiritual bliss in the Hereafter; 6) material
prosperity as an aid to the good life; 7) the joys of having righteous
offspring.*

[4] "Not so the wicked but they are like the chaff which the wind
driveth away." After the Psalmist has explained the nature of the
happiness of the righteous, he declares that of the wicked the opposite is true. Not only do they fail to find the happiness and tran-
quillity of the righteous (in this connection he says "not so the
wicked"), but they are compared to the very opposite of a tree. They
are not like the chaff when it is together with the grain and which
protects the grain, for that kind of chaff is not driven away by the
wind, since the grain acts as a shield. They are rather like: "chaff
which the wind driveth away," the chaff from which the grain has
been removed so that the wind can blow it away. For as long as the
masses are attached to the righteous to surround and protect him
as the chaff the grain, he is their protection. But this cannot happen
if, like the chaff without the grain, they are on their own. The significance of the parable lies also in this, that just as winnowing the
chaff from the grain has the purpose of cleansing and refining the
grain by removing the waste, so, too, there is purpose in the destruction of the wicked, the purpose being to prevent them con-
taminating the righteous. Hence the next verse says: "Therefore the
wicked shall not stand." "Therefore" has the meaning of "in order
that" they (the wicked) should not stand in the congregation of the
righteous to be associated with them.

*Malbim's analogy is a bit forced here and is more homiletical than
a real attempt at discovering the meaning of the text. It is perhaps
fair to say that this is true of many of his interpretations, for all
their brilliance.*

[5] "Therefore the wicked shall not stand in the judgment, nor
sinners in the congregation of the righteous." "Therefore the wicked
shall not stand in the judgment" even on their own. "Nor sinners"
who sin because of the fierceness of their desires and are, conse-

quently, less blameworthy than the "wicked." Although these, on their own, will stand when they are judged on their own, for they will be able to present as an excuse that it is the nature of flesh to turn to lust, as it is said: "Behold, I was brought forth to iniquity" (Psalms 51:7), and it is said: "So He remembered that they were but flesh" (Psalms 78:39). Nevertheless, they will not stand "in the congregation of the righteous," that is, when they are judged in comparison with the righteous. For then they will be pronounced guilty when it is shown to them that the righteous did succeed in controlling their passions and prevailing over their lusts.

The "wicked" who sin because of their base philosophy, as above, have no hope. But the "sinners" who sin because they lack self-control will not be dealt with so harshly. They have an excuse which is accepted, so that they are able to "stand in the judgment." But they cannot be entirely exonerated and when they are judged together with the righteous, whose lives demonstrate that self-control is possible, they cannot "stand."

[6] "For the Lord knoweth the way of the righteous; but the way of the wicked shall perish." "Knoweth" here refers to the attachment of that which is perceived by one who perceives, as it is said: "For I have known him to the end, that he may command his children and his household after him" (Genesis 18:19), that is to say, he is attached to My knowledge. This can only happen to those things that are eternal and changeless. These can become attached to the One who is Eternal and Changeless. Now it is the way of the righteous that they tread the path of perfection leading to the House of God, loving the Lord and becoming attached to Him. The righteous man becomes inseparable from the knowledge of God and becomes eternal, as God is Eternal. Therefore, the righteous are immortal, but the way of the wicked leads to the depths of Sheol, to those things that waste away and are impermanent. They have no attachment to the knowledge of God and, consequently, they perish ultimately and it is as if they had never existed.

Malbim attempts to explain the significance of God "knowing the way of the righteous." His metaphysical interpretation is that the good man pursues all his life the knowledge of God and he thus becomes "attached" to God, as it were, so that he shares God's eternity.

Baruch Epstein

What are the various ways of misleading others?

The remarkable Russian Jewish scholar Rabbi Baruch Epstein was born in 1860 and was murdered by the Nazis in 1942. Epstein was not a professional Rabbi, but earned his living as a bank manager. His work on the Pentateuch, Torah Temimah, "Perfect Torah," enjoys great popularity. Epstein's book is based on the idea that the Rabbinic interpretations of Biblical verses, although they frequently seem at variance with the plain meaning of the text, are, in fact, implied in the text. He collects all the more important Rabbinic comments to a particular verse and then gives his own interpretation, with the aim of showing how the sayings are at one with the text. Hence the title: "Perfect Torah," i.e., the Written Torah (= the Bible) and the Oral Torah (= the teachings of the Rabbis) form, in reality, one, perfect and whole Torah. Epstein's work is thus both an anthology and a commentary. He comments here on: "Thou shalt not curse the deaf, nor put a stumbling-block before the blind, but thou shalt fear thy God: I am the Lord" (Leviticus 19:14). Epstein gives a valuable list of Rabbinic teachings on the verse and then gives his own interpretation of them. We have headed the Rabbinic texts with the letter A and Epstein's own comments with the letter B.

(I)

"Nor put a stumbling-block before the blind." What does "Before the blind" mean? It refers to someone who is in the dark (literally "blind") about some matter (and you must not mislead him). If he takes your advice, do not advise him to his disadvantage. For instance, do not advise him to set out on his travels early in the morning, your intention being that bandits should rob him. Do not advise him to set out on his travels at noon, your intention being that he should get sunstroke. You may argue: "I am giving him sound advice," but it is all a matter of the heart, as it is said: "But thou shalt fear thy God."

This passage is from the early Midrash known as Torat Kohanim, "The Law of the Priests" (or Siphra, see the example from this in the first volume of this series). The "blind" of the verse is not taken literally, but as referring to the man who does not clearly see the way he should behave. If you mislead him when he asks for your advice then you are, in fact, putting a stumbling-block before him. You may wish to harm him but, frightened to do this openly, you offer him harmful advice. For instance, you say to him that if he goes out on his business travels early in the morning, he will get there before his competitors. This, in itself, is quite sound advice, but supposing you know that bandits lurk there early in the morning when few people are about, then you are guilty of this offense. The meaning of "it is all a matter of the heart" is that sometimes it is impossible for anyone to know whether your intentions are good or evil, but you know in your heart and God knows. Therefore it says: "but thou shalt fear thy God" as if to say, you may succeed in fooling your neighbor, but you cannot fool God.

"Nor put a stumbling-block before the blind." Rabbi Nathan said: How do we know that a man must not hand over a cup of wine to a Nazirite or give a limb torn from a living animal to a son of Noah? Scripture teaches us this when it says: "Nor put a stumbling-block before the blind."

Rabbi Nathan was a second century Palestinian teacher. He takes "blind" to mean blind to goodness, i.e., as referring to one who wishes to commit a sin. If he does, you must not be the means of causing him to sin; you must not provide him with the opportunity of sinning, because if you do you are putting a "stumbling-block" before him. Rabbi Nathan gives two examples. A Nazirite is a man who takes a solemn vow not to drink wine. Obviously he must keep his vow and he must not drink wine. If, therefore, he asks you to hand him some wine which he intends to drink and so break his vow, you must not do so. The Rabbis speak of seven laws which are binding even on Gentiles, not only upon Jews. Gentiles in this context are referred to as "the sons of Noah," the father of the human race after the Deluge. (See the section on Hazzekuni in this volume). One of these seven is that forbidding the eating of a limb torn from an animal while the animal is still alive (a cruel practice that was evidently unknown in Rabbinic times). Supposing a "son of Noah" asks you for this forbidden food, then you might perhaps argue, why should I be concerned if he wants to sin? But if you do hand him the forbidden food, then you cause him to sin and so you offend against our verse.

"Nor put a stumbling-block before the blind." It was taught: Where is there a hint in the Torah that graves have to be marked? Abaye said: "Nor put a stumbling-block before the blind."

Abaye was a fourth century Babylonian teacher. Priests (kohanim) are not permitted to come into contact with a corpse or a grave (see Leviticus 21:1-6). Consequently, graves should be marked as such, so that the priests will take care not to trespass on the forbidden ground. This is called only a "hint" since here, unlike in the other examples, the "stumbling-block" is placed before the "blind" in a much more indirect manner.

"Nor put a stumbling-block before the blind." This verse refers to one who strikes his grown-up son.

An interesting application of the idea that it is forbidden to cause another to sin. If a father chastises his grown-up son, the latter might be tempted to retaliate and he would then offend against the fifth commandment. Consequently, it is an offense for a father to strike his grown-up son. The next passage quoted by Epstein is from the Babylonian Talmud and pursues the same theme as this passage. Since it has been quoted in full in the first volume in this series it is omitted here.

"Nor put a stumbling-block before the blind." Rab Ashi owned a forest. He sold it to fire-worshippers. Rabina said to him: But does this not offend against: "Nor put a stumbling-block before the blind?" He replied: Most wood is used for ordinary heating purposes.

Rab Ashi, the famous Babylonian teacher, died in the year 427. He was a rich man with a number of estates. Babylon in his day was part of the Persian Empire, with Zoroastrianism as the state religion. Fire-worship involved the kindling of fires in the name of the Zoroastrian religion. This was idolatry from the point of view of Judaism, and so it could have been argued that by selling them the forest Rab Ashi was causing them to sin; he was putting a "stumbling-block" before the "blind." His defense was that if it could be known for certain that they would use the wood of the forest for idolatrous purposes, it would indeed have been wrong to sell them the forest. But wood is not generally used for fire-worship, but for such innocent purposes as heating the home. Therefore, Rab Ashi was justified in selling them the forest and he was under no obligation to conclude that they wished to use the wood for idolatrous purposes. In the case of the Nazirite, for instance, it is only forbidden to hand him the wine if he intends to drink it.

"Nor put a stumbling-block before the blind." Both the man who lends money on interest and the man who borrows offend against the verse: "Nor put a stumbling-block before the blind."

It is strictly forbidden to lend money on interest, but, say the Rabbis, it is also a severe offense to borrow money on interest. Therefore, in addition to the special offense of which lender and borrower are guilty, each causes the other to sin and this falls under the heading of our verse. If no one would borrow money on interest, no one would lend and if no one would lend, no one would borrow.

"Nor put a stumbling-block before the blind." Rab Judah said in the name of Rab: Whoever lends another person money when no witnesses are present offends against: "Nor put a stumbling-block before the blind."

Rab was the great early third century Babylonian teacher, Rab Judah his pupil. To lend money where there are no witnesses or

*where there is no bond, for example, might encourage the borrower
to deny that he had, in fact, borrowed the money. Thus one who
lends money to another without witnesses or bond can in some
sense be said to be putting a "stumbling-block" before the "blind."*

**"Nor put a stumbling-block before the blind." Rabbi Phinehas ben
Jair entered through the gateway of Rabbi's house and noticed
there some white mules. He said: "This man has the angel of death
in his house." When Rabbi heard of it, he offered to sell the mules
but Rabbi Phinehas said to him: "Nor put a stumbling-block before
the blind."**

*Rabbi is Rabbi Judah the Prince, the editor of the Mishnah (see the
first volume in this series). White mules were dangerous beasts and
Rabbi Phinehas refused to enter Rabbi's house because he held that
it is forbidden for a man to have anything dangerous in his house.
A man who has white mules in his house entertains, as it were, the
"angel of death" in his house. Rabbi offered to sell them, but just
as he was not allowed to have them so, too, other persons were not
allowed to have them. Consequently, by selling them to others he
would cause them to sin and our verse would apply.*

(II)

**The *Torat Kohanim* and the Talmud in all the examples we have
quoted understand our verse as referring to one who causes another to sin or who misleads another, and not as referring literally
(as do the Sadducees, as stated in tractate Niddah) to one who
places a stumbling-block in the way of a physically blind man. The
commentators explain the departure from the plain meaning of the
verse because, they argue, if the verse were intended in the literal
sense it should have said "Nor *place* a stumbling-block." The expression: "Nor *put* (literally "give") a stumbling-block" suggests, therefore, one who gives another person advice but conceals in his heart
that it is, in fact, misleading. According to this way of looking at it,
the term "blind" denotes one blind of heart, as in the verse: "His
watchmen are all blind" (Isaiah 56:10) where the meaning is blind to
the truth. Hence the Rabbis understand the verse as referring to one
who causes another to sin or who misleads him.**

For the Sadducees, see the section on Ibn Ezra in this volume. The Sadducees understand our verse literally. It simply means what it says, that one should not place an obstacle in the path of a blind man so that he will fall over it. But the Rabbis interpret the verse figuratively, and understand it in the sense of giving misleading advice or causing another to sin, as in the examples quoted. What compelled the Rabbis to depart from the literal meaning? Epstein quotes the commentators as replying that the verse does not say "place" but "give" (Hebrew tittén), *hence the verse means: "Nor give a stumbling-block before a man blind to sin or folly." This is the view of many commentators. Epstein himself favors a different view which he now proceeds to expound.*

But it seems to me that the various Rabbinic expositions do not, in fact, reject the plain meaning of the text but simply state that causing another to sin and misleading him are also implied in the verse, since what difference is there between causing the body of another to fall or causing his soul to stumble? Since the term "blind" is used in Scripture both of one physically blind and of one spiritually or intellectually blind, the verse embraces both types. The Sadducees only disagree with the Sages in one thing. The Sadducees limit the verse to causing another's body to stumble and they do not apply it to his soul.

The other commentators, quoted by Epstein, argue that so far as the Rabbis are concerned, the verse refers only to the kind of stumbling-block mentioned in the examples given. Thus the debate between the Sadducees and the Rabbis is on whether the verse has to be understood literally or figuratively, whether the "stumbling-block" is a real or a figurative one, and whether the term "blind" means one physically blind or intellectually (or spiritually) blind. Epstein's view is rather that the Rabbis, too, accept the plain literal meaning of the verse. They do not deny it at all, but simply make it more embracing. Hence, for Epstein, the Sadducees say that the verse must *only be taken literally, whereas the Rabbis do not say that it must* only *be taken figuratively, but that it must be understood in both senses.*

It seems to me further that one is obliged to say that the verse retains its literal meaning. This is because we find in Deuteronomy the verse: "Cursed be he that maketh the blind to go astray in the way" (Deuteronomy 27:18). But it would not be right for him to be cursed unless the Torah had previously stated an explicit prohibition, just as in all cases where the Torah records a punishment there is always a preceding explicit prohibition. Even though it is true that Rashi to the verse in Deuteronomy also refers it to one who gives bad advice but there, surely, the verse does not lose its literal meaning. The Zohar, too, says that the verse in Deuteronomy is intended to be taken literally.

For the Zohar, see the second volume in this series. For Rashi see the beginning of this volume. Epstein's point is that if the commentators he quotes are correct, then our verse refers only to causing another to sin or misleading him and this means that there is no explicit prohibition against the physical act of placing an obstacle in the path of the physically blind. And yet in Deuteronomy one who does this is cursed and it is a general principle, according to the Rabbis, that there is never found in the Torah a statement of any punishment for an offense that is not recorded elsewhere explicitly. Therefore, our verse must refer also to the physical act, as Epstein has argued.

We are now in a position to understand the association of the two prohibitions in our verse: "Thou shalt not curse the deaf, nor put a stumbling-block before the blind." Scripture gives the example of two unfortunates who can be harmed without their hearing or seeing that which affects them.

According to the commentators, there is no association between the two halves of the verse, since the first is to be taken literally and the second only figuratively. But if Epstein's interpretation is accepted, then all is clear. The deaf person cannot hear the curse and so to curse him is to take advantage of his deafness, and the blind person cannot see the stumbling-block and so to place it in his path is to take advantage of his blindness.